THE SINO-JUDAIC

BIBLIOGRAPHIES

OF

RUDOLF LOEWENTHAL

BIBLIOGRAPHICA JUDAICA 12

A bibliographic series of the Library of
Hebrew Union College-Jewish Institute of Religion
3101 Clifton Avenue, Cincinnati, Ohio 45220
Edited by Herbert C. Zafren

1 Rudolf Glanz. *The German Jew in America.* An Annotated Bibliography Including Books, Pamphlets and Articles of Special Interest. 1969
2 *Judaica.* A Short-Title Catalogue of Books, Pamphlets and Manuscripts Relating to the Political, Social and Cultural History of the Jews and to the Jewish Question, in the Library of Ludwig Rosenberger, Chicago, Illinois. 1971
3 Bernard Grossfeld. *A Bibliography of Targum Literature.* 1972
4 *Judaica.* Supplement [to No. 2 above]. 1974
5 Werner Weinberg. *How Do You Spell Chanukah?* A General-Purpose Romanization of Hebrew for Speakers of English. 1976
6 Martin H. Sable. *Latin American Jewry: A Research Guide.* 1978
7 Shimeon Brisman. *A History and Guide to Judaic Bibliography* (Jewish Research Literature, Vol. 1). 1977
8 Bernard Grossfeld. *A Bibliography of Targum Literature.* Volume Two. 1977
9 Vera Basch Moreen. *Miniature Paintings in Judaeo-Persian Manuscripts.* 1985
10 Nahum Waldman. *The Recent Study of Hebrew: A Survey of the Literature with Selected Bibliography.* Forthcoming
11 Shimeon Brisman. *A History and Guide to Judaic Encyclopedias and Lexicons* (Jewish Research Literature, Vol. 2). 1987
12 *The Sino-Judaic Bibliographies of Rudolf Loewenthal.* 1988. (In association with the Sino-Judaic Institute)

The
SINO-JUDAIC
BIBLIOGRAPHIES
of
RUDOLF
LOEWENTHAL

Edited by MICHAEL POLLAK

HEBREW UNION COLLEGE PRESS
Cincinnati
in association with
The SINO-JUDAIC INSTITUTE
Palo Alto, California
1988

Library of Congress Cataloging-in-Publication Data

Loewenthal, Rudolf.
  The Sino-Judaic bibliographies of Rudolf Loewenthal.

  (Bibliographica Judaica ; 12)
  Reprint (1st work). Originally published: The Jews in China, in the Yenching journal of
social studies, v. 1, no. 2, January 1938.
  Reprint (2nd work). Originally published: The Jews in China, an annotated bibliography.
Peking? 1940.
  Reprint (3rd work). Originally published: The early Jews in China. Peking : Catholic
University of Peking, 1946.
  1. Jews—China—Bibliography. 2. China—Ethnic Relations—Bibliography. I. Title.
II. Series
Z6373.C5L5725 1988   016.3058'924'051   88-24420

[DS135.C5]
ISBN 0-87820-910-7   Manufactured in the United States of America

CONTENTS

INTRODUCTION

The three Sino-Judaic studies published by Rudolf Loewenthal[1] in Beijing between 1939 and 1946 represent the first substantial efforts ever made to compile a comprehensive bibliography of the widely dispersed literature that has accumulated on the subject throughout the dozen or more centuries in which there has been a Jewish presence in China.[2]

The importance of Dr. Loewenthal's contributions to the study of Sino-Judaic history can scarcely be overstated. One need only turn the pages of virtually any serious publication in the field that has been issued since the late 1940s to appreciate how much its author owes to the introductory essays, the bibliographical listings and annotations, and the extended citations that are to be found in the Loewenthal studies.

Today, unfortunately, these seminal works are almost as hard to come by as many of the scattered source materials they list. All three of these works were published in a China torn by war, a fact which may well explain why they were printed in very small numbers and on inferior paper that has all too quickly fallen victim to the ravages of time. As an inevitable consequence, few libraries currently own any of the Loewenthal Sino-Judaic bibliographies, while those that do tend to be understandably reluctant to risk further damage to their brittle holdings by passing them through a photocopying machine. Researchers in Sino-Judaic studies who are unable to gain direct access to the Loewenthal texts, or to facsimiles thereof, are therefore compelled to resort to whatever derivative sources happen to become available to them. In so doing, they naturally run the risk of inheriting and perpetuating the errors of omission and commission that may have been introduced by the intermediary sources to which they have had recourse. A case in point is that of a doctoral candidate at a Brazilian university who, lacking personal access to any of the Loewenthal publications, was left with no alternative but to base substantial portions of his dissertation upon materials extracted from the incidental remarks of authors who had not been handicapped in the same manner. As may readily be understood, his dissertation, when completed, was not as free from error as it might have been. Nor did its contents suggest that its author was even remotely aware of what he would quickly have realized, had the Loewenthal works been available to him — that, in short, considerably more was known about his topic than he suspected.[3]

It is for these reasons — the obvious scholarly importance of the Loewenthal bibliographies, their limited availability, and the drastic physical deterioration they have suffered — that the Library of the Hebrew Union College and the Sino-Judaic Institute have joined hands in sponsoring this lithographic reprint of the 1939-1946 editions.

The career of Rudolf Loewenthal reflects the chaotic world conditions in which it evolved. Born in Schwerin-Mecklenburg, Germany, in 1904, he worked between 1923 and 1929 for publishing houses in France and Germany, and in 1933 received a doctoral degree in economics from the University of Berlin. Almost immediately, the advent of Hitlerism drove him from his native land to a haven in the Far East. Arriving in China, he was appointed in 1934 to a teaching position at Yenching University, in Beijing, serving also on its library staff. Within a few years, he acquired Chinese citizenship, added Chinese and Russian to an already extensive linguistic repertory, and developed an outstanding reputation as an expert in Sino-Soviet relations.

Rudolf Loewenthal's tenure at Yenching University lasted until 1947, when the successes of the Maoist military forces drove him into a second exile, this time in the United States. Here he busied himself in research and teaching, first at Cornell University and later at Georgetown University. After becoming an American citizen (1957), he worked in a number of capacities for the United States Information Agency, specializing in the creation of bibliographies and other publications dealing with China, Africa, Turkey, and various Arabic national groups and institutions. Later, he became associated with several commercial firms engaged in the development of computer-related translation programs. During this period, he and his wife Ariadne, a Slavonic specialist at the Library of Congress, designed one of the earliest systems for the computerized translation of Russian technical journals into English. His marriage, incidentally, brought him a fourth citizenship, and this for the reason that in grateful recognition of the pioneering work done by a grandfather of Mrs. Loewenthal on the development of the icebreaker — and, moreover, to memorialize that gentleman's decision, as captain of a foundering prototype of this vessel, to go down gallantly with his ship — the city fathers of Vladivostok had bestowed honorary citizenship in their municipality upon all his descendants in perpetuity, as well as upon whatever spouses they might acquire. As part of this legacy, Russian national citizenship was automatically conferred upon each beneficiary. What could never have been foreseen, of course, was that, decades later, when Rudolf Loewenthal was called upon to testify before a succession of United States Senate committees on the complexities surrounding the three-sided relationships existing between the United States, China, and Russia, it would turn out that the expert witness whose counsel was being sought had held citizenship in all three of the powers under discussion.

The scholarly record of Rudolf Loewenthal is exceptionally impressive. Aside from his Judaic-related writings, he has published extensively, both as author and translator, on such matters as the growth of foreign-language and religiously-oriented periodicals in China and elsewhere in the Far East; Russo-Islamic and Sino-Islamic studies; Russian-held collections of materials dealing with Arab, African, and Turkic peoples; biographical data concerning numerous outstanding Russian intellectual and political figures; and the like. He also founded and edited the *Central Asian Collectanea*, and served with distinction on the editorial board of *Monumenta Serica*.

The principal Sino-Judaic publications of Rudolf Loewenthal which deal with the autochthonous Jews of China, excluding those of his articles which have appeared in a variety of encyclopedias, are:

1. "Literatur vegn di Yidn in Khine" ("Literature concerning the Jews of China"), *Yedies fun Yidishn Visenshaftlekhn Institut*, Wilno (November-December 1937). A initial listing of seventeen titles compiled by Dr. Loewenthal for M. Birman.

2. "The Jews in China: a Bibliography," *Yenching Journal of Social Studies* vol. 1, no. 2 (January 1939), pp. 256-91.

3. "The Jews in China: an Annotated Bibliography," *Chinese Social and Political Science Review* vol. 24, no. 2 (July-September 1940), pp. 113-234. Reprinted, 1940, with minor changes and new pagination: [1-4], i-iv, [119]-261.

4. "The Early Jews in China: a Supplementary Bibliography," *Folklore Studies* vol. 5 (1946), pp. 353-98.

5. "The Nomenclature of Jews in China," *Monumenta Serica* vol. 12 (1947), pp. 97-126. A revised and substantially enlarged version of this study appears in Hyman Kublin's *Studies of the Chinese Jews* (New York, 1971), pp. 53-84.[4]

6. "Jews and China in Eighteenth-Century Literature," *Historia Judaica* vol. 12 (1950), pp. 67-76.

7. "An Imaginary Illustration of the Kaifeng Jewish Synagogue," *Oriens Extremus* vol. 19 (December 1972), pp. 95-99.[5]

In contrast to the Jews who lived in the western regions of Asia, such as those in Babylonia and Persia, the Jews of China were always very few in number and enjoyed no more than occasional contact with their brethren in foreign lands. For that matter, the outside world seems to have assumed that the very minor Jewish presence in China that had been noted by several Arab and

Christian travelers in the interval between the ninth and the fourteenth centuries no longer existed. Not until 1605, when the discovery of the survival of a centuries-old Jewish enclave in the old Song capital city of Kaifeng was announced by the Jesuit missionary Matteo Ricci, did the West realize that there was still a Judaic diaspora, however attenuated, on the far side of the Great Wall of China. By 1605, moreover, there had been absolutely no communication between the Jews of China and the rest of world Jewry for at least three generations, and, as it turned out, there would be none until the second half of the nineteenth century.

Given their exceedingly small numbers and their lengthy isolation in so remote a corner of the globe, it is not at all surprising that relatively few documentary materials or oral reports concerning the Jews of dynastic China — whether of a primary or secondary nature, or of Chinese origin or Jewish origin — were ever transmitted to the West, and that rather little was written about the subject in either the West or the East.[6]

It is quite understandable, accordingly, that when Rudolf Loewenthal committed himself to the daunting challenge of compiling the first comprehensive census of Sino-Judaic historical data that had ever been attempted, he was not faced with the frustrating problem which bibliographers in other disciplines must so often address — that of deciding which of their masses of potential listings must be discarded if their projects are not to become too cumbersome for practical use. For Dr. Loewenthal, the problem was not one of weeding out the unimportant, the peripheral, or the questionable, but of finding and cataloguing whatever relevant titles he could — even those whose relevancy seemed quite minimal — so that his readers would at least know that these titles existed.

To counteract the difficulties that would obviously be engendered by the choice of so undiscriminating a standard for the selection of his entries, Dr. Loewenthal adopted an exceedingly liberal annotational policy that on the whole makes it possible for the reader to determine whether individual entries are of sufficient interest and credibility to justify further investigation. Unfortunately, however, the ongoing hostilities during which Dr. Loewenthal's three bibliographies were compiled made it impossible for him to acquire and examine at first-hand every item that was eventually entered in his listings.[7]

Later writers have also made a point of recording virtually every pertinent bibliographical item that came to their notice, while attempting, as Dr. Loewenthal did, to caution the reader about accepting any that they suspected of being erroneous or spurious.[8] Fortunately, the situation has been drastically altered since Kaifeng, effectively sealed off to foreign visitors for decades, was reopened to them eight or nine years ago. Large numbers of tourists, a few sinologists, and, not infrequently, a journalist or two have now had the opportunity to travel to the city and meet some dozens of the several hundred remaining descendants of its ancient Jewish community. Because of all this, and for other reasons which need not be gone into here, we have in recent years been regaled by an extraordinary outpouring of scholarly and popular books and articles regarding the story of the Jews in China. Understandably, these are of very uneven quality — ranging as they do from the factual to the utterly absurd.

The present reprinting of the Loewenthal 1939-46 studies represents the first phase of a contemplated two-part Sino-Judaic project which, it is hoped, will culminate in the publication of an annotated bibliography that will not only take notice of the more recent additions to the literature but will also include many of the older items which escaped the attention of Dr. Loewenthal nearly a half-century ago.

When we consider the sharp increase in the quantity of the Sino-Judaic publications with which we now must deal, it becomes obvious that the time has arrived to apply a more rigorous set of standards to the way we go about determining what deserves a lasting place in the literature and what does not. In brief, it no longer makes sense to preserve every fish that swims into the Sino-Judaic bibliographical net. Presumably, the planned, updated bibliography noted above will be compiled with this in mind.

In view of the fact that the entries contained in Dr. Loewenthal's 1939 bibliography were merged (alphabetically, by author), into his second, the 1940 "Annotated" work, only the Introduction and the Preface of the 1939 work are reprinted herein. The 1940 (second version) and 1946 editions, on the other hand, are reprinted in full. For the convenience of the reader, the original pagination has been retained and augmented by a sequential numbering system printed in bracketed numerals.

In the preface to his *Studies of the Chinese Jews*, published in 1971 and dedicated to Dr. Loewenthal, the late Hyman Kublin made the following comment:

> Some of the materials reprinted in this volume originally appeared in journals whose condition has unfortunately deteriorated over the years. While every effort has been made to reproduce such material with as much clarity as possible, the results in some instances have not been as had been hoped. For this shortcoming, I ask the indulgence of the reader. My guiding consideration has been that a usable reproduction of a rare study is worth more than an original which may soon be extinct.

Because the camera work for the printing of the present volume is for the most part being done from photocopies made from crumbling, discolored offprints of the original texts, the reader will readily understand that Dr.

Kublin's apologia is as germane here as it was in the case of the work for which he wrote it.

I wish to express here my sincere thanks to the several individuals whose contributions to the preparation of this book proved to be both invaluable and indispensable: to Dr. Loewenthal, for authorizing the Hebrew Union College Press and the Sino-Judaic Institute to reissue his bibliographies, and for providing certain of the materials which have been included in this Introduction; to his longtime friend George Barclay, for providing additional data; to Leo Gabow, who originally conceived the project of republishing the Loewenthal studies and did so much to bring it to fruition; to Albert E. Dien and Donald Daniel Leslie, to whom I was able to turn repeatedly for counsel in matters dealing with Chinese culture and language; and to Herbert C. Zafren, whose constructive criticisms and skills as a librarian were of greater assistance than he can possibly know.

Michael Pollak

Dallas, Texas
July 1988

NOTES

1. Dr. Loewenthal's earlier publications, including the works reprinted here, record their author's surname as Löwenthal, the original German-style spelling.

2. The Loewenthal bibliographies list several hundred individual titles, many times more, that is, than the number ordinarily found in the Sino-Judaic works of earlier authors. Thus, C. G. von Murr's *Versuch einer Geschichte der Juden in Sina* (Halle, 1806) and James Finn's, *The Jews in China* (London, 1843) each contain bibliographies consisting of fewer than two dozen entries. Dr. Loewenthal, moreover, provides appendices including a body of exceptionally valuable materials extracted not only from sources that had previously appeared in print, but also from documentary sources that had not.

3. See Nicholas Mu Yu Chen's doctoral dissertation, *A Communidade Israelita de Khai Fon* (São Paulo: Universidade de São Paulo, 1976). The bemusing allusions to Dr. Loewenthal as a Catholic priest (i.e.: "*Padre* Loewenthal"; see pp. 82 and 101-02, n. 14) are further manifestations of Dr. Chen's regrettable but apparently unavoidable dependence upon intermediate sources rather than upon the Loewenthal texts themselves.

4. Kublin (p. 55) notes that this study was originally printed in *Collectanea Commissionis Synodalis* vol. 17 (May-December 1944), pp. 354-370, but that, "owing to the Pacific War only some ten copies of the issue" were preserved.

5. For listings of Dr. Loewenthal's bibliographical works on the Occidental Jewish press in China, see Shlomo Shunami's *Bibliography of Jewish Bibliographies* (Jerusalem, 1969), pp. 108-09.

6. Two long-lost bibliographical treasures for which the hope of retrieval is not yet entirely gone are the books written about Judaism (in Chinese) ca. 1663 by two outstanding Chinese-Jewish leaders, the brothers Zhao Yingcheng and Zhao Yingdou. The title of Yincheng's work is *A Record of the Vicissitudes of the Holy Scriptures*; that of Yingdou is *A Preface to the Clarification of the Way*. As far as is known, the former was never printed. The latter, however, is probably the unnamed volume which was described by the Italian Jesuit Jean-Paul Gozani in the first quarter of the eighteenth century as a printed work that the Jewish community presented to the local authorities (presumably to newly inducted officials) for the purpose of letting them know who and what their Jewish townsmen were. It is not inconceivable, moreover, that other hitherto unrecognized source materials of both Chinese and Jewish origin may in time be brought to light.

7. These hostilities also put a halt to the publication of one of Dr. Loewenthal's most important bibliographical works, a 400-page index to Henri Cordier's *Bibliotheca Sinica*. This occurred when the Japanese, having seized Tientsin, confiscated the printing plant in which the volume was then on press. Because paper shortages and other production problems made it impractical to start work again on the index at war's end, it remains even now unpublished. However, two copies of the author's typescript are presumed to be in the possession of Yenching University.

8. *Cf.*: Leslie, D. D. *The Survival of the Chinese Jews* (Leiden, 1972); Pollak, Michael. *Mandarins, Jews, and Missionaries* (Philadelphia, 1980); and Leventhal, Dennis A. *Sino-Judaic Studies* (Hong Kong, 1985).

The SINO-JUDAIC BIBLIOGRAPHIES of RUDOLF LOEWENTHAL

The Jews in China: A Bibliography

Preface

The present bibliography was started as a by-product of an earlier article on *The Jewish Press in China* (title no. 70). The author traced many articles and books concerning the subject which were largely unreliable and in many instances contradictory. The information on the Jews in China was frequently based upon second, third, or even fourth-hand material without due acknowledgement of the original source. The author attempted in vain to find a suitable compiler for a still unwritten, complete history of the Jews in China.

It is hoped that the present collection of material will encourage and enable someone to take up this task. If the present bibliography should prove helpful toward that end, the purpose of the effort will have been fulfilled.

The literature on this fascinating subject has appeared in many languages and is scattered all over the world. The author is greatly indebted to the Yenching University Library for its generous co-operation; particularly to Mr. T'ien Hung-tu (田洪都), who kindly offered the necessary facilities. Special acknowledgement is due to Mr. Ch'en Hung-shun (陳鴻舜), assistant librarian, and Miss Margaret L. Waller, former assistant librarian of this university. They both furnished the compiler with a large number of titles. In addition, Mr. Ch'en supplied the Chinese terms concerning the Jews.

Moreover, the author is greatly indebted to Mr. Shlomo Shunami, librarian of the Jewish National and University Library, Jerusalem, for sending numerous titles. Dr. E. Urbach, formerly of the Jüdisch-Theologisches Seminar, Breslau, who will soon also join the above institution, likewise furnished titles and extracts from various articles. In both cases the titles sent by them have been indicated in the bibliography.

Dr. William B. Pettus, director of the College of Chinese Studies, Peking, kindly opened his library to the compiler, who traced there a number of new titles. Mr. T. C. Hu (胡道靜), formerly librarian of the History Compilation Bureau of Greater Shanghai (上海市通志館編纂) kindly checked and copied some articles from the old Shanghai newspapers which were not available locally.

Mr. M. Birman, manager of the Far Eastern Jewish Central Information Bureau, Harbin, also gave the author data by mail concerning several titles. Mr. Aba S. Izgur, headmaster of the Tientsin Jewish School has kindly translated and transcribed the Hebrew and Yiddish titles. Finally, the author owes thanks to his numerous colleagues and friends who on various occasions offered him advice and suggestions.

Rudolf Löwenthal (羅文達)

Yenching University

[3]

Introduction

According to the information available at the present time, there is no reason to believe that any large number of Jews settled in China before the 12th century, though individuals may have entered the country before that date. Statements to the contrary have been either unfounded or based upon misinterpretations of facts. Religious enthusiasm has often carried authors away and encouraged wishful thinking.

The first foreigner to visit the Jewish community was the Jesuit, Aleni, who came in 1613 at the repeated request of his superior, Matteo Ricci. J. L. Liebermann (or Libermann) who went there in 1857, was the first Jew from outside to call on the community. He was followed in 1866 by the Protestant missionary, W. A. P. Martin.

The number of Jews in China in former times has apparently been grossly exaggerated. If there had been as large numbers of them as some writers were inclined to believe, probably more references to Jews would have been found in Chinese literature. The only Chinese publication, one written by the Kaifeng Jews themselves, is mentioned by Finn:*

> "It is stated, that they (the Jews) have written no books about themselves but one, which they keep and exhibit to the Gentiles whenever their religion is called in question."

At present the number of Jews in China amounts to about 15,000 people, of whom about 90% are of Russian or former Russian nationality. 8% come from either Europe or America and 2% from Iraq and India. Most of them live in the three cities of Shanghai, Tientsin and Harbin, but small groups are also to be found in other cities. The present hostilities, however, have changed the old statistics to such an extent that reliable data cannot be given.

Meanwhile, the early Jewish immigrants to Kaifeng were either wiped out or assimilated by their Chinese and Mohammedan neighbours. This process of absorption has apparently been complete, and· the features of the alleged Jews on the photographs taken by various visitors do not reveal any definite similarity to those of the original immigrants. The persons concerned might belong either to the Chinese race or to one of the Mohammedan ethnic groups.

The lot of the Jews in China was not always easy and has changed considerably with the vicissitudes of the history of this country. Floods and droughts, famines and wars affected the Jews as they did the rest of the population. Such events, as well as assimilation, have caused the disappearance

---

* James Finn, *The Jews in China*, London. 1843. p. 46. *Cf.* title no. 39.

[4]

of the first Jewish settlers. Again, the present hostilities have told on the various Jewish communities which have suffered severe losses in places like Shanghai and elsewhere. In spite of her own difficulties, however, China has given shelter to numerous foreign Jews, and the European persecutions of the last four years have brought a large number of professional men to China.

During November, 1938, approximately 500 German and Austrian Jews arrived in Shanghai after their release from a German concentration camp. Another 3,000 to 4,000, about one-quarter of German and three-quarters of Italian nationalities, are expected there in the near future. 1,000 of them are supposed to have arrived in Shanghai before the end of 1938.

The Jewish Relief Committee of Tientsin has prepared for the accomodation of nearly 2,000 refugees in the British and French Concessions, but apparently difficulties have arisen concerning their landing on occupied territory.

The treatment of the Jews in China has always been fair and impartial, at no time has there been any discrimination against them, and even some anti-Semitic propaganda imported directly or indirectly from Europe has not been able to alter the traditional tolerant attitude of the Chinese people towards other religions and races.

What Perlmann wrote in 1913, still holds true.

> "I must add .... in justice to the old civilized Chinese nation, that the Jews in China have never had to complain of intolerance; they were never under exceptional laws; they were never persecuted or despised for their religion. They always enjoyed full rights like the Chinese."

Many different names have been used for signifying the Jews and their faith.

1	朮 忽	*Chu-hu*
2	竹 忽	*Chu-hu*
3	主 鶻	*Chu-ho*
4	主 吾	*Chu-wu*
5	朮 忽 持	*Chu-hu-t'ê*
6	朱 乎 得	*Chu-hu-tê*
7	諸 呼 得	*Chu-hu-tê*

This group of names represents the phonetic rendering of the Arabic word *Djuhud* (Jew). It was first identified by Palladius (see title no. 91). Some of these and of the following terms were compiled by Noyé.[1]

8	猶 太	*Yu-t'ai*
9	攸 持	*Yu-t'ê*

These two terms are phonetic renderings of European words for Jews. Particularly the term no. 8 is now commonly used.

---

[1] E. Noyé, "Les juifs en Chine." (*Le Bulletin Catholique de Pékin,* Peking. 22:268. December, 1935. p. 650-651.) *Cf.* title no. 89.

10 刀 筋 敎   *Tao-chin-chiao*
11 挑 筋 敎   *T'iao-chin-chiao*

The third group of names signifies "the sect which extracts the sinews", alluding to prescriptions of slaughtering animals.[2]

12 藍 帽 (子) 回 回   *Lan-mao-(tzu)-hui-hui*

"Mohammedans with blue turbans."[3] This name was given to the Jews in order to distinguish them from the Mohammedans who used to wear other colours. According to Noyé this term is still being used around Sian.[2]

13 回 回 古 敎   *Hui-hui-ku-chiao*

"The ancient Mohammedan (Hui-hui) religion", is a term mentioned by Milne.[4]

14 一 賜 樂 業 敎   *I-szu-lê-yeh-chiao*

"The religion of *Israel*"; this phonetic rendering of the word *Israel* is now frequently used.

15 天 竺 敎   *T'ien-chu-chiao*

"The religion which came from India", a term which was chosen because the first Jewish immigrants came either from or through India. It was dropped by the Jews during the persecutions of Christians, so that they might not be confused with the Catholics (天主敎), and persecuted as such. The Catholics had adopted a name of the same sound, though of a different meaning and written in different characters.[5]

16 天 敎   *T'ien-chiao*

The term, "the religion of Heaven" was used formerly, but has been abandoned.

17 希 伯 來   *Hsi-po-lai*

The phonetic rendering of the word *Hebrew*.

18 *Mussauites*, "followers of Moses", derived from *Mussau*—Moses (摩 西 *Mo-hsi*). This term is mentioned by Yule in the *introductory notice* to "The journey of Benedict Goes from Agra to Cathay."[6]

---

[2] Marshall Broomhall, *Islam in China*. London. 1910. p. 176. *Cf.* title no. 16a.

[3] S. M. Perlmann, *The history of the Jews in China*. London, 1913. p. 25. *Cf.* title no. 96a.

[4] William C. Milne, *Real life in China*. 2nd ed. London, 1858. p. 411. *Cf.* title no. 80a.

[5] W. A. P. Martin, *A cycle of Cathay*. 2nd ed. New York. 1897, p. 277. *Cf.* title no. 74.

[6] Henry Yule, *Cathay and the way thither*. London, 1916. v. 4, p. 175; (cf. title no. 129e).

19 幹 脫   Kan-t'o

This term which means "money" or "usurer", according to some Japanese authors refers also to Jews, more particularly to Jewish money-lenders in Kansu. According to other authors this is not so. As no reliable facts have been established concerning the word, it is still doubtful whether or not it refers to Jews.

20 敎 經 敎   Chiao-ching-chiao

"The religion which teaches the Scriptures."

[7]

THE JEWS IN CHINA

An Annotated Bibliography

Rudolf Löwenthal

羅 文 達

Yenching University

Reprinted from
THE CHINESE SOCIAL & POLITICAL SCIENCE REVIEW
PEKING.

Dedicated to

Professor William Hung

洪 煨 蓮 （業）

of Yenching University

in appreciation of his friendship and inspiration

Reproduction of the title page of the Yiddish newspaper *Der Weiter Misroch* or *The Far East*. It is printed in Hebrew type; without indication of vowels. It appeared in Harbin thrice weekly, from 1921 to 1922, with a circulation of from 700 to 800 copies. This publication has been the only one of its kind in the Far East. Original size: 55 × 35 centimetres.

PREFACE

The first edition of this bibliography appeared in the *Yenching Journal of Social Studies**) in January, 1939. It was started as a by-product of an earlier article on *The Jewish Press in China***) which appeared in 1937. While the first issue of the bibliography contained 145 titles, the number of titles in the present second issue amounts to 258. Moreover, numerous corrections and additions have been inserted. Many of the articles were based upon second, third, or even fourth-hand materials, frequently without due acknowledgement of the original source.

The literature on this fascinating subject has appeared in many languages and is scattered all over the world. The author is greatly indebted to the Yenching University Library for its generous co-operation; particularly to Mr. T'ien Hung-tu (田洪都), who kindly offered the necessary facilities. Special acknowledgement is due to Mr. Ch'en Hung-shun (陳鴻舜), assistant librarian, and Miss Margaret L. Waller, former assistant librarian of this university. They both furnished the compiler with a large number of titles. In addition, Mr. Ch'en supplied most of the Chinese terms concerning the Jews.

Moreover, the author is greatly indebted to Mr. Shlomo Shunami, librarian of the Jewish National and University Library, Jerusalem, for sending numerous titles. Dr. E. Urbach, formerly of the Jüdisch-Theologisches Seminar, Breslau, who will soon also join the above institution, likewise furnished titles and extracts from various articles. In both cases the titles sent by them have been indicated in the bibliography.

Dr. William B. Pettus, director of the College of Chinese Studies, Peking, kindly opened his library to the compiler, who traced there a number of new titles. Mr. T. C. Hu (胡道靜), formerly librarian of the History Compilation Bureau of Greater Shanghai (上海市通志館編纂)

---

*) *The Yenching Journal of Social Studies*, Peking, vol. I, no. 2; January, 1939; p. 256-291.

**) Cf. title no. 113.

[12]

kindly checked and copied some articles from the old Shanghai newspapers which were not available locally.

Mr. M. Birman, manager of the Far Eastern Jewish Central Information Bureau, Harbin, also gave the author data by mail concerning several titles. Mr. Aba S. Izgur, headmaster of the Tientsin Jewish School has kindly translated and transcribed the Hebrew and Yiddish titles. Finally, the author owes thanks to his numerous colleagues and friends who on various occasions offered him advice and suggestions.

Dr. George R. Loehr of Yenching University kindly helped the author with various suggestions and with the translation of Italian titles.

Thanks are also due to Mr. Julius Leavitt, Chief of the Catalogut Division of the Library of Congress, Washington, D.C. Mr. Leavite kindly supplied the author with several additional titles and photostas of the articles.

July 29, 1940.

TABLE OF CONTENTS

LIST OF ABBREVIATIONS

The letters on the left side of the titles indicate the sources from which the information has come.

Cor   Cordier, Henri. *Bibliotheca Sinica.* Paris, 1904-1907. (title no. 26).

Fi   Finn, James: *The Jews in China.* London, 1843. (title no. 39).

Je   *Jewish Encyclopedia.* New York—London, 1912. (title no. 27),

Mö   Möllendorff, P. G. and O. F von—: *Manual of Chinese bibliography.* Shanghai, 1876. (title no. 82).

Mu   Murr, Christoph Gottlieb von—: *Versuch einer Geschichte der Juden in China.* Halle, 1806. (title no. 86).

RA   Andree, Richard: *Volkskunde der Juden.* Bielefeld, 1881. (title no. 5).

Shu   Shunami, Shlomo; librarian of the Jewish National and University Library Jerusalem. (through correspondence).

Sk   Skachkov, P. E.: *Bibliography on China.* Moscow-Leningrad, 1932. (title no. 111).

Ur   Urbach, Dr. E.; formerly of the Jüdisch-Theologisches Seminar, Breslau. (through correspondence).

*   This symbol indicates that the compiler has not seen the books or articles concerned and has been unable to trace any details about their contents.

IV

INTRODUCTION

DISCOVERY OF THE JEWISH SETTLEMENT IN CHINA
AND THEIR TREATMENT IN THE LITERATURE
CONCERNED

Considerable interest in the early Jewish settlement in China has been displayed since the beginning of the 17th century. Although, or perhaps because, very little information was available, many fantastic theories about the time of their arrival and their activities have been developed. Frequently such theories were coloured by wishful thinking on the part of their authors in order to prove their favourite ideas.

When and where started this interest in the Jews? It began in 1605, when the Kaifeng Jew Ngai T'ien (艾田) visited the Jesuit missionary and scholar Ricci in Peking. From then on to the closing years of the 19th century, foreigners exclusively took an interest in this strange dispersed group.

Up to 1891, ten people had visited Kaifeng with the express purpose of studying the local Jewish community. Among them were two Chinese, acting, however, on behalf of foreigners.

The first and most important group investigating the Jewish community consisted of Catholic missionaries, or, more exactly, of Jesuit Fathers. To them we owe most of the historical data. The visitors were Aleni (1613), Domenge (1722) and Gaubil (1723). Longobardi and Fernandez, who went to Honan in 1619, did not actually go to Kaifeng.

After a period of more than 125 years, Protestant missionaries became active. In 1850 Bishop Smith of Victoria, in conjunction with the Rev. Dr. Medhurst, acting for the Society in London for promoting Christianity among the Jews, dispatched two Chinese emissaries there: K'iu T'ien-sang and Tsiang Yung-chi. These were followed by the Rev. Dr. W.A.P. Martin (1866), Bishop Schereschewsky (1867), and the Rev. Mills (1891).

A-merchant, by the name of Liebermann from the then Austrian Silesia, was the first European Jew to visit his co-religionists. His visit was followed in 1900 and in subsequent years by efforts of the Shanghai Jewish committee to rescue the remnant in Kaifeng.

In addition to these three groups, a German colonel named Lehmann seems to have visited the Honan Jews in 1899. However, the facts concerning this visit are contradictory and the compiler has been unable to verify them or to obtain the original sources.

The interest of many of the authors who reported their findings again and again and embellished them with unsubstantiated theories was in most instances theological. The Catholic and Protestant missionaries felt that the presence of Jews in China was a sign that God had spread his word to the remotest corners of the earth. It was too good a proof justifying their vocation to be missed. The second motive was presumably that of conversion of this small group. This would seem the more natural, as the Jews at the time of Ricci—as later on during the visit of Schereschewsky—thought they were dealing with co-religionists, until the difference was explained to them. The process of absorption by the Chinese and Mohammedan population had, however, already proceeded so far that the expectation of conversion was never fulfilled.

In the case of Jewish visitors and writers it was largely the fascination of having an early historical connection with the old Chinese culture which caught their imagination.

A fourth group, whose influence must not be underestimated, was that of the early etymologists who tried their hand at sinology and phonetics. In their great enthusiasm some of them developed theories for which their contemporary colleagues still blush.

The Chinese for the most part were unaware of the presence of this small remnant. Hung Chün (洪鈞), scholar and diplomat (÷ 1893),

[18]

became interested in Jews. He erroneously also identified the *Wo-t'o* as Jews. The *Wo-t'o* were, however, Mohammedan commercial organizations under the Yüan dynasty, whose activities were often rather discreditable. Following the publication of Hung's work (see title no. 92) in 1897, interest in the Jews was aroused among Chinese scholars. His views have more or less been accepted as truth, because no one inquired about the true meaning of the original Mongol term. A number of Chinese and Japanese scholars developed imaginary theories similar to those of their Western colleagues.

First Entry Of The Jews Into China

The views on the entry of the Jews into China vary greatly. The stone inscription of 1663 in Kaifeng mentions the Chou dynasty (1122-244 B.C.) as the time of their arrival. Pelliot[1] and other authorities attribute this early date to a faulty interpretation of the inscription of 1489. The inscription of 1512 as well as oral tradition places their entry in the Han dynasty (206 B.C.—220 A.D.) This opinion, with numerous variations has been held by a large number of authors.

The possibility that some Jews may have arrived in the Han dynasty cannot be denied. However, no evidence is available to support that surmise and it appears improbable according to the available information. The oldest stone inscription of 1489 mentions the arrival of the Jews under the Sung dynasty (960-1278). The assumption that they had then arrived at the capital (at that time P'ien-liang, the present Kaifeng) after having lived for some time in other parts of China is unfounded, because the texts are silent on this subject. Tobar attempted to reconcile both views by assuming that two migrations had taken place, one under the Han dynasty and another under the Sung dynasty.

---

[1] P. Pelliot; review of Tobar, *Inscriptions juives* in the *Bulletin de l'Ecole Française d'Extrême-Orient*, Hanoi; v. 1, 1901, p. 263-264. (Cf. title no. 188.)

Whatever the merits of this surmise are, we have at present no evidence that the Jewish settlers came to China before the 12th century, as was mentioned above.

Pelliot assures us that the Jews came to China by the sea route and not overland, as some authors claim. This view is also held by Chavannes and Laufer. It accounts for the presence of a Jewish colony at Ningpo during the 15th century. The passage on this point by Pelliot reads as follows:—[1]

"...Cette première et fondamentale inscription, celle de 1489, nous atteste l'existence à Ning-po au XVe siècle, d'une communauté juive qui envoya deux exemplaires du *Pentateuque* aux correligionnaires de K'ai-fong-Fou. Or, Ning-po, où il y a encore une rue de Persans, fut de tout temps sans doute, mais surtout sous les T'ang et les Song (VIIe-XIIIe S.) une des grandes échelles de l'Extrème-Orient. A Ning-po, comme dans toute cette région de l'embouchure du Yang-tze, aventuriers et commerçants debarqués des larges jonques persanes, gens de tous races et de tous cultes, manichéens et mazdéens, musulmans et nestoriens, se heurtaient a des frères venus par l'autre route, par le Turkestan et le Kansou. Il serait étrange que les Juifs se fassent seuls tenus en dehors de ce courant puissant, et que, venue au debut de notre ère, quand ces relations n'étaient pas établies, leur colonie ignorée de l'histoire fût assez vivace après quinze siècles pour fournir d'exemplaires du *Pentateuque* la synagogue de K'ai-fong-Fou."

Laufer, thirty years later came to exactly the same conclusion:-[2])

"In company of Arabic and Persian Mohammedans the Jews must have made their first appearance in China, for the various stages of their migration can be traced with a fair degree of exactness; we meet them in the same ports of southern China as the Arabs and Persians ; at Zaitun (the Arabic name for Ts'üan-chou-fu in Fukien Province), Ning-po, Hang-chou, Nanking, Yang-chou, finally advancing into the metropolis of the Northern Sung, K'aifung, and in the fourteenth century also in Peking. It is not necessary to assume that there was but a single stream of their immigration into China: more probably they poured in gradually, in small detachments, but they always entered China from India over the maritime route at the southern ports, not, as was formerly believed without reason, over the land route by way of Central Asia. The first immigration may be assigned to the ninth or tenth century."

2   B. Laufer; *A Chinese-Hebrew manuscript*, in *The American Journal of Semitic Languages and Literature*; 46:3, April, 1930, p. 193-194, (Cf. title no. 108.)

Laufer offers in addition an etymological explanation for his claim that the Jews did not enter China before the 9th or 10th century :-[3]

"......the name of the Jews,..........as it is on record in the annals of the Yüan dynasty.........is a very exact phonetic transcription of New Persian *Djuhūd* or *Djahūd* with initial palatal sonant, while in Middle Persian the word is *Yahut* corresponding to Hebrew *Yehūdi* and Arabic *Yahūd*. The change of initial *y* into *j* is peculiar to New Persian. For the Chinese it was just as easy to transcribe *ya* as *dja* or *dju*, but the fact that they transcribed *Djuhūd* goes to show that they heard the New Persian form and that they could not have learned the name of Jews before the tenth century."

THE JEWISH POPULATION IN CHINA
THE KAIFENG SETTLEMENT

As most of the early Jews entered China originally for trading purposes there is little reason to believe that their number was ever very large. Taking an average of five persons per family, the number of original settlers at Kaifeng, who arrived during the 12th century, may have been around 350; making an allowance for numerous children the 500 mark would hardly have been exceeded. During the next five centuries the number of families increased from 70 to 200, through natural reproduction, through further immigration, or through intermarriage. Most likely all three factors were instrumental in the increase of the population. Since the beginning of the 18th century the Jewish population of Kaifeng has never passed the 1,000 mark. Meanwhile they have either been wiped out by natural disasters, such as inundations of the Yellow River, and by wars, or they have been absorbed. Hence, it seems that today no pure Jews have been left in that place, if any at all. The Catholic missionary Scarella reported as early as 1880 from Honan that the last survivors of the Jewish community in Kaifeng had disappeared[4] : —

"Depuis cette époque (1843, when Finn had reported the presence of seven remaining families), les derniers survivants ont disparu et, il y a quelques années, il n'y avait plus qu'une femme, mariée à un Tartare du pays."

---

[3]　*Ibid.*, p. 192-193.
[4]　L. Pfister, *Notices biographiques et bibliographiques*, (see title no. 155) v. I, p. 470.

JEWISH IMMIGRANTS INTO CHINA DURING
THE 19th AND 20th CENTURIES

While the first Jews to settle in China were of Perso-Indian origin, since the 19th century Jews from other parts of the world have entered this country.

At present the total number of Jews in China amounts to approximately 28,000. Though exact figures are not available, their distribution is estimated as follows:

Harbin	5,000
Shanghai	20,000
Tientsin	2,000
Balance of China	1,000
Total...............	28,000

Until 1937, the Jews who came from Western Europe, America Iraq and India numbered only about 1,000. At that time 700 of these were in Shanghai: 250 of various European nationalities, 50 American, and 400 from Iraq and India. The last-mentioned were usually British subjects. In Tientsin, on the other hand, there were less than 100 from both Europe and America. A few more were scattered in other Chinese cities.

Due to persecution in Europe, commencing in 1933, Jews began to filter into China. However, during the last quarter of 1933 and through the first half of 1939, a steady stream of refugees poured into Shanghai from Germany, Austria and—to a small extent—from Italy. During the second half of 1939, the various local authorities stopped this influx, which had reached the remarkable figure of 16,000 persons. Since then, this last open harbour for refugees has been practically closed to further immigration, in order not to aggravate the problems of the much tried port city.

[22]

THE JEWISH POPULATION FIGURES ACCORDING TO VARIOUS SOURCES

Title no.	author	reference	place	date	no. of clans	no. of families	no. of persons
132	Mishkowsky	Sze inscription of 1489	Canton	878/79 12th cent.			40,000*
53	Diaz	Longobardi, Fernandez	Kaifeng		16	70**	350-500
		inscription of 1663	Honan	1619			10,000***
108	Laufer	register	Kaifeng	1642		200	
108	Laufer	Gozani	Kaifeng	1660/70	7		
(178)	Smith	K'iu, Tsiang	Kaifeng	1704	7		712****
(124)	Martin		Kaifeng	1850	7		
167	Schere-schewsky		Kaifeng	1866			1,000
(155)	Pfister	Scarella	Kaifeng	1867			300-400
135	Möllendorff		Kaifeng	1880			200-300
180	Sopher	Lehmann	China	1895			1
108	Laufer		Tang-chwang	1899			175+
21	Berthelot		Kaifeng	1901		50	500++
	Compiler	estimate	Kaifeng	1905		6	200
243	Franck		China	1916			250
180	Sopher	Wong	Kaifeng	1923	7	8	72
100	Ko		Kaifeng	1924			1,000-2,000
	Compiler	estimate	China	1929			100-200
	Compiler	estimate	China	1933			99
			China	1940			70-80,000+++
							7,000-8,000
							28,000++++

* According to historical tradition 120,000 Jews, Arabs (Mohammedans) Christians, and Parsees were killed during that rebellion; the surmise that 40,000 of them were Jews is entirely arbitrary and most unlikely.

** These were the original settlers in Kaifeng.

*** This figure represents presumably an overestimate.

**** The register contains the names of 453 men and 259 women; many of the latter were of Mohammedan or pure Chinese stock. Laufer estimates the total at about 1,000 people, including children.

+This figure refers presumably to Hongkong and Shanghai. There the Jews were represented by 21 companies.

+ + This alleged discovery of a Jewish community is probably a misunderstanding.

+ + + This figure is highly exaggerated. The total for all China hardly exceeded 8,000, of whom between 6,00 and 7,000 resided in Harbin. These figures would also be more in line with the author's statement that there were 1,000 Jews in Shanghai, 140-150 in Hongkong and 200 in Kaifeng. These three estimates appear to be accurate.

+ + + +This number includes about 16,000 German and Austrian nationals and some 10,000 Russian or former Russian nationals.

Only a few professional men and women have had the opportunity of going into the interior of the country, because — apart from the language difficulties — a high degree of adaptation to local conditions is necessary. Tientsin and Peking have been able to absorb approximately 100 refugees. As these two cities are located in Japanese occupied territory, the military authorities have prevented further immigration. Simila r steps were taken in Manchuria.

Jewish residents who are former subjects of the Tzarist Russian Empire have largely acquired different nationalities because of the political changes after the Russian Revolution. Those who did not become Soviet citizens or who lost their nationality, mostly became Polish, Latvian, Esthonian and Lithuanian citizens. A small number acquired Chinese citizenship. Socially and culturally they are, however, a comparatively homogeneous group, whose contacts are primarily based upon the Russian language. They number about 11,000, most of whom entered China after 1918, taking refuge in Harbin. From there many went to Tientsin and Shanghai, particularly after the occupation of Manchuria in 1931/32.

As to languages, the Jews fall into three main groups: those who use English, German and Russian. English is used by those from America and the British Empire, as well as—more or less freely—by wide circles of citizens of other nationalities. English is, therefore, the foremost medium of international communication, although probably not more than 600 Jews in China consider it as their mother tongue.

The German group, largest of all, consists of more than 16,000 people originating from Germany and Austria. The overwhelming majority of them are recent immigrants.

The Russian-speaking community is second in size. Approximately 11 000 people of Russian or former Russian citizenship belong to this third group. They frequently use Yiddish as a secondary language,

[24]

which may be transliterated into either the Hebrew or the Latin alphabet. Hebrew itself is hardly used at all, and then only in its classical form. Probably not more than $\frac{1}{2}\%$, and certainly not more than 1%, can read it. Hebrew is presumably more common with them than with the other two groups.

The difficulties of mutual understanding between the English and German-speaking communities on the one hand, and those speaking Russian on the other, have created a certain language barrier. This has been partly bridged over, while coöperating in relief work for the newly arrived refugees.

NOMENCLATURE

Many different names have been used to signify the Jews, their faith and their language:-[5]

1	朮 忽	Chu-hu
2	朮 忽 特	Chu-hu-t'e
3	竹 忽	Chu-hu
4	主 鶻	Chu-ho
5	主 吾	Chu-wu
6	朱 乎 得	Chu-hu-te
7	諸 呼 得	Chu-hu-te

This group of names represents the phonetic transcription of the New Persian *Djuhud* or *Djahud* (Jew).[6] It was first identified by Palladius[7].

8	猶 大	Yu-t'ai
9	猶 泰	Yu-t'ai
10	攸 特	Yu-t'e

---

[5] In the article by E. Noyé, "Les Juifs en Chine," a collection of Chinese names for the Jews has been made from various sources. (*Bulletin Catholique de Pékin*; 22:268, December, 1935, p. 650-651.-Cf. title no. 143.) - Other names from various sources have been added in the present survey.

[6] B. Laufer, "A Chinese-Hebrew manuscript," *op. cit.*, p. 193-194.-Cf. title no. 108.

[7] Palladius, "Elucidations of Marco Polo's travels." (*Journ. N..C. Br. R.A S.*, new series v. 10. 1876, p. 38.-Cf. title no. 145.)

These three terms are phonetic renderings of European words for Jews. Particularly the term no. 8 is now commonly used.

| 11 如德亞 | Ju-te-ya |

This is the phonetic rendering for "Judea."

| 12 刀筋教 | Tao-chin-chiao |
| 13 挑筋教 | T'iao-chin-chiao |

This group of names signifies "the sect which extracts the sinews," alluding to prescriptions of slaughtering animals.[8]

| 14 藍帽(子)回回 | Lan-mao-(tzu)-hui-hui |

"Mohammedans with blue turbans."[9] This name was given to the Jews in order to distinguish them from the Mohammedans who used to wear other colours. According to Noyé this term is still being used around Sian.[5]

| 15 真回回 | Chen-hui-hui |

"True Mohammedans," popular contemporary name of the Kaifeng Jews.[10]

| 16 (回回)古教 | (Hui-hui) Ku-chiao |

Mailla mentioned the term "ku-kiao (古教), Loi ancienne" in his Description générale de la Chine." Later on, Milne called attention to the term Hui-hui ku-chiao, or "Old Mohammedan Religion."[12]

| 17 天竺教 | T'ien-chu-chiao |

"The religion which came from India," a term which was chosen because the first Jewish immigrants came either from or through India. It was dropped by the Jews during the persecutions of Christians, so that they might not be confused with the Catholics, and persecuted as

8   M. Broomhall, *Islam in China*; London, 1910, p.176.-Cf. title no. 28a.
9   S.M. Perlmann, *The history of the Jews in China*, 1913, p. 25. Cf. title no. 154a.
10 This term was furnished by the courtesy of Dr. Hellmut Wilhelm, Peking.
11 Mailla, *Histoire générale de la Chine*, v. 13. Paris, 1785, p. 616.—Cf. title no. 246.
12 W. C. Milne, *Real life in China*; 2nd ed., London, 1858, p. 411.—Cf. titles no. 131a and 251c.

such.[13]. The Catholics had adopted a name of almost the same sound, though of a different meaning and written in different characters: *T'ien-chu-chiao* (天主教).

    18   天教   *T'ien-chiao*

The term, "the religion of Heaven" was formerly used, but has been abandoned,

    19   教經教   *Chiao-ching-chiao*

"The religion which teaches the Scriptures."

    20   一賜樂業   *I-szu-le-yeh*

    21   以色列   *I-se-lieh*

Phonetic renderings of the word "Israel", of which only the first one is commonly used.

    22   希博萊   *Hsi-po-lai*

The phonetic rendering of the word "Hebrew".

    23   益廸士(的)   *Yi-ti-shih-(ti)*

Phonetic transcription of the word "Yiddish".

    24   輯安會   *Chi-an-hui*

    25   又稱   *Yu-ch'eng*

    26   猶殖民主義   *Yu-chih-min-chu-i*

    27   信本猶殖民主義者   *Hsing-feng-yu-chih-min-chu-i (-che)*

Modern terms for "Zionism" (nos. 23-25) and "Zionist" (no. 26).[14]

    28   *Mussauites*, "followers of Moses", derived from *Mussau*— Moses (*Mo-hsi* 摩西). This term is mentioned by Yule in the *Introductory Notice* to "The journey of Benedict Goes from Agra to Cathay."[15]

    The term *Wo-t'o*, (斡脫), according to some authors, applies to Jews (The character *kan* 幹 is often wrongly substituted for the character *wo*

---

13   W.A.P. Martin, *A cycle of Cathay*, 2nd. ed., London, 1897, p. 277; (title no. 125).– Cf. also Smith-Medhurst, *A mission of inquiry*, p. 449; (title no, 178).

14   *Webster's collegiate dictionary.* Shanghai, 1933. (英漢雙解.韋氏大學 字典.)

15   H. Yule, *Cathay and the way thither*; London, 1916, v.4, p. 175.—Cf. title no. 215e.

in the term *Wo-t'o)*. This thesis was apparently brought up and supported by Hung Chün (洪 鈞).[16] Other Chinese and Japanese author have taken over this view without questioning its accuracy.

Pelliot has mentioned the term twice in the *T'oung Pao*, explaining clearly its derivation. *Wo-t'o* is the Chinese equivalent for the Mongolian word *ortoq* and the Turkish word *ortaq*. This name applies mainly to "Mohammedan commercial organizations".[17] Pelliot further explains that the "Mongols entrust Mohammedans with the investment of their money, as they do not engage in trade themselves.[18]

The *Rev. P.* Antoine Mostaert, *C.I.C.M.*, Peking, the well-known expert on the Mongol language, kindly made available to th-author the meaning and derivation of the Mongol term *ortoq*. His letter of July 22nd, 1940, giving the detailed information in question is as follows:—

"Le mot turc *ortaq* est donné par le vocabulaire turco-arabe de Mahmoud Kachgari (fin du XIe siècle). Il y a le sens de 'Genosse'. Voir C. Brockelmann, *Mitteltirkischer Wortschatz nach Mahmūd Al-Kašүaris Divān Luүat At-Turk*, *Bibliotheca Orientalis Hungarica* I, Budapest-Leipzig, 1928, p.128."

"Le même *ortaq* existe encore à présent en turc osmanli, où il a conservé le même sens de 'compagnon'. Dans une note de la page 907 de sa *Grammaire de la langue turque (osmanli)*, J. Deny écrit: *ortaq* signifie aussi 1) (chez les écrivains de l'histoire mongole) 'marchand' 2) 'chacune des femmes d'un même mari.'"

---

[16] Hung Chün (*hao* Wen-Ching 文 卿), born in Soochow in 1839, passed the imperial examinations with the highest honours (*chuang yüan* 狀 元) at the age of thirty years. After having served in the civil service he became in 1888 Chinese envoy to Germany, where he resided, being simultaneously accredited to Russia, Austria and the Netherlands. In 1890 he was recalled to assume the post of Secretary of State in the War Ministry. This position he held to the time of his death in 1893.

[17] Paul Pelliot: "Notes sur le 'Turkestan' de M. W. Barthold." (*T'oung Pao*, Leyden. 1930. v. 27, p. 33, fn. 1.) "Dans les textes chinois de l'époque mongole, on trouve souvent la mention d'une catégorie de gens appelés 斡 脱 *wo-t'o* (altéré dans bien des cas en 斡 股 *Kan-to*) . . . *wo-t'o* représente une prononciation *ortoq* de *ortaq*, nom connu des associations commerciales qui étaient organisées surtout par les Musulmans."

[18] Paul Pelliot: *Sao-houa, Sauүa, Sauүal, Saguate.* (*T'oung Pao*, Leyden. v. 32, 1936, p. 232 (end of footnote 4 from p. 231.) " ... les mongols ne se livrent pas aux commerce, mais confient leur argent aux Musulmans pour le faire fructifier (c'est le système connu des *wo-t'o*, turc *ortaq* V mo. *ortoq*) ... "

"Ce mot *ortaq* a passé en mongol et il se rencontre en mongol médiéval sous la
même forme et avec le même sens de 'compagnon'. Voir N. Poppe, Mon-
golskii Slovar' Mukaddimat Al-Adab, Moscou-Leningrad, 1938, p. 271a."

"Dans un document mongol datant de la fin du XIVe siècle et conservé dans
le Hua-i-i-yü 華夷譯語 (IIb, f. 4v.), on rencontre l'expression *bedzirged
orto'ud*, qui dans la traduction interlinéare est rendue par les mots 商 賈 *Shang-
ku*. Le mot *bedzirged* est le pluriel d'un mot **bedzirgen* emprunté au turc. Cf. le
mot turc *bezirgān* 'marchand' dans N. Poppe, *op. cit.*, pp. 158, 246, 302). Quant
à *orto'ud*, c'est un pluriel de forme mongole du mot *ortoγ*, laquelle forme *ortoγ*
sort de **ortaγ* par labialisation de la voyelle *a* sous l'influence de la voyelle de la
première syllabe."

"Notre mot est resté vivant jusqu'à présent chez les Mongols Kalmouks qui
lui donnent le sens de 'Gemeinschaft,Teilnehmer' (G. J. Ramstedt, *Kalmückisches
Wörterbuch*, Helsinki, 1935, p.290a.)"

"Quant au mongol écrit, quoique le dictionnaire de Kovalevskii ignore le
mot, nous le trouvons dans le *Dictionnaire mongol-japonais* de Suzue et Shimonaga
où il est traduit par 'association' et écrit *ortoq*."

It is not surprising that Jews have frequently been confused with
Mohammedans in Chinese popular opinion. The Jews who originated
from Persia were related in customs and theological terminology to the
Mohammedan minority. Particularly, however, they had in common
the abstinence from pork. This was the more conspicuous as pork represents the main meat diet of the Chinese population.

In the popular belief the Jews were apparently taken for another
Mohammedan sect, as is indicated by the nomenclature. The Jews
were called *Lan-mao Hui-hui* 藍帽回回 or "Mohammedans with the
blue turban" (cf. term nc. 14) and *Hui-hui Ku-chiao* 回回古教 or "Old
Mohammedan Religion" (cf. term no. 16). They are still called *Chen
Hui-hui* 真回回 (cf. term no. 15) in Kaifeng. The Jesuit report of 1770,
"Mémoire sur les Juifs établis en China"[19]) points in the same direction:

"Les Chinois appellent les juifs qui demeurent parmi eux Hoaihoai
(回 伫). Ce surnom leur est commun avec les mahométans.'

Another factor apt to confuse the issue has been that during the
Yüan dynasty and at other times many of the alleged "Jews" were
presumably more or less Judaized Asiatic tribes. This has been claimed

---

[19] See *Lettres édifiantes*, Panthéon littéraire, v.4, p. 141; cf. title no. 231.

by A.H. Godbey in his *The Lost Tribes, A Myth* (cf. title no. 78) According to him many Central Asiatic tribes nominally became Jews; *i.e.*, they limited themselves to the adoption of a few customs or of some war cries. This view, if true, would also explain the fact that in spite of persistent rumours of the presence of numerous Jewish tribes it has never been possible to obtain any tangible proof.

ATTITUDE OF THE CHINESE PEOPLE
TOWARDS THE JEWS

The treatment of the Jews in China has always been fair and impartial, at no time has there been any discrimination against them. What Perlmann wrote in 1913 concerning the traditional tolerant attitude of the Chinese people, still holds true:—[20]

"I must add ... in justice to the old civilized Chinese nation, that the Jews in China have never had to complain of intolerance ; they were never under exceptional laws ; they were never persecuted or despised for this religion. They always enjoyed full rights like the Chinese."

---

[20] S. M. Perlmann, *The history of the Jews in China*, London, 1913, p. 37.— Cf. title no. 153.

BIBLIOGRAPHY

1   Adler, Elkan N.: ["Supplement to explanations to prayers by Neubauer."] (*Jewish Quarterly Review*. 1897, v. 10, p. 624.)

Reference to prayers obtained by the Chinese emissaries of the Bishop of Victoria in 1850; (see title no. 178). Dr. Neubauer had previously written explanations in the *Jewish Quarterly Review*; (see title no. 142).

Ur 2   Adler, Elkan N.: "A Jewish merchant in China at the beginning of the tenth century." Vienna, 1933, (Abhandlungen zur Erinnerung an Hirsch Perez Chajes. The Alexander Kohut Memorial Foundation. p. 1-5.)

This article refers presumably to the merchant Sulaiman. (See title no. 86.)

Cor 3   Adler, Marcus [N.]: "The Jews of China." 1900, 4 p. Lecture; from the "Jewish Chronicle," June 22, 1900.

4a Adler, Marcus N[athan]: "Chinese Jews". (*The Jewish Quarterly Review*, London. 13:49. October, 1900, p. 18-41; with 3 illustrations.) Reprinted by Horace Hart, Printer to the University, Oxford, 1900. 24 p.

"A lecture delivered at the Jews' College Literary Society, Queen Square House, London, June 17, 1900."

After a brief historical introduction, based on the reports of the early Jesuits, the author gives an abstract of the stone inscription of 1489, and translations of the inscriptions dating from 1512 and 1663.

Accepting the inscription of 1489 as genuine, Adler writes: "It is supposed that the settlement took place soon after the year 34

A.C.", after the Babylonian persecutions. He goes on to say:
"Others hold that the settlement took place thirty-five years later,
after the fall of Jerusalem. It is quite possible that the Jewish
colony in China may be of even older date. Having regard to
the fact that the trade route of ancient times from China and India
was not exclusively maritime, but crossed the steppes and highlands
of Central Asia, and then passed through Media, Mesopotamia
and Syria, it is not at all impossible that sections of the ten tribes
of Israel may have found their way to China, as we believe they
did find their way to Cochin China." (p. 23.) Later he again
expresses this opinion: ".... there is nothing to show that the
ancient congregations in China were not descended from the ten
lost tribes." (p. 35.)

He also accepts the erroneous view that the allusion in Isa. xlix.12
to "the land of Sinim" refers to China. (p. 24.)

Pages 25 to 30 contain a detailed description of the interior and
exterior of the synagogue, including three drawings prepared by
Father Domenge. It is also mentioned that the synagogue was
rebuilt in 1279, 1489, at the beginning of the 17th century and in
1653.

Pages 31 to 41 describe the efforts of Westerners to establish
contacts with the Jewish community of Kaifeng. Pages 33 to 53
represent a digression, being an examination of the scriptures of the
community.

While the various visits to the Kaifeng community have been
reported in several publications, the written communications are less
well-known. Hence, Adler is quoted as follows: "I found
among the MSS. in the British Museum an elaborate letter written
in elegant Hebrew by the Haham Isaac, the son of the well-known
David Nieto, dated Adar 1,5520, that is, the year 1760 (B.
M. additional MSS. 29868), in which, in the name of the

London Jewish Community he affectionately addressed his brethren
dwelling in the furthermost East, imploring them to tell him as to
their condition and their origin.   He subjoins a list of questions
which he asks them to answer.   Appended to this document is a
letter, unsigned, addressed by the writer at the request of his
friend, Mr. David Salamons, to a member of the East India Company, asking him for his good offices in getting the letter delivered
to the Jewish community in China."   (Cf title no. 231.)

"My brother, Elkan Adler, has called my attention to a book
written originally in Hebrew by a Morocco Rabbi—Moses Edrehi
by name—which was translated into English and published in
1836.   Nieto's letter is given in full, and Edrehi states 'an answer
to the letter was received, and it was couched in the Chinese and
Hebrew languages.'   The original was placed in the museum at
the India House.   Edrehi says he could not find it.   I regret to
say I have had no better success."   (p. 31.)

Another letter was written by James Finn (1842), who subsequently
became British Consul at Jerusalem.   He did not receive a reply
until 1870.   (p. 31-32; cf. title no. 65.)

Further data are given concerning the visits to Kaifeng of J L.
Liebermann (1867) and Dennis J. Mills (1891), and of a visit to
Honan by the German Colonel Lehmann, who met some Jews.
(p. 37-38.)

The remaining pages contain a reproduction of further correspondence, as evidence of a renewed effort on the part of
foreign Jews to get into contact with the Kaifeng community.
The concluding letter, dated March 13, 1900 (5660 A. M.), is
signed by S. J. Solomon, David Ezekiel Abraham, and forty-four
other members of the Jewish community in Shanghai.   This Hebrew letter was sent, with a Chinese translation (prepared by Dr.
Jedkins of the I. M. Customs), to Kaifeng.   It offered the Kaifeng
community its help and implored them "not to part with the scrolls

(of the Law) still left'' to them, and also requested them to send two or three men for questioning, with an offer to pay all their expenses. These men eventually were sent.

In spite of its historical shortcomings, which were generally shared at that time, this article offers a reliable account of the events leading to the renewed rescue activities of Jewish circles up to June, 1900. In particular, the sections dealing with the correspondence of foreign Jews with the Kaifeng community contain information not found elsewhere.

4b Adler, Marcus N.: *Die Juden China.* Berlin, 1900.

4c Adler, Marcus N.: *Hayehudim Be'China.* Meturgam me'anglith al yedei Elhanan Segal. Vilna, (5661) 1901. (Hebrew translation). 36p.

Adler, Marcus N.: *The Jews in China.* Translated from the English by Elhanan Segal. Vilna, 1901. 36p.

Translations of the above article.

RA 5 Alexander, J.: *The Jews.* London, 1870. p. 111 f.

Ur 6 Andree, Richard: *Volkskunde der Juden.* Bielefeld, 1881. p. 244-248.

Critical summary of the history of the Chinese Jews. Several sources, not mentioned elsewhere, are quoted in this place.

Cor 7 Annaud, A.S.: "The Jewish colony." (*London and China Telegraph*, Supp. Oct. 31, 1893, p.2.)

8a Bainbridge, Oliver: "Chinese Jews." (*The National Geographic Magazine*, Washington. 18:10. October, 1907. p 621-632; with 7 illustrations.)

8b [Bainbridge, Oliver]: "Les Juifs Chinois." (*A travers le Monde*, Paris. vol. 14, 1908, p. 280.)
French translation of the above title.

[34]

9 Balfour, Frederic Henry: *Waifs and strays from the Far East.* London—Shanghai. 1876. Ch. XIX, p. 202-208: "Chinese Jews."

The author fully accepts the view that the Jews came to China during the reign of the Chou dynasty (1122-249 B. C.). As proof of his contention he produces analogies between Chinese and Jewish legends. He first refers to the claim of the memorial tablets "that the mythical Chinese hero P'an-ku Shih 盤古氏 is identical with Adam." He then continues: " . . . we find in some old books the story of a woman who was turned into a statue while fleeing with her family, because she looked back: of the descent of manna; of the Sun being stopped in its course by a General to complete a victory, and of a rock producing water upon being smitten with a stick." These and similar traditions were supposedly brought to China by Jews, and later became incorporated into the ancient Chinese literature.

About the contemporary conditions of the Jews he says: "There are colonies of Jews at Hangchow, Soochow, and elsewhere, possessing, or having possessed, many precious relics of their ancient ritual. The Soochow Jews have, we are informed, received much generosity from their wealthy co-religionists, the Sassoons." (p. 204-205.)

The last section contains in part the report of Dr. W.A.P. Martin on his visit to the Jewish community of Kaifeng. (p. 205-208.) (Cf. titles no. 124-126.)

10 Ball, J. Dyer: *Things Chinese.* 5th ed., rev. by E. Chalmers Werner. Shanghai, 1925. p. 307-308. "Jews". (4th ed. appeared in 1903).

Copies of Hebrew MSS. were obtained from the Kaifeng community. They were deposited in "institutions, such as the City

Hall Library in Hongkong, the British Museum, and the Bodleian." It is assumed that the Jews entered China during the 7th century A. D.

11 Ball, James Dyer: *The Celestial and his religions: or the religious aspect of China*; being a series of lectures on the religions of the Chinese. Hongkong, 1906. (Kelly & Walsh.) Lecture VI, p. 159-180: "A remnant of the scattered race." In his account the author mentions the first historical reference to the Jews (1352 A.D.), when they were asked to join the forces of the declining Mongol dynasty. (p. 152.) This statement is, however, inaccurate. References to the Jews during the Yüan dynasty are to be found in 1329, 1340 and 1354. He then reports on Semmedo's information, received in Nanking from a Mohammedan. (p. 157.) Towards the end he mentions Bishop Schereschewsky's visit to Kaifeng (p. 178.)

Cor 12 Barrow, John W.: "On a Hebrew Ms. of the Pentateuch, from the Jewish Congregation at Kai-fung-fu in China," by Mr. John W. Barrow of New York; presented by Dr. Martin Communication to the *American Oriental Society*, May, 1869, *Journal*, 9:2, p. liii.)
" . . . In the 26th Chapter of Davidson's "Biblical Criticism" (ed. 1866, pp. 366-370), reference is made to the collation of another synagogue roll from the same source, with similar results. Dr. Lee in the "Prolegomena in Biblia Polyglotta Londinensia Minora," gives extracts from Koegler's 'Notitiae S.S. Bibliorum Judaeorum in Imperio Sinensi' (Halle, 1805) in which the Kai-fung-fu manuscripts are discussed "

13 Bartoli, S J., Daniello, *Delle Opere del Padre Danie'lo Bartoli della Compagnia di Gesu*. Turin, 1825. v 16, book 2. no 201, p. 386-389 "Abboccamento d'un Giudeo Letterato di Caifûn col P. Ricci: e dell'avvenuto fra essi."

no. 202, p. 389-390. "De' Giudei nella Cina: dove, e quando venutivi."

no. 205, p. 393-395. "Lettera del P. Ricci a' Cristiani antichi, e a' Giudei di Caifùn, senza niun frutto."

The facts in the above sections are based upon the information supplied by Ricci. Bartoli misinterpreted him blatantly in one instance, as may be seen from the following quotations and their English translations: —

Bartoli, v. 16, p. 394. "Era costui per età presso a decrepito, e sì indiscreto co' sudditi, e, fosse zelo o natura, sì rigido ne' comandi, che sentiva del tiranno più che del Sacerdote: massimamente gravandoli sotto pena dell' anima, a non mangiare altre carni, che de gli animali vittimati, o uccisi per le sole sue mani: al che fare sì conduceva sì di rado, che ne arrabbiavano della fame "

He (the rabbi of Kaifeng) was on account of his age almost decrepit and so inconsiderate of his flock, and by zeal or by nature so severe in his commands that he appeared to be more of a tyrant than a priest. He especially prohibited them under the penalty of losing their souls from eating any other meat than that of the animals sacrificed, or killed by his hands alone. This, however, he did so seldom that they became enraged on account of hunger.

Ricci, v. 2, p 473. "E sopratutto questo si doleva delle obbligationi che l'archisinagogo gli poneva, come di non mangiare niente di carne che non fosse di animale ammazzato per sua mano, dicendo che quivi a Pacchino, se avessero voluto guardar questo, sarebbono morti di fame."

And especially he (Ngai) complained of the restrictions which the rabbi placed on them, such as not eating any meat of animals which had not been killed by his own hand, saying that here in Peking, if they had wished to abide by this regulation, they would have died of hunger.

[37]

14 Basnage, Jacob Christian: *The history of the Jews from Jesus
    Christ to the present time* . . . . being a supplement and
    continuation of the History of Josephus. Translated into
    English by Tho. Taylor, A. M., London, 1708.

"T'is pretended farther that the ten Tribes appear, and make a
figure in China.   The Jew we have spoken of, and who, being
deceived by the Jesuit Raci, worship'd the Virgin, maintain'd that
there were at Pequin ten or twelve Families of Israelites and
a Synagogue which had cost them ten Thousand Crowns to repair.
He asserted, that they had been settl'd in this Province about five
hundred Years, and that they religiously preserv'd one of the Five
Books of Moses, which he call'd the Sepher Thora.   He could
not read Hebrew, having neglected the Study of it in his youth;
by which negligence, he was excluded from the Offices and
Government of the Synagogue, which his Brother exercis'd because he understood the Language, but he repeated the Stories of
the Old Testament, particularly those of Abraham, Judith and
Esther.   He added, that there were in the Capital of the Province
of Chequiam, a great many Synagogues, and Israelite Families;
for they give themselves that Name, because being the Posterity
of the ten Tribes, they knew not that of the Jews.   This account
has two things true in it, one, that there are in China, some Jewish
Families; the other, that they have there some secret Synagogue.
There are also two things false, one, the Antiquity this Israelite
pretended to.   And indeed who could depend upon the sincerity
of this Israelite who was ignorant of what related to the Ancient
History of his Nation?   The other Falsity is that those who
might have pass'd into China for Traffick, made a considerable
part of the ten Tribes and the Title of Israelites, which this Jew
gave 'em, was sufficient to prove it."   (Reprinted in S Mendelssohn, *The Jews of Asia*, p. 159-160; cf. title no. 239).

15 Benjamin of Tudela: *Travels of Rabbi Benjamin, son of Jonah,
    of Tudela*: *through Europe, 'Asia and Africa; from the
    ancient kingdom of Navarre, to the frontiers of China.*—
    Faithfully translated from the original Hebrew; and enriched
    with a dissertation and notes . . . . . . by the Rev. B. Gerrans.
    London, 1783.

p. 102, 125, 127-128, fn. 1. Tibet (Tuboth or Thibeth) mentioned.

p. 143-144. China (*Zin*) mentioned; fairy tale description of how
to get there. Cf. also fn. 9 on. p. 143.
The first edition of the *Travels* was printed in Hebrew at Con-
stantinople as early as 1543. Up to 1811, sixteen editions in
various languages were published. Since then numerous further
editions have appeared. The first Latin translation by Benoit
Arian Montan was issued in 1575. Another Latin translation,
with the Hebrew text in the margin, was published in 1663 by
the emperor Constantin.

Cordier has listed the most important editions in his *Bibliotheca
Sinica*, v. 3. 2nd ed. 1906-1907, col. 1953-1955. There he
has also reproduced the French translation of the passage concerning
China (col. 1954) from the *Recueil* of Bergeron, 1735, I, col.
55-56.

16 Benjamin, Israel Josef (Benjamin II): *Acht Jahre in Asien und
    Afrika. Von 1846 bis 1855* . . . . . . Mit vergl. Notizen aus
    Benjamin de Tudela. . . . . . Hannover, 1858. (Publ. by the
    author) p. 156-158 and 160-163.

The author went to Canton, where he heard of the "Havaists,"
people who lived near the Yellow River. They were believed to
be Jews. Health reasons compelled the author to leave China so
that he could not make personal investigations.

[39]

The French letter of the Grand-Rabbi Aaron Arnauld of Strasbourg (dated Nov. 13, 1855), with an extract from a letter by his nephew, is also reproduced. In this letter the information concerning the Jews in China is summarized. The writer mentioned the Hebrew MSS. in the hands of English missionaries, claiming that they had been taken away from Kaifeng under false pretenses and that the Jewish community refused to sell them.

The last part contains the reprint of an article which had appeared in the *Zeitung für Norddeutschland* on March 1, 1858, evening issue. It refers to the visit of the two Chinese emissaries who were sent to Kaifeng in 1850 (cf. title no. 178).

17 Berger, Philippe: "Jewish manuscript." (*T'oung Pao*, Leyden. Ser. 2, v. 11, 1910. p. 709-710.)

Jewish MS. found by the Pelliot mission and the Hebrew-Persian MS. found by Stein.

18 Berger, Ph[ilippe] et M[oïse] Schwab: "Le plus ancien manuscrit hébreu." (*Journal Asiatique*, Paris. 11ème ser., v. 2. July-August, 1913. p. 139-175.)

Detailed philological analysis of the Hebrew MS. brought back by the Pelliot mission. The MS. was communicated to the Académie des Inscriptions et Belles-Lettres at its session on July 1, 1910 (Cf. Comptes rendus des séances, 1910, p 317-318.) The authors conclude that this document is the oldest Hebrew MS., dating it between the VIIIth and IXth centuries. It contains the prayer of a traveller for protection. One line in the text is damaged through folding and almost lost, and no date or signature is given. The MS. is supposed to be very similar to that found by Sir Aurel Stein. In the first part the historical development of the Hebrew is explained and the style of the text is compared to other early literature. Next the text of the version, its corrected (rectified) Hebrew transcription and translation are given, followed by detailed comments on each line.

19 Berthel, E. M.: "Chinese Hebrews." (North-China Daily News, Shanghai May 22, 1924 p. 4, col. 1-3.)

In reply to the article "Chinese Hebrews" in the N. C. D. N. of May 19, 1924.

20 Berthel, E. M.: "The Jewish colony of Honan." Personal experiences of the Israelitish remnant in Kaifengfu: Two ancient tablets and the story they tell. (dated May 19, 1924). (North China Herald, Shanghai. v. 151, no. 2965. June 7, 1924, p. 371, col. 1-3.)

In reply to two articles which appeared in the North-China Daily News on May 14 and 19, 1924.

21 Berthelot, Ph.: "Notes sur les résultats scientifiques d'une mission diplomatique en Chine." (Bulletin de l'Ecole Française d'Extrème-Orient. Hanoi, 1905. v. 5, p. 412-414. III. "La colonie juive de K'ai-fong et les stèles de la synagogue." Communication faite à l'Académie des Inscriptions et Belles-Lettres le 17 mars 1905. (Extrait des Comptes-rendus).

The author had the opportunity to stay in Kaifeng, to study the two steles and to talk to the heads of the six then remaining families. He says that according to the oldest inscription of 1489 the Jews had come to China during the Sung dynasty; i.e., between 960 and 1126. "MM. Chavannes et Pelliot ont accepté ces dates et estiment que, venant de l'Inde, ces juifs avaient nécessairement pris la route de mer. Cette opinion est relativement nouvelle, car les sinologues ont souvent fait venir les juifs en Chine par voie de terre dès le début de l'ère chrétienne; leur historiographe, le P. Tobar, dans son volume des Variétés sinologiques, cherche a concilier les deux thèses en supposant que deux colonies sont venues en Chine à des époques différentes, l'une sous les Han, l'autre sous les Song." "Quoi qu'il en soit, l'examen des stèles juives actuellement existantes révèle plusieurs particularités dignes d'interêt et inquiètantes au

[41]

point de vue de leur ancienneté. . . . Sur le rebord de droite de la mare . . . se dresse une grande stèle chinoise posée sur un dé de pierre grossièrement orné et haut de Om50.   La stèle est couverte de caractères sur ses deux faces: un relevé attentif, les reproductions du P. Tobar sous les yeux, m'a prouvé que sur la face antérieure de la stèle était gravé l'inscription de 1512, et, sur la face postérieure, l'inscription de 1489:   ce fait est d'autant plus surprenant que les auteurs, depuis les maîtres indigènes délégués en 1850 à K'ai-fong-fou par une société religieuse de Londres, ont toujours présenté les deux inscriptions comme distinctes, allant jusqu'à indiquer que l'une des stèles se trouvait dans la maison de l'un des Juifs dans une cuisine, et l'autre près des lieux d'aisance. . . . J'ai pris moi-même les estampages qui, comparés à ceux publiés par le P. Tobar, sont identiques, présentant les mèmes trous, les mèmes caractères manquants, les mêmes brisures de la pierre: il a publié une photolithographie de l'inscription de 1512, comme provenant d'un décalque pris par des Jésuites au XVIIIe siècle, et de celle de 1489, comme prise récemment par des // envoyés des missionaires italiens de Ho-nan.   La stèle actuelle n'a pas l'air ancien, et le Juif chinois qui m'accompagnait me dit qu'elle datait de 70 ans environ, et de l'époque de la destruction de la synagogue."   (p. 412-413.)

"Sur la côté gauche de la mare se dresse une seconde stèle presque illisible: quelques caractères déchiffrables indiquent sa date (1679) et son titre: "Inscription lapidaire contenant l'histoire de la salle des ancêtres"; elle a été longtemps conservée dans une salle obscure de la maison du Juif Tchao et n'avait pas été signalé jusqu'ici par les voyageurs sur l'emplacement de la synagogue: c'est en effet en mars 1904 seulement, quelques mois avant mon arrivée, qu'un ingénieur americain, M. Jenks, venu pour étudier les mines d'argent du Ho-nan, s'adressa au vice-roi pour le prier de faire sortir la stèle qui fut placé au jour et appuyée contre le mur extérieur de

la maison où elle était enfermée; elle se trouve ainsi sur le bord de
la mare."

"Quant à la quatrième inscription signalée par les auteurs, celle de
1663, que le P. Brucker avait indiquée comme figurant sur une
stèle distincte, il ne m'a pas été possible d'en retrouver la trace:
les Juifs affirment qu'il n'existe pas d'autre stèle que les deux
élevées sur le terrain de la synagogue . . . "

"J'ai rapporté longuement . . .ces quelques constatations, confirmées
par les estampages que j'ai pris, pour indiquer exactement ce qui
subsiste des documents du passé, mais sans songer à contester
l'authenticité mêmes des stèles de 1489 et 1512, puisque M.
Devéria avait retrouvé à la Bibliothèque nationale une copie ancienne
de la première inscription. Peut-être la stèle actuelle n'est-elle
qu'une reproduction des inscriptions du XVe et du XVIe siècles."

The author had the opportunity of meeting the 72 members of the
community. He remarked about them: "Les traits caractéris-
tiques de la race ne sont pas marqués chez eux, ainsi que l'indiquent
mes photographies; d'ailleurs une telle constatation serait peu
probante, car le type israélite accentué est très répandu en Chine."
(p. 413.) This passage is followed by further interesting details
concerning the members of various Jewish families.

22 Бирман, М.: (Еврейская Жизнь, Харбин. но. 15-17, 1924.)
    Birman, M.: ["Jews in China."] (*Hebrew Life*, Harbin, nos.
    15-17; 1924.)

23 Birman, M.: ["The Jews in China."] (*Der Tog*, New York.
    December 26-31, 1926.) (In Yiddish.)

24 Bleyhöffer, B.: ,,Chinesische Juden." (*Ostasiatische Rundschau*,
    Hamburg. 14:20. October 16, 1933. p. 449-451.)
    One of the many summaries of the history of the Chinese Jews.
    The inaccurate details were checked and pointed out by Jäger;
    (see title no. 96).

[43]

25 Borchardt, Paul: "L'itinéraire de Rabbi Benjamin de Tudèle en Chine." (*T'oung Pao*, Leyden. Série II; vol. 23, 1924. p. 31-35.)

The author has analyzed critically the travel route of Rabbi Benjamin and considers the report to be reliable.

26 Bridgman, E. C.: "Jews in China: Notices of those in the East by Josephus, Peritsol, Benjamin of Tudela, Manasseh, and the Jesuits." (*The Chinese Repository*, Victoria, Hongkong. 3:8. August, 1834. p. 172-175.)

*27 Bronne, L.: *The story of the Jews.* Transl. by Ni Hsiuchang. Shanghai, 1939.—Cf. title no. 254.
倪秀章譯：猶太民族史，上海，民國二十八年出版.（商務印書館）

28a Broomhall, Marshall: *Islam in China.* London, 1910.
p. 31 and 50. Alleged massacre of more than 120,000 Arabs, Jews and Christians at Canton in 878.
p. 50, fn. 2. First arrival of Jews in China.
p. 55. Kublai Khan's attitude towards the Jewish religion.
p. 175-176. Chinese nomenclature of the Jews.
p. 222. Merging of the Jewish with the Chinese population in Honan and North Anwhei.

28b Broomhall, Marshall (editor): *The Chinese Empire: A general and missionary survey.* London, (preface 1907).
Guinness, C. I. M., G. Whitfield: "The province of Honan." p. 159. The Jewish community in Honan.
Appendix II, p 428-432. Extract of: *A lecture delivered by Marcus N. Adler,* etc , (see title no. 4a).

29 Brown, H. F.: "Are the Jews God's people?" (*Shih Chao Yüeh Pao*, Shanghai. 35:5. May 1, 1940. p. 18-21; with 5 ill. inside the front cover and 1 ill. in the text)
博郎：談猶太人.（時兆月報,上海,第三十五卷五期,第十八至二十一頁.一九四〇年五月一日）
The article has a purely theological character.

Cor 30 Brot[t]ier, Gabriel: *C. Cornelii Taciti opera recognovit ... Gabriel Brotier*, Paris, 1771. v. 3, p. 567-580: "De Judaeis Sinensibus."

"The dissertation on this subject is omitted in the later editions." Extracts from the letters by the Catholic missionaries Gozani, Domenge and Gaubil.
Cf. also "Mémoire sur les Juifs établis en Chine" (title no. 230d).

Cor 31 Buxton, L. H. Dudley: *China, the land aud the people* Oxford, 1929. (Clarendon Press.) p. 52.
"But the type (of the Jews) to a certain extent still survives."

Fi 32 Calmet: *Calmet's Dictionary of the Bible.* London, 1823. v. 4, p. 251.

33 Chang Hsiang-wen (Wei-hsi): "A visit to the stone inscriptions in Kaifeng." *(Nan Yüan Manuscript Series* —The China Geographical Society. Peiping, 1935. v. 4, p 8-9.
張柏文 (薇西): 大梁訪碑記. (南園叢稿. 北平. 中國地學會鉛印本, 民國二十四年, 卷四8-9頁.)

34 Chang Hsing-lang (Liang-ch'en): "Early intercourse between China and the Jews" *(Historical facts concerning early contacts between China and the West.* Catholic University Series no. 1, Peiping, 1930. v. 4. 2nd article, 40 p, separate pagination.)
張星烺(亮塵): 古代中國與猶太之交通. (中西交通史料匯篇. 北平. 民國十九年. 輔仁大學叢書第一種, 第四冊 40頁.)

The article represents a careful study of the problem. It begins with an analysis of the foreign and Chinese sources and proceeds to give a detailed account of the history of the Kaifeng Jewish community during the Ming and Ch'ing dynasties. Close attention has been paid to the various stone inscriptions. Pages 4 to

20 are devoted to the *Wo-to* 斡脫 who since the time of
Hung Chün (1897) have been erroneously identified as Jews.
(Cf. *Introduction*). The author has accepted this view in his
article, although recently he has changed his opinion on the subject. The author himself points out, in his article, the fact that
in the *Yüan Tien Chang* 元典章 three persons with distinctly
Mohammedan names mentioned in a document were referred
to as Jews. He thinks that they might have been Moham-
medanized Jews. (p. 10.) Cf. also suppl. vol. 6, p. 584.

35 Chao Ming-i (transl.): *In the dark*. Shanghai, 1933 (or ear-
    lier). (Modern Book Store.)
    Translation of four plays.
    趙明堃：在黑暗中，上海．(現代書局．)

36 Ch'en Chien: "The world crisis in relation to the secret plans of
    the Jews." (*Chung Kuo Kung Lun*, Peking. February, 1940.
    2:5, p. 13-24.)
    Section 9, p. 23-24. "The Jews and the China Incident." 猶太
    與中日事變之關係．
    陳諓：世界動亂與猶太之國際陰謀．(中國公論．北京）

37 Ch'en Yüan and Yeh Han: *Study on the Israelitic community in
    Kaifeng. — Commentaries on the stone inscription of the
    Israelites*. Shanghai. 1st ed , 1923; 3rd ed., 1925. (Com-
    mercial Press) 69 p.

    The booklet is out of print. On the pages 1-18 the three stone
    inscriptions of 1489, 1512 and 1663 are reproduced. The main
    article by Ch'en Yüan is to be found on the pages 19-63. Com-
    mentaries on two stone inscriptions are given by Yeh Han on the
    pages 65-69.

    陳垣，葉瀚 (同撰)：開封一賜樂業教考．上海 民國十二年．(商務印書館).

38 Ch'iao-yüeh-se, Ssu-ch'a-lao-tzu: "Jewish refugees." (*Kuo I*, Nanking. 1:2. February 15, 1940. p. 65.)

Three reproductions of wood-cuts by a German: "Kitchen," "Service for the dead" and "Bachelors' quarters".

(德) 喬約惡. 斯查勞终: 猶太難民. (國藝, 南京. 第一卷第二期; 民國二十九年二月十五日; 第六十五頁.)

39 Christie, Dugald (ed. by his wife): *Thirty years in Moukden, 1883-1913*. London, 1914. (Constable & Co, Ltd.) p. 166-167. Story of a Russian Jew, resident of London, who was compelled, while on a visit to Russia, to join the Russian forces during the Russo-Japanese war in 1904.

Cor 40 [Cibot, *S.J.*, Pierre-Martial]: "Mémoire sur les Juifs de la Chine." Pékin, 28 oct. 1770.

"Mémoire inédit du P. Cibot publie par le P. Sommervogel dans les *Etudes religieuses*, 2le année, 5 Sér., XII, nov. 1877, pp. 748-758. Voir également dans les *Mémoires concernant les Chinois*, XV, pp. 52-58: "Digression sur le tems où les Juifs ont passé en Chine." Par le P. Cibot."

" . . . Le P. Cibot y résume ce qu'on a fait pour se procurer, mais en vain, une copie de la Bible des Juifs chinois, et ce qu'on pourrait fair pour y réussir." (Pfister, *Notices biographiques et bibliographiques*, v. 2, p. 899, no. 53.)

41 Cibot, *S J.*, Pierre-Martial: "Parallèlle des moeurs et usages des Chinois avec les moeurs et usages décrits dans le livre d'Esther." (*Mémoires concernant l'histoire, les sciences . . . . des Chinois; par les missionnaires de Pékin*. Paris, v. 14, 1789, p. 309-516; v. 15, 1791, p. 1-207.)

The author compared the literary meaning and the historical implications of the passages concerned in the book of Esther with the customs of the Chinese.

[47]

42 Clark, Grover: *The Great Wall Crumbles.* New York, 1935. (The MacMillan Co.) p. 17, 25 and 80.
The author mentions the early Jewish settlers in China, stating that they came from the Mediterranean region in the Han dynasty.

* 43 Cohn, Israel: *Journal of a Jewish traveller.* London, 1925. p. 115-122.

44 Coleridge, *S.J.*, Henry James: *The life and letters of St. Francis Xavier.* 4th ed, London, 1935. p. 378-379.
Xavier mentioned in his letter of May 10, 1546, to Rome that he had heard in Malacca from a Portuguese that in the middle of China there were people who abstained from swine's flesh and kept many festival days in a very solemn manner. The Portuguese had heard the story from a Chinese friend and Xavier wondered whether these people were Christians observing Jewish rites, or Jews.

Cor 45 [Cordier, Henri] signed *Old Mortality:* "The Jews in China." *(Shanghai Budget,* September 13, 1873.)

Cor 46 [Cordier, Henri], signed *Kao:* "Les Juifs en Chine." *(Le Gaulois,* vendredi. 7 fev. 1890.)
"Article signé KAO (Henri Cordier) en réponse à un article du même titre, du Général Tcheng Ki-tong, paru dans le même journal, le dimanche, 2 fév. 1890."
"L'article de Tcheng a été réimprimé, pp. 219-229, de son vol. intitulé *Mon Pays,* 1892."

Cor 47 Cordier, Henri: "Les Juifs en Chine." *(L'Anthropologie,* no. 5. Sept.-Oct. 1890, pp. 547-551.)
Reprinted from *Le Gaulois* (cf. title no. 46) with a bibliography.

Cor 48 Cordier, Henri: *Les Juifs en Chine.* Paris, 1891. (Léopold Cerf.) 14 p.

[48]

"A Monsieur *Joseph Derenbourg* en l'honneur de son 80e anniversaire, 21 août 1891.—Tiré à 100 ex. dont deux sur papier du Japon,"

49 Cordier, Henri: *Bibliotheca Sinica*. Dictionnaire bibliographique des ouvrages relatifs à l'empire chinois. 2nd rev. and enlarged ed. Paris, 1904-1907.
vol, 2, col. 1353-1360, "Judaisme"; col. 931, letter of Nov. 5, 1704 from Kaifeng by Gozani; col. 936, ,,Mémoire sur les Juifs établis en Chine".
vol. 3, col. 1953-1955, "Benjamin de Tudèle."
vol. 4, col. 3136, ,,Judaisme."
vol. 5 (supplément tome 1, 1924), col. 3779-3780, ,.Judaisme."
All the important titles on the Chinese Jews have been included in the present bibliography, but a number of insignificant references have been omitted.

50 Couling, Samuel: *The Encyclopaedia Sinica*. Shanghai, 1917.
p. 47, article: "Benjamin of Tudela."
p. 262, article: "Jews in China."

RA 51 Crawfurd: ["Jews in China."] (*Journ. Ethn. Soc.* New Ser. v. 3, p. 106.)
The author stated that the Chinese Jews did not differ from the indigenous population and that "they are only Jews by religion."

Ur 52 Delitzsch, Franz: *Zur Geschichte der jüdischen Poesie vom Abschluss der heiligen Schriften des Alten Bundes bis auf die neueste Zeit.* Leipzig, 1836. (Tauchnitz) p. 58-62.
Details about the history, customs and language of the Kaifeng Jews; largely based upon information furnished by the early Catholic missionaries.

53 Diaz, *S.J.*, Emmanuel (Manuel); surnommé l'ancien: "Relatione dell' anno 1619; Macao: 7.XII.1619." (In: *Relatione*

delle cose piu notabili scritte ne gli anni 1619, 1620 and 1621.
Dalla Cina. Al molto Rev in Christo P. Mutio Vitelleschi
Preposito Generale della Compagnia di Giesu. In Roma,
per l'Erede di Bartolomeo Zannetti. M.DC.XXIV. Con
licenza de' Superiori. p. 3-61.)
A report concerning the most noteworthy events written in the
years 1619, 1620 and 1621 from China to the Very Rev. P.
Mutius Vitelleschi, General of the Society of Jesus. Rome,
1624. (Bartolomeo Zannetti Heirs.)

The contribution of Father Diaz contains references to the Jews
in Honan on p. 38-39 and p. 41-42. In 1619, Father Longobardi
and Friar Giovanni Fernandez went to Honan, where the number
of Jews was estimated to be about 10,000. This number, however, was on the decrease.
References to the above work are to be found in Rob. Streit,
O.M.I. Bibliotheca Missionum, Aachen, 1929, v. 5, p. 755,
no. 2124, and p. 734-736, no. 2110. Cf. also Henri Cordier,
Bibliotheca Sinica. Paris, 1885, v. 2, col. 1648; and
Sommervogel, *Bibliothéque,* Brussels-Paris, 1892, v. 3, col. 43.
The attention of the compiler was drawn to this title through the
courtesy of the *R.P.* Henri Bernard, *S.J.*

54 Du Halde, J[ean] B[aptiste]: *Description géographique,*
    historique . . . . de l'empire de la Chine. Hague, 1736. v. 3,
    p. 77-78.
"Juifs en fort petit nombre à la Chine."

55 Duvigneau, C.M., A.-B.: *Les Sinim d'Isaie seraient-ils les*
    Chinois? Peiping, 1936. (Imprimerie des Lazaristes.) For
    private circulation only. (IV) + 64 p.

Based on notes taken while reading the literature concerned. The
problem was raised repeatedly in the *Bull. Cathol.* The printing
was done in order to try out a new linotype machine which had

been bought by the Lazarist printing office at the time. (Cf. preface, May 15, 1936.)

After a thorough study of the problem and of the literature concerned the author firmly rejects the possibility that the prophecy of Isaiah (XLXIX, 12), mentioning *Sinim*, refers to China. One must be grateful to the author for having so painstakingly examined the theological literature on the subject and analyzing the problem so clearly. This pamphlet should be helpful in refuting the wishful assumption that the Jews arrived in China prior to our era. No historical facts are available at the present time to support that belief.

56 Duyvendak, J.J.L.: "Early Chinese studies in Holland." *T'oung Pao*, Leyden. 32:5. April, 1936. p. 329-340.)
Record of the early conception of the relation between the Chinese and Hebrew languages. This theory has been proved to be without foundation.

57 Edkins, Joseph: *China's place in philology*. London, 1871.
    p. 72. The Semitic language system younger than the Chinese one.
    p. 90-91. Semitic 'relative" compared with the Chinese "equivalent".
    p. 253-254. Some Semitic and Chinese similarities.
    p. 390-391. Characteristics: Chinese, *order*; Semitic, *life*.

58 Edkins, *Rev.* Joseph: *Religion in China*. London, 1878, revised edition 1893. (Trübner.) p. 181-183. "The Jewish community of Kaifeng."
Edkins conversed in Shanghai with three Jews from Kaifeng. One of them was "a literary graduate." According to the author the first Jewish immigration into China took place between 200 B.C. and 220 A.D.

[51]

Mu 59 Eichhorn: *Einleitung in das alte Testament.* 1st ed. Leipzig
1781. pt. 2, p. 131-136.

Brief abstract of the publication by Koegler; (see title no.
101 a-b)

60a Ezra, Edward Isaac: "Chinese Jews." (*The East of Asia
Magazine,* Shanghai; "North-China Herald" Office. v. 1,
1902. p. 278-296; with 10 illustrations.)

The author accepts the view that the Jews entered China during
the first century A.D. by way of Khorasan and Samarkand.
However, he objects to the view that the Chinese Jews were
descended form the Ten Lost Tribes. The author then mentions
the Arab travellers Abu Zayd and Ibn Batuta, Ricci and the
early Catholic visitors of the Kaifeng community. He continues
with a complete account of the foreign visitors during the second
half of the 19th century, up to 1902.

The author gives a description of the synagogue, of the literature
and inscriptions in Kaifeng. He reports on the efforts of the
foreign Jews on behalf of the Kaifeng community. In April,
1901, a Kaifeng Jew went to Shanghai with his son. Another
delegation of eight Jews arrived there in March, 1902. They
were received in the house of the author, who questioned them.
The information obtained was embodied in a report to the Rescue
Society. The planned establishment of a Jewish Mission and
the rebuilding of the synagogue, however, never materialized.

The article is very valuable for its pictures and for the full account
of the visits to Kaifeng by foreigners between 1850 and 1902.
The illustrations of the old site of the synagogue, of the last com-
memorative stone and of the Jewish visitors from Kaifeng are
particularly useful. They have been frequently reproduced by
other authors without due acknowledgment.

60b Ezra, Edward Isaac: „Chinesische Juden." (*Földr. Közlem.*, Budapest. vol. 33, 1905. p. 1-12.)
Hungarian translation of the above title.

61 Ezra, Edward Isaac: *Chinese Jews*. Shanghai, 1925.—
Cf. title no. 180.

62 Fang Hao: "The Jewish community of Chekiang province." (*Kuo Fêng*, Nanking, 8:9-10, October, 1936. p. 84-86.)

Summary of the subject; largely based upon foreign sources.
方豪：浙江之猶太教(國風，南京. 第八卷 第九期至十期,第84-86 頁，民國二十五年，十月.)

63 Finn, James: *The Jews in China, their synagogue, their scriptures their history*, &c. London, 1843. 86 p.

The author, who lived for many years in China and later was British Consul in Jerusalem, lists in his booklets 19 titles concerning the subject. He also mentions the rather unfriendly attitude of some of the early Jesuit missionaries who were charged by Rome with the investigation of the matter. Julius Aleni visited the synagogue in 1613, as the first foreigner.

The pamphlet is carefully written and contains some interesting information. Most of it can now be obtained from other sources, after almost 100 years have expired and many additional facts have been brought to light.

64 [Finn, James]: "The Jews in China." (*The Chinese Repository*, Victoria, Hongkong, 14:7. July, 1845. p. 305-334 and 14:8. August, 1845. p. 388-395.)
Summary of the book by Finn; (see title no 63).

[53]

Shu 65 Finn, James: *The Orphan Colony of the Jews in China.*
London, 1872. (Nisbet & Co.)

66 Foster, Arnold: *Christian progress in China.* London,
1889. (Religious Tract Society.) Appendix, p. 247,
255. "The Jews in China."

Taken from: "*Williams, Middle Kingdom* 4th ed., vol.
II, pp. 287-288." (Cf. titles no. 202-203.)

"The Orphan Colony of Jews in China, by James Finn,
M. R. A. S. London (Nisbet), 1872, p. 52-59 and
67-69, condensed and in part re-written, and p. 98-
104." (Cf. title no 53.)

67 Froger, François (Ernst Arthur Voretzsch ed.) *Relation
du premier voyage des François à la Chine en 1698.
1699 et 1700 sur le vaisseau "L'Amphitrite".*
Leipzig, 1926. (Verlag der Asia Major.) p. 140.

"*Juifs a la Chine.*—Je sçay qu'on a trouué quelques juifs
a la Chine et il n'y a pas longtemps qu'il s'en trouua
un a Tçi-nin-tchéou dans la province de Chan-toun que
entendant parler de Jesus Christ, il est vray, dit il que
nos Peres l'ont crucifié, a quoy il ajouta le Blaspheme:
mais je n'ai jamais veu ny oüy dire que personne eut veu
des Liures Hebreux ny traduits de l'Hebreu entre leurs
mains. Au reste je ne sçay si ces Juifs étoient naturels
de la Chine, et s'il y en a ils sont en si petit nombre
qu'il n'y a pas d'aparence qu'ils ayent pû conseruer leurs
liures."

68a Fuchs, Walter: "The Chinese Jews of K'aifengfu."
(*T'ien Hsia*, Shanghai. 5:1. August, 1937. p. 27-
40. With 8 plates of the Temple, of the Scriptures
and of a Chinese Jew with his son.

The article represents a good summary of the subject, the illustrations are the same as those in the article by Ezra and in the *Jewish Encyclopedia* (see titles no. 60a and 102).

68b Fuchs, Walter: "Chinese Jews of K'aifengfu." (*China Digest*, Shanghai, May, 1939. p. 16-20.).

Condensed from *T'ien Hsia.*—Cf. title no. 68a.

Cor 69 G., J.W.: "On the Jews in Khai-fung-fu." (*Journal of the American Oriental Society.* 3:1. p. 235 f.)

"On lit p. 240 de cet article: '*The Illustrated London. News* of Dec. 13, 1851, contains a statement of the preceding facts, together with portraits of Chaou Wan-kwei and Chaou Kin-ching, two Israelites brought from Khai-fung-fu to Shanghai, where the former is studying Hebrew with an English Missionary.' "

70 Gaillard, S. J., Louis: *Croix et swastika.* Shanghai. 1st ed., 1893; 2nd ed, 1904. (Variétés sinologiques, no. 3.) Second part, ch. 3, §1, p. 134-139.

The information in this section is mainly based on the *Lettres édifiantes* (see title no. 230). The author accepts the view that the Jews came to China during the Han dynasty. Those at Sian claim to be descendants of the tribe of Aser.

71 Garnier, A.J.: *Chinese versions of the Bible.* Shanghai, 1934. (Christian Literature Society for China.)

This pamphlet contains details about the Chinese translations of the Old Testament by Catholics and Protestants.

The activities of Bishop Schereschewsky, who was of Jewish descent, are appraised on p. 40, 41-43, 47, 49-50.

[55]

賈立言, 馮雪冰: 漢文聖經譯本小史　上海, 1934. (鹿學會.)
Chinese translation of the above title by A. J. Garnier
and H.P. Feng.

Cor　72　Gaster, M.: "Note on the inscriptions of the Chinese
Jews." (*Babylonian and Oriental Record.* 6:12'
June, 1893. p. 288.)

Fi　　73　Gaubil, *S. J.*, Antoine: *Traité de la chronologie
chinoise.* Publ. by de Sacy. Paris, 1814. p. 264.

Cor　74a Glover, A.K.: "The tablet inscriptions of the Chinese
Jews discovered at Kai-fung Fu (China), in 1850."
(*Babylonian and Oriental Record:*—
　　　　　5:6, June, 1891, p. 138-141;
　　　　　5:7, July, 1891, p. 161-164;
　　　　　5:8, August, 1891, p. 179-182;
　　　　　6:9, March, 1893, p. 209-213.)

Cor　74b　Glover, *Rev.* A. Kingsley: *The tablet inscriptions of
the Jews in China.*—Being the records of the Jews
of China discovered in the year 1850, in the city of
Kai-Fung Fu, on the Hoang-ho river, by the agents of
the London Missionary Society at Shanghai, China.
—Reprinted from the author's papers in the
"Babylonian and Oriental Record", 1891, with
additional notes and comments by Prof. Dr. de
Lacouperie. Appleton, Wis, 22 p.

"Suivie de: Appendix on the Commerce of the An-
cients, Showing the routes of Jewish dispersion in the
Far East.—Reprinted from the author's papers in
"Menorah Monthly" (1888), 14 p."

Cor　74c Glover. *Rev.* A, Kingsley: "The tablet inscription of
the Jews in China," (*Biblia.* v. 7. October, 1894.)

[56]

"M. Glover a réédité les inscriptions de 1489 et 1512 avec la traduction du Dr. Medhurst dans la revue juive *Menorah* de 1888 à 1891, et la première de ces deux inscriptions avec la traduction du même Dr, Medhurst dans la revue *Transaction of the Meriden Scientific Association*, vol. 7, 1895; p. 13-31." (Tobar, *Insc. Juives*, p. 35 note.)

Cor   74d   Glover, A. Kingsley: "Tablet of 1488. A table recording the rebuilding of the Temple of Truth and Purity." (*Biblia, A Monthly Journal of Oriental Research*, Meriden, Conn. 8:4. July, 1895. p. 91-107.)

Cf. *Biblia.* October, 1894,

Cor   75   Glover, *Rev.* A. Kingsley: "Testimony of the Chinese Jews to the date of the exodus." (*Biblia.* 7:6. September 6, 1894.)

Cor   76   Glover, *Rev,* A. Kingsley: *Jewish-Chinese papers.* Appleton, Wis. [1894].

"The Chinese discovery of America.—The Jews of India.—The manuscripts of the Jews of India and China.—The tablet inscriptions of the Jews of China— with commentary.—The commercial activity of the ancients in the East."

"Articles parus dans *Menorah* et dans.le *Magazine of American History.*"

JE   77   Glover, A. Kingsley: *The Jews of the Extreme Eastern Diaspora. (The Menorah,* IV-VI; *The Babylonian and Oriental Records,* 1893, V-VI.)

[57]

78   Godbey, Allen H.:   *The lost tribes, a myth.*   Durham
     North Carolina, 1930.   (Duke University Press.)

Ch. 13. p. 368-425.   "Persian, Turkoman, Mongol, and
Chinese Jews."   (Illustrations contain a plate: "Chinese
Jews of Kaifeng" from the *Jewish* Encyclopedia.)

The author has expressed his views as follows: "It seems
that we must recognize several origins of Judaism in
China, and that we must begin by recognizing Israelite
trade with China as early as the eighth century B.C."
(p. 369, cf. also p. 373.)   "The Old Testament....
gives us ample justification for a host of reminiscences of
ancient Israelite activities in Central Asia. Since the
Jewish Khazar dynasty adopted Jewish names, we recognize that this records the retirement into Chinese Tartary
of the Khazars who were driven from Russia early in the
tenth century of our era; and in the stories of the immense
spread of the ten tribes in Central Asia we recognize that
the Judaization of the population, which had begun fifteen
hundred years earlier, was probably increased by Khazar
official activity." (p. 371.)

The author mentions Wolff's findings on the Khiva Jews,
part of whom had emigrated to China. (Cf. title no.
205a-c). He also points out that 'Wood mentions a
nameless Jewish traveller who had spent years about the
Aral and Caspian and in China gathering records of 'lost
tribes', (*Journey to the source of the Oxus,* pp. 280 ff.)
and he heard of some in Kashmir and Thibet." (p. 371.)

The author has come to the conclusion that Stein's discovery of the Judaeo-Persian fragment, dated by Margoliouth 708 A. D., "proves that the Jewish trader spoke
Persian and that he was probably a Judaized Persian;

that his correspondent used the same language and script."
About the Hebrew fragment found by Pelliot in Turkestan which, according to Schwab, dates from the eighth
century, the author says: "It is a simple Selichah or
devotional sheet, composed of passages from the Psalms
and prophets. But it is written on paper,—which at that
time was made only in China. This old junkheap where
the fragment was found , therefore, tells us that Jewish
merchants from China were using that caravan route
then."

The author further mentions that "the Spanish Jewish
traveller, Soliman of Andalusia (875-900 A.D.) records
that he found in all the large cities of China Jews who
understood Hebrew, and who received him hospitably."
(p. 397.) Apparently this Soliman or Sulaiman was,
however, a Mohammedan. (Cf. titles no. 18, 79, 86,
and 170.)

79 Goeje, J. de -: "Un roman géographique." (T'oung
       Pao, Leyden. v. 3.   March, 1892. p 94-97.)
    The author rejects Schwab's view that Sulaiman, the
    merchant, was a Spanish Jew, and not an Arab. (Cf.
    titles no. 18, 78, 86, and 170.)
    "Je présume qu'il (Schwab, the compiler) n'a inventé
    la fiction du voyageur juif que pour exciter l a curiosité et
    pour inviter à la lecture." (p. 97.)

80 Goodrich, L[uther] C[arrington], and C H. Fenn:
       A syllabus of the Chinese civilization and culture.
       2nd ed, New York, 1934. (The China Society of
       America, Inc.)
    p. 22, XII, 7. "Jewish contacts under the T'ang."
    The bibliography contains two titles referring to the Jews.

[59]

81 Graves, *Rev.* Rosewell Hobart (Chi Hao-pi): *Geo-graphy of Judea* (Palestine). Shanghai, 1882. (I Chih Shu Hui Fa Shou..) (In Chinese.) 137 leaves.

紀好丕: 猶太國地理志, 光緒八年. (益智書會發售.)

Written as a tool for theological studies.

82 Grosier, *Abbé* : *Description générale de la Chine.* Paris, 1787. v. 2, Ch. 7, p. 246-258. "Juifs établis à la Chine." The chapter deals with the Kaifeng Jewish community. For complete details cf. Mailla, title no 246.

Cor 83 Guignes, Christian Louis Joseph de—: "Observations sur plusieurs familles juives établies anciennement à la Chine." [Lues le 15 janvier 1790.] (*Mém. de Litt. tires des registres de L'Ac. des Insc. et Belles-Lettres,* v 48, 1808, pp. 763-770.)

84 Guignes, Christian Louis Joseph de—: *Voyages à Péking. Manille et l'Ile de France, faits dans l'intervalle de années 1784 à 1801.* Paris, 1808. v. 2, p. 334. "Juifs".

A few general remarks from Catholic sources. Cf. also by the same author title no. 83.

85 [Hardoon, S. A.]: *Mr. Hardoon, in commemoration.* Shanghai, 1931. 16 vols., bound in 12. (Chung Kuo Fang Ku Yin Shu Chü; for private circulation only.)

v. 1. Pictures.—v. 2. Picture inscriptions.—v. 3. Government decorations.—v. 4. Character and private life.—v. 5. Career.—v. 6. Gravestone inscription.—v. 7. Funeral pictures.—v. 8. Obituary scrolls.—v. 9. Funeral speeches.—v. 10. Scroll with funeral odes.--v·

[60]

11. Funeral scrolls with classical quotations. —v.12.
Family scrolls.—v.13. Scrolls by Chi Chüeh-mi
(姬觉彌).—v. 14. Scrolls asked for from outsiders. —
v. 15. Silver anniversary of the wedding and birthday.
—v. 16. Funeral reception.

Hardoon, born in 1851 in the Iraq, went in 1873 to
Hongkong and during the following year to Shanghai.
He married a Buddhist Chinese girl. His enormous
fortune was largely acquired through opium trade. At
the time of his death, in 1931, he was British subject.
哈同先生榮哀錄　上海, 民國二十年. 中國仿古印書局. 仿宋聚珍
版印本, 十六卷, 十二冊一函.

86　Hasan ibn Yazid, Abu Zaid, al Sirafi (Sulaiman, the merchant):

a　Ferrand, Gabriel (translator): *Voyage du marchand arabe
Sulaymân en Inde et en Chine*, rédigé en 851, suivi
de remarques. Paris, 1922.
p. 89. The Great Khan showed a picture of Moses to
the Arab traveller.
Translation from the Arabic. Cf. also review by Paul
Pelliot in *T'oung Pao*, v. 21, 1922. p. 399 ff.

b　Reinaud, Joseph Toussaint (translator): *Relations de
voyages faits par les Arabes et les Persans dans l'Inde
et à la Chine, dans le IXe siecle de l'ère chretienne.*
Texte arabe imprimé en 1811 par les soins de feu
Langlès . . . . . . traduction francaise . . . . . . par M. Reinaud. Paris, 1845.
v. 1, p. 84. The Great Khan showed the picture of
Moses to the Arab traveller.
The original Arabic text is contained in the work.

c　Renaudot, Eusebius (translator): *Anciennes relations des
Indes et de la Chine de deux voyageurs mahométans*

qui y allèrent dans le IXe siècle, traduites de l'Arabe par Eusèbe Renaudot.   Paris, 1718.

Ancient accounts of India and China by two Moham-medan travellers, who went to those parts in the 9th century. (English translation of Renaudot's French version.) p. 183-199.   An enquiry concerning the Jews discovered in China.

d 劉半農 (劉復), 劉小蕙: 蘇萊曼東遊記. 上海 1937.
　　(中華書局.) 134 p.

In part translated into Chinese by Liu Pan-nung (*alias* Liu Fu) and Liu Hsiao-hui.

Schwab (title no. 170) and Godbey (title no. 78) claim that Sulaiman was a Spanish Jew.   This assumption is refuted rightly, it appears, by de Goeje.

This book is the composite work of two writers.   The first author is unknown.   He wrote in 851, quoting a Sulaiman who had been to China.   The second part was written by Abu Zaid of Siraf.   There exist three French versions of the work; the earliest of these has been translated into English.

Cor 87 Hirsch, Henri: *Les Juifs de la Chine.* Paris, 1844. 24 p. Extracts from the *Archives israélites de France,* from January to May, 1844.

88 Hirsch, Leo: „Die Juden von Kai-Fung-Fu." (*C.V.-Zeitung,* Berlin.   June 30, 1938. p. 8.) .
Brief summary of the Jewish history in Kaifeng.   The plan of the old synagogue was reproduced from the *Philo-Lexikon.*

89 Hodgkin, H.M.: "Work amongst European refugees." (*Chinese Recorder,* Shanghai.   February, 1940. 71:2 p. 81-85.)

[62]

'The article deals mainly with contemporary Jewish refugees in Shanghai.

90 Hsü Tsung-tse: "A general discussion of the Kaifeng Jewish community." (*Revue Catholique*, Shanghai. 25:4. January, 1936. p. 194-202.)

The photograph of a Hebrew MS is reproduced as a frontispiece of the issue. The information is based upon foreign sources.

徐宗澤: 開封猶太敎概論. (聖教雜誌, 上海. 民國二十五年 四月. 第二十五卷, 第四期, 194-202 頁.)

91 Huang I: "A study on the Chinese Jews." (*Wén Hua Chien Shê*, Shanghai. 1:4. January, 1935. p. 74-78.)

黃義: 中國猶太人考. (文化建設. 上海, 民國二十四年一月. 第一卷 第四期, 74-78頁.)

92 Hung Chün: *Supplement to the translation of the history of the Yüan dynasty.* 1897. Section 29: "A survey on the various religious sects during the Yüan dynasty." The leaves 1-3 deal with the Jews.

The full Chinese text concerning the Jews, together with its English translation is reprinted in the *Appendix* III. To Hung Chün is due the erroneous identification of the *Wo-t'o* 斡脫 as Jews. Hung's mistake can be traced throughout the related Chinese and Japanese literature. Concerning its proper interpretation cf. *Introduction*.

洪鈞: 元史譯文證補. 光緒二十三年. 第二十九卷 元世各教名考 第一至第三頁.

93 Hyamson, Albert M.: "China (Jews in)" (In: *Encyclopedia of Religion and Ethics*, ed. by J. Hastings New York—Edinburgh, 1910, v. 3, p. 556-560.)

The article represents a historical account of the Jews in China, with extracts from the stone inscriptions, etc.

Although the views about the date of arrival of the early
settlers are obsolete, the brief bibliography at the end
of the article is useful.

94 Ibn Battuta: *Travels in Asia and Africa. 1325-1354.*
Translated from the Arabic and selected by H.A.R.
Gibb. London. 1929. p. 293. Jews in Hangchow.
Cf. also Yule-Cordier; (see title no. 215).

Cor   95 Isaac, I.A.: *Short account of the Calcutta Jews, with a
sketch of the Bene-Israels, the Cochin Jews, the Chinese
Jews, and the Black Jews of Abyssinia.* Calcutta, 1917,
5 pts.

96 Jäger, F.: ,,Zur Frage der chinesischen Juden." (*Ostasia-,
tische Rundschau*, Hamburg. 15:7. April 1, 1934. p.
160-164.)
Critical study on the history of the Chinese Jews, made in
reply to the inaccurate article by Bleyhöffer; (see title no.
24)
A Latin summary of the article was prepared by P.
Maurus, *O.F.M.*, Hungkialou. (*Digest of the Synodal
Commission*, Peiping. 8:7-8. July-August, 1935. p. 638-
645.)

JE   97 Katz Albert: "Jews in China." (*Israelitische Monatsschrift*, 1898, nos. 1-4.)

Shu   98a Katz, A[lbert]: *Die Juden in China.* Berlin, 1900 (Publ.
by the author.) 31 p.

Sk   98b Кац, А.: Евреи в Китае. Перевел с.нем. Лев Майзель.
С дополнениями переводчика и с планом синагоги
в Кай-Фун-Фу. Варшава, губ. тип., 1900. 37 стр.
Katz, A[lbert]: *The Jews in China.* Transl. from the
German by Lev Maizel; with annotations by the
translator and a plan of the synagogue in Kai-fung-fu.

[64]

Warsaw, 1900. 37 p.

"Historical outline and present condition of the Jews
in China."

Fi   99 Kennicott, Benjamin: *Biblia Hebraica.* Oxford, 1776.
         "Dissertatio generalis", p. 65.

100 Ko Sui-ch'eng: "The scattering of the Jewish people and
         their national movement." (*The Eastern Miscellany,*
         Shanghai, 26:20. October 25, 1929. p. 113-123.)

The author has attempted to analyze the conditions of the
Jews throughout the world. The information contained in
the article is quite unreliable. This is sufficiently demons-
trated by the fact that the author has accepted as truth
and reproduced in part the notorious fake of the ,,Protokolle
der Weisen von Zion" ("*Zionist Protocols*").

A brief section is devoted to the Jews in China (p. 116-
117). Their number is given as between 70,000 and 80,000
(1929). One-tenth of this figure would probably have been
nearer the truth at that time.

葛綏成: 猶太人口的分佈和其民族運動的概況. (東方雜誌. 上海.
第二十六卷第二十號第一一三至一二三頁.)

101a Kögler, *S.J.*, Ignaz: "Notitiae SS. Bibliorum Judaeorum
         in Imperio Sinensi." (*Journal zur Kunstgeschichte
         und allgemeinen Litteratur,* Nürnberg. pt. 7, 1779;
         p. 240-252.—Supplement in pt. 9, 1780; p. 81-92.)

101b Kögler, *S. J.*, Ignaz: *Ignatii Koegleri S.J. Notitiae SS.
         Bibliorum Judaeorum in Imperio Sinensi.* 2nd enlarged
         ed. with additions by C.T. de Murr. Halle, Saale,
         1805.(I.C. Hendel) 80 p.

Reprinted in Murr, *Geschichte der Juden;* (see title
no. 140). Cf. also Murr's supplement (title no. 141)

[65]

102 [Kohler, Kaufmann — and Henri Cordier]: "China [Jews in]." (*The Jewish Encyclopedia.* 1st ed., 1903,. 3rd [American] ed. New York and London, 1912. v. 4, p. 33-38; with three illustrations.)

The article represents a careful study of the subject and contains all the information which was available at the time. The bibliography at the end of the article is more extensive than any of the previous ones.

103 Kroker, Bruno: "The Chinese Jews of Kai-feng." (*The China Journal,* Shanghai. 29:3. September, 1938. p.141-146; with 6 p. of illustrations, reproduced from photographs by Harrison Forman.

Brief summary of the history of the Kaifeng Jews.

104 Krueger, Hans E.: „Kaifoeng, die alte chinesische Judenstadt." (*Ostasiatischer Lloyd,* Shanghai, February 19, 1938. p. 4.)

Brief account of the history of the Kaifeng Jewish community and their synagogue.

105 Kuan Pin: "The Jews of Kaifeng" (*History and Geography Weekly,* no. 100; supplement to the *Ta Kung Pao,* Tientsin. August 28, 1936. p. 11.)

Summary of the subject, based upon some Chinese and foreign sources.

關斌: 開封的猶太人. (史地周刊. 第一百期, 11 頁 大公報, 天津. 民國二十五年八月二十八日.

106 Kuwabara, Jitsuzo: *Collection of essays on oriental cultural history.* Tokyo. 1934.

p. 303-304 (cf. also p. 406). Attempt to prove the early presence of Jews in China from certain personal names.

p. 318-322. Jews in China. This section is largely based upon foreign sources.

桑原隲藏: 東洋文明史論叢. 東京 昭和九年. (弘文堂書局.)

Cor 107 Laufer, Berthold: ,,Zur Geschichte der. chinesischen
Juden " *Globus*, Braunschweig. 87:14. April 13,
190⁷. p. 245-247.)

This article represents the results of investigations made in
China in 1903. At that time the author had occasion to
meet several Chinese Jews. He laid his results before
the International Congress for the History of Religions
held at Basel, Switzerland, in September, 1904. His
findings were subsequently published.

108 Laufer, Berthold: *A Chinese-Hebrew manuscript, a new
source for the history of the Chinese Jews. (The
American Journal of Semitic Languages and Literature.*
46:3. April, 1930. p. 189-197.—Read at the meeting
of the American Oriental Society at Cambridge, April
3, 1929. Also reprinted for private circulation.)

The article is based upon a manuscript containing a register
of the Jewish congregation of Kaifeng, drawn up between
the years 1660 and 1670, giving first the names of male
individuals, then those of women, both in Hebrew and
Chinese. The manuscript is in the possession of the
Hebrew Union College of Cincinnati which owns a collection of Hebrew manuscripts originating from the Jews in
Kaifeng. The article is essential for any study on the
problem.

Cf. also review by A.C. Moule in the *T'oung Pao*,
Leyden. Ser. 2, v. 28, 1931. p. 125-128; and in the
same volume p. 176-177. Moule supplements some facts
concerning Ngai Tien, Ricci's informer.

109 Lehmann: "Jews in China." (*American Hebrew*, January 12, 1900; taken from the *Chicago Inter-Ocean*,
December 31, 1899.)

The article was written by Lehmann, a colonel in the German army stationed at Kiauchou, and not by J. J. Liebermann, as wrongly given. (Cf. M. N. Adler "Chinese Jews", p. 37-38, and 39; title no. 4a; and Mendelssohn, *The Jews of Asia*, p. 156; title no. 239.)

Cor   110   Lehmpful, H.:   „Eine jüdische Kolonie in China."(*Zeitschrift für Missionskunde,* Heidelberg. v. 18, 1903, p. 175-177.)

Cor   111   Lévy, Louis: "Les juifs en Chine." *(L'Univers siraélite.* 1901; no, 28, March 29; no. 29, April 5; no. 30, April 12.)

RA   112   Liebermann, J. L. "Jews in China."Report of the Anglo-Jewish Association for 1879; reprinted in *Jewish Chronicle,* London, July 11, 1879, and in *Israel's Watchman,* August, 1879, p. 248.)

"In July, 1867, a Jew, named J. L. Liebermann visited the city.   He wrote a long Hebrew letter of what he saw to his father in Bielitz, then in Austrian-Silesia. This letter was translated by Dr. Löwy, and appeared in the report of Anglo-Jewish Association for 1879." (M.N. Adler: "Chinese Jews", p. 37; cf. title no. 4a.)

Liebermann was the first European Jew to visit his Chinese co-religionists.   His "Notes" were published in the *North China Herald,* Shanghai, on October 3, 1879.

113   Löwenthal, Rudolf (羅文達):   "The Jewish press in China."   (*Nankai Social & Economic Quarterly,* Tientsin. 10:1. April, 1937. p. 104-113 and chart. —Reprinted with additions in the *Digest of the Synodal Commission,* Peiping. 10:7-8. July-August, 1937. p. 684-691.)

A second enlarged revision of the article has appeared in the book: *The religious periodical press in China* published under the auspices of the China Synodal Commission. Peking, 1940; p. 251-265.

According to the survey 36 Jewish periodicals in English German, Russian, and Yiddish were established in the three cities of Shanghai, Tientsin and Harbin. The oldest magazine was started in Shanghai in 1904.

114 Löwenthal. Rudolf (羅文達): "The Jews in China: A bibliography." (*The Yenching Journal of Social Studies*, Peking. 1:2. January, 1939. p. 256-291.)
The bibliography consists of 145 titles in various languages. These are supplemented by a historical introduction and a person and subject index.

JE 115 Lopez: *The Portuguese in Malabar.* Lisbon, 1898. p. 82.

116 Lowrie. *Rev.* W. M.: "On the fulfillment of the prophecy of Isaiah concerning the land of Sinim." *(The Chinese Repository*, Victoria, Hongkong. 13:9. September, 1844. p. 467- 469. "The Jews in China."
Theological interpretation about the time of arrival of the first Jews in China, which, according to the author, dates from 258 B. C. — Cf. also Noyé, title no. 143.

117 Lu Yen (transl.): *Collection of Jewish short stories* Shanghai, 1926. (Kai Ming Book Store.)
Stories by Sholom Alechem, I. L. Perez, D. Pinski.
魯彥：猶太小說集.海上 （開明書局.)

118 Lung Ta-chün: "The problem of Jewish immigration in China " (*Hsin Shih Chi*, Shanghai. 1:6. September 16, 1939.)

[69]

龍大均: 猶太人移居中國問題 (新世紀. 上海. 第一卷第六期 民國
二十八年九月六日.)

119 Ma   Li-se and Le Po-lang (Rrench authors); Chou Shou-
chüan (translator):   *The Jewish lamp.*   Shanghai. 1st
ed., 1917; 5th ed., 1928.   (The Chinese Book Store.
76 p.

瑪利瑟. 革勃朗著 ; 周瘦鵑譯: 猶太燈. 上海, 民國六年初版. 民國
十七年五版 (中華書局.)

This detective story of Sherlock Holmes has been translated
from the French into Chinese (Wen Yen). It had
become quite ·popular, as not less than five editions
appeared between 1917 and 1928.

120a MacGillivray, D.: "The orphan colony of Honan."
(The Chinese Recorder, Shanghai. 48:1. January,
1917. p. 37-42.)

Brief abstract of the history of the Kaifeng Jews and of
the visits by the Catholic and Protestant missionaries.
The author accepted the view that the Jews had come to
China 1,800 years ago.

120b MacGillivray, *Rev.* D.: "The Jews of Honan: A
tragic story of submergence. (A fresh study of the
stelae.)'' *(The Journal of the North-China Branch
of the Royal Asiatic Society,* Shanghai. v. 49, 1928.
p. 22-49; with 2 plans of the Kaifeng synagogue from
Tobar, *Inscriptions.)*

The article is devoted to the stone inscriptions of the former Kaifeng synagogue.

121a McLeod, N.: *Epitome to the ancient history of Japan,
including a guide book.* Nagasaki, 1875. p. 35-36.

121b McLeod, N.: *Illustrations to the epitome of the ancient history of Japan.* Tokyo, 1879.

121c McLeod, N.: *Korea and the ten lost tribes of Israel;* with Korean, Japanese and Israelitish illustrations. Yokohama-Tokyo, 1879. p. . .

The three books were printed for private circulation. The author, an early British missionary in Japan, made fantastic statements concerning the Ten Lost Tribes, whose descendants the Japanese were supposed to be. He likewise claimed that remnants of the Jews were scattered over China and Korea. A wild imagination has led the author to an incoherent theory and surprising historical distortions.

122 Mann, Erika and Klaus: *Escape to life.* Boston, 1939. (Houghton Mifflin Company.)
p. 219-222. "Jews in Shanghai" This section deals with Jewish refugees.

123 Margoliouth, D. S.—; with an introductory note by M.A Stein and communications from W. Bacher, A. E. Cowley, and J. Wiesner: "An early Judaeo-Persian document from Khotan in the Stein Collection, with other early Persian documents." (*The Journal of the Royal Asiatic Society of Great Britain and Ireland,* London, 1903. Article XXVI, p. 735-760, with a photographic reproduction of the document.)

The *Introductory Note* by Stein contains an account of the acquisition of the document. In it is also reproduced Wiesner's expert opinion on the antiquity and genuineness of the document. This report was dated May 23, 1903. It is followed by Margoliouth's explanations. He claims that the document is 200 years older than any other

[71]

Judaeo-Persian document as yet known and about 100 years older than any Persian document. Towards the end Cowley's observations on the palaeography of the document are given. Finally, the text is reproduced, together with the modern Hebrew transliteration, followed by the translation into English and by notes, part of which were furnished by Bacher. A photographic reproduction of the document (without pagination) concludes the article. The Persian document written in Hebrew characters, published by Margoliouth, was found on January 5, 1901, during Stein's archaeological exploration in Chinese Turkestan under the orders of the Goverment of India (1900-01). The document represents a mutilated letter, of which 37 lines have been partly recovered. According to its contents, style of writing, paper, etc., it has been dated 718 A. D. (Cf. also titles no. 136 and 182.)

124   Martin, W. A. P.:   "Account of an overland journey from Peking to Shanghai, made in February and March 1866." (*Journal of the North-China Branch of the Royal Asiatic Society*, Shanghai.   New series, No. III, December, 1866. Art. II, p. 26-39.

"Dr. Martin addressed the Society, describing his Journey, at a special meeting on the 29th of March.   He subsequently at the Society furnished this condensed statement for publication."

Section II, p. 30-33, contains the author's observations of the Jewish community at Kaifeng. At the time of his visit the Jewish population was estimated at from three to four hundred. "They were unable to trace their tribal pedigree; keep no register, and never on any occasion assemble together as one congregation." (p. 32.)

The article also contains an explanation of the reason the Jewish community of Kaifeng has been called the "orphan colony." It is the analogy of their position with a famous rock nearby. "Near the margin of the Poyang lake there stands a lofty rock, so peculiar and solitary that it is known by the name of the "little orphan." The adjacent shore is low and level and its kindred rocks are all on the opposite side of the Lake, whence it seems to have been torn away by some violent convulsion and planted immoveably in the bosom of the waters." (p. 33.)

Reprinted also in Martin's: *The Chinese, their education, philosophy, and letters.* New York, 1881. p. 287-306. "Account of a visit to the Jews in Honan, February, 1866."

125 Martin, W.A.P.: *A cycle of Cathay.* 2nd ed. New York Chicago-Toronto, 1897; 3rd. ed. 1900.
Ch. 4, p. 265-279. "Visit to a colony of Jews "
The author visited Kaifeng in 1866.

126 Martin, W.A. P,: "The Jewish monument at Kaifung-fu " *(Journal of the North-China Branch of the Royal-Asiatic Society,* Shanghai. v 37, 1906 p. 1-20.
The author describes his visit to the Kaifeng Jewish community in 1866. He found the community in a "deplorable condition."

The first eight pages of the article are devoted to historical considerations, while the remaining pages contain translations of the two stone inscriptions, dating from 1489 and 1512.

127 Menahem, M. Ben: "Mandschurei un die Jiden." *(Die jid. Emigracie,* Berlin, v. 5. 1929. p. 6-8.) (in Yiddish), "Manchuria and the Jews."

[73]

Shu 128 Menashe ben Israel: *Mikweh Israel.* Amsterdam. (5658) 1898. (in Hebrew).

        Menashe ben Israel: *Refuge of Israel.* Amsterdam. 1898. (1st ed.)

Cor 129 Michaelis, Johann David: *Orientalische und exegetische Bibliothek.* Frankfurt, 1771; pt. 5, p. 70; pt. 9, p. 40. 1780; pt. 15, no. 26, p. 25 ff, & no. 238.

        Brief abstract of the publication by Kögler; (see title no. 101 a-b).

      130 Milne. *Rev. W[illiam].*: "Notice of a seven months. residence in the city of Ningpo, from December 7th, 1842, to July 7th, 1843." *(The Chinese Repository,* Victoria, Hongkong. 13:2. February, 1844. p. 79.)

        Information concerning the Kaifeng Jews, solicited from a Kaifeng Mohammedan.

131a Milne, William C.: *Real life in China.* 2nd ed. London, 1858.

        Pt.4, ch. 2, p. 403-411, "Colony of Hebrews in the interior." With facsimile of a Hebrew MS.

131b Milne, William C.: *La vie réelle en Chine.* 2nd ed. Paris, 1860. Transl. by André Tasset from the English.

        Pt. 4, ch. 2, p. 341-348. "Colonie d'Hébreux à la Chine."

        This section is mainly based upon the findings of the Smith-Medhurst emissaries; (see title no. 178).

      132 Mishkovsky, Noiah: ,,*Ethiopie, Yiden in Afrike un Asie.* Chicago, 1936. Ch. 9, p. 131-160. ,,Di Yiden in Chine" fun mein Reise arum die Welt. (Yiddish in Hebrew type).

Mishkowsky, Noach (New York): *Ethyopia, the Jews in Asia and Africa.* Chicago, 1936. (Morris Ceshinsky, Publ. 2720 W. Division St.)

Ch. 9, p 131-160. "The Jews in China" from my trip around the world.

The author spent four years in Manchuria and Mongolia. He also went to Shanghai. During his stay in China he met two Chinese Jews on the Chinese Eastern Railway. They assured him that they were of Jewish descent, though they knew neither the Jewish rites, nor the Hebrew script. One of them, however, a sales agent for crockery, had marked his goods with Chinese characters, supposedly corresponding to the numbers of the Hebrew alphabet. The author met also a Chinese Jew (or a Jewish Chinese in the French Concession of Shanghai who served as attend) ant during the prayer meetings in the synagogue.

The author then summarized a lecture delivered by the "Marquis" Sze in 1931 before the Tientsin Jewish Club "Kunst", the results of which were also published in the local press. The lecture contained a number of apparently misleading and unsubstantiated facts: (1) About 40,000 Jews were allegedly killed during a pogrom in Canton- (Probably Sze refers to the rebellion lasting from 878 to 879, when many Chinese and 120,000 Jews, Christians and Mohammedans were killed in Canton. This massacre had not the character of a pogrom, and the figure concerning the Jews appears highly exaggerated.) (2) Sze claimed that the Jews had come to China around 200 B. C. from Persia via India. — (3) During the 17th century a Manchu emperor ordered that the Jews should be distributed throughout the 40 provinces, and that this order was complied with. — (4) Sze made vague references to Chinese literature mentioning the Jews, He also claimed that many temples without idols were a proof of their previous presence.

Finally, Mishkowsky gave an account of contemporary Jewish communities in Manchuria, for instance, in Mukden, Hailar and Harbin, and of others in Tientsin, Shanghai, Canton and Hongkong.

133 Möllendorff, P. G. and O. F. von—: *Manual of Chinese bibliography.* Shanghai, 1876. p. 221-222.
Titles no. 2952 to 2967; the section contains a few references, not mentioned elsewhere.

134 Möllendorff, P. G. von—: ,,Das Land Sinim." *(Monatsschrift für Geschichte und Wissenschaft des Judentums.* v, 38, 1894. p. 8-9.)

The Hebrew word *Sini* China or the Chinese (sing.) and *Sinim* the Chinese (plur.) (Jes. 49, 12) was formerly derived from the name of the feudal state of "Thsin" (秦). Victor von Strauss replaced it by the character 人 ("man or Chinese"), but the author rejects this suggestion.

135 Möllendorff, P. G. von—: ,,Die Juden in China." *(Monatsschrift für Geschichte und Wissenschaft des Judentums.* v. 39, 1895. p. 327-331.)

The author described the various visits to the Kaifeng Jewish community. The second part of the article contains the Hebrew transcription and the German translation (from an English translation) of the original Arabic report by a Jewish friend of the author. The report, dating from January 30, 1895, deals with the Jewish community in China. At that time there were 21 companies and about 175 Jews in China. They were merchants, dealing in yarn, cotton and opium, Their languages were Arabic, Hindustani and English. Their synagogue was ,situated on Foochow Street of the Shanghai settlement.

136 Moule, A.C.: *Christians in China before the year 1550* New York and Toronto, 1930. (Society for the Promotion of Christian Knowledge, London.)
p. 1-9. Well annotated summary of the early history of the Jews. p, 23, fn. 35; p. 76, 86, 119, 134, 201, 218, 221, 224, fn. 17; and 258, Jews in China are mentioned.
Indispensable for any critical study on the subject. The author mentions on p, 2, fn, 4 a mutilated Judaeo-Persian fragment found at Dan-dan-uiliq by Sir Aurel Stein and a little MS of the 9th century in square Hebrew letters which was found by Pelliot.

137 Mowrer, Edgar Ansel: *Mowrer in China.* Harmondsworth, Middlesex, 1938. (Penguin Special No. 14, Penguin Books Ltd.)
p. 93. "The Canadian Episcopal Cathedral, sheltering two priceless bronze tablets of ancient Chinese Jewry, had been ruined..." This statement must be corrected in so far as the church was damaged, but the stone (not "bronze" tablets previously had been brought into safety.
Cf. also Mowrer's: *The dragon wakes.* A report from China. New York, 1939. p. 99.

*138 Müller, F.W.K.: „Abklatsche der Inschriften aus der Synagoge von K'ai-fung-fu." *(Zeitschrift für Ethnologie*, Berlin. vol. 37, 1905. p. 438. (1/4 p.)

139 Münsterberg, Oskar: *Chinesische Kunstgeschichte.* 2nd unrevised edition. Esslingen a. N., 1924. p. 198-200;

with two illustrations, nos. 160 and 161 on p. 200 and 201.

A description of the Jewish synagogue at Kaifeng with its monuments, etc., based upon *The Jewish Encyclopædia* (title no. 102) and Yule, *The book of Ser Marco Polo* (title no. 156b). London, 1903, vol. 1, p. 346-347.

140   Murr, C. hristoph] G ottlieb' von — (editor): *Versuch einer Geschichte der Juden in China.* Nebst P. Ignaz Köglers Beschreibung ihrer heiligen Bücher in der Synagoge zu Kai-foug-fu. Halle, 1806. Anastatic reprint made in 1874. (J. C. Hendels Verlag) 77 p.

This booklet, which first appeared in 1806, was at that time the most complete account of the history of the Jews in China. It contains on the pages 5 to 12 a very useful bibliography; on pages 13 to 20 the history by the editor is to be found. On the pages 21 to 40 letters by the P. Gozani are reproduced. The third part on pages 41 to 56 consists of information gathered by the P. Ignaz Kögler, Superior of the Catholic Missions in China and Japan; (see title no. 101 a-b). On the pages 56 to 77 other authors have been quoted and the editor has furnished further commentaries.

According to the information, available at his time, Murr believed that the Jews had come to China in 217 B. C. The work was compiled in a scientific spir t and has helped clarify the facts. Though obsolete, the booklet is still an interesting historical document.

Mu 141   Murr, C. G. von — : "Nachtrag zu den Köglerischen Notitiis. "(New *Leipziger Journal*, Leipzig. pt. 1, 1793; p. 147-149. — Supplemented by some remarks of the Kanzleirat Olav Gerhard Tychsen, Rostock, in pt. 2, 1799; p, 303-308.)

Shu 142 Neubauer, A]dolf]: "Jews in China." *(Jewish Quar-*
terly Review, London. 8:29. October, 1895. p. 123-
139.)

Reference to prayers obtained by the Chinese emissaries of
Smith and Medhurst in 1850; (see title no. 178). Cf.
also the supplement to the explanations by Elkan N. Adler
(title no. 1).

143 Noyé, O. F. M., E.: "Les juifs en Chine." *(Le Bulletin*
Catholique de Pékin, Peiping.

22:267. November, 1935. p. 587-599;
22:268. December, 1935. p. 649-652;
23:269. January, 1936. p. 22-29;
23:270. February. 1936. p. 77-88.)

The author has come to the conclusions: (1) that the Jews
had trade with China at the time of King Solomon (1082-
975 B.C.); (2) that the passage in Isaiah: "Ecce isti de
longe venient, et ecce illi ab aquilone et mari, et isti de
terra australi" (49,12) refers to China; (3) that the Jews
came to China before 164 B.C.

Even if one does not agree with all the conclusions, the
abundance of facts which have been carefully compiled
and arranged make the article helpful for any study on
the subject.

144 Oko, Adolph S.: "Acquisition of Chinese-Hebrew MSS
by the Hebrew Union College, Cincinnati, Ohio."
(North-China Daily News, Shanghai, May 19, 1924,
p. 6, col. 8. cf. also "Hebrews in China" ib., May 14,
1924, p, 7, col. 4; and "Chinese Hebrews," May
22, 1924, p. 4, col. 1-3.)

Prof. Oko, librarian of the Hebrew Union College,
acquired the MSS which had formerly been in the possession of the London Society for promoting Christianity

among the Jews. Emissaries of this society had visited the Kaifeng Jewish community as early as 1850; (cf. title no. 178). The Kaifeng MSS were written in the Jewish-Persian dialect and bound in Chinese silk.

145 Palladius, *Archimandrite:* "Elucidations of Marco Polo's travels in North China drawn from Chinese sources." (*Journal of the North-China Branch of the Royal Asiatic Society*, Shanghai. New Ser. no. 10, 1876.) p. 38. First reference to Chinese Jews in Chinese documents.

"The Jews are mentioned for the first time in the *Yuen shi* under the year 1329.....Mention of them is made again under the year 1354....In both cases they are named 朮 忽 *Chu-hu* (Djuhud)."

146 Paravey; *Chevalier* de — (1787-1871): *Dissertation abrégée sur le nom antiqueet hiéroglyphique de la Judeé; ou, traditions conservées en Chine, sus (sic,* the compiler) *l'ancien pays de Tsin, pays qui fut celui des céréales et de la croix.* Paris, 1836. (Treuttel et Wurtz, et Th. Barrois, Libraires.) 27 p.; with two illustrations.

"Cet article est extrait du Numéro 70 des ANNALES DE PHILOSOPHIE CHRETIENNE, rédigées sous la direction de M. *A. Bonnelly,* de la Societé Asiatique de Paris."

The author starts with the assumption that the name of *Ta-tsin* 大秦 applies to the Syrians in Palestine and to Palestine itself. He then attempts to prove, with a considerable stretch of imagination, that China is a Jewish or Syrian colony.

Cor 147 Parker, Edward Harper: ["Chinese Jews."] (*The China Review,* Hongkong. 25:6. June-July, 1901, p. 300-301.)

148 Parker, Edward Harper: *China and religion.* London, 1905.

> p. 12. Taoist influence on the Jews.
>
> > p. 151. Jewish women were prohibited from marrying with their uncles — Jews were ordered to take part in the defence of the empire.
> >
> > Ch. 8, p. 164-177; cf. also p. 179. "The Jews"; summary of the history of the Jewish colony in Kaifeng.
>
> Cf. also review by Pelliot in the *Bulletin de L'Ecole Française d'Extrême-Orient,* Hanoi. v. 6, 1906, p. 413-414.

RA 149 Pégralb: "Jews in China." *(Bull. de la soc. de géogr.* October, 1869. p. 335.)
The author was pro-vicare of the Catholic mission in Honan province.

150 Pelliot, Paul: "Le juif Ngai, informateur du P. Mathieu Ricci." *(T'oung Pao,* Leyden. Ser. 2, v. 20, 1921. p. 32-39.)

The author identified the informer as the licentiate 艾山 Ngai T'ien.

Cor 151 Perlmann, S. M.: "The Jews in China." *North-China Herald,* Shanghai. January 2, 1909. p. 35-38.)

Cor 152 Perlmann, S. M.: *The Jews in China.* London, 1909. (I. Narodicsky Printer.) 24 p.
An abridgement of the "Jews in China" appeared in "The International", November, 1908.

153 Perlmann, S. M.: *Hassinim (The Chinese),* Chinese life, manners and customs....With an Appendix. *The Jews in China,* being a complete record of their past history

and present conditions in the Celestial Empire. London, 1911; with illustrations. 264 p. (in Hebrew).

154a Perlmann, S. M.: *The history of the Jews in China.* London, 1913; with 1 illustration. 95 p.
I. "The Jews in China. General view."— II. "The Jewish memorial stones and their lesson."

A level-headed and just account of the problem. The author avoids the pitfalls of imagination to which so many other writers have succumbed.

Cor   Notice: *London and China Express,* Suppl., April 4- 1913, p. 1.

Sk   154b Перлман, С. М.: "Евреи в К. "Перев. с. англ. И. Петелина. Вестник Азии. 1909, 1, стр. 113-236.)
Perlmann, S. M.: "The Jews in China." Transl. by I. Petelin. (*Vestnik Asii.* v. 1, 1909; p. 113-236.)
This title was traced in Skachkov's bibliography (no. 5540). It seems improbable that the translation should have appeared before the original English edition, but the compiler had no possibility of checking the dates, as the Russian edition was not available locally.

155 Pfister, *S. J.,* Louis: *Notices biographiques el bibliographiques sur les Jésuites de l'ancienne Mission de Chine 1552-1773.*

Tome I, XVIe & XVIIe siècles; tome II, XVIIIe siècle. Shanghai, 1932-1934. (Imprimerie de la Mission Catholique; variëtës sinologiques, nos. 59 and 60.)

Aleni, *S. J.,* Jules (1582-1649, Italian); no. 39, v. 2, App., Addenda et Corrigenda, p. 16*, to be supplemented in v. 1, p. 126. Reference to his visit to the Kaifeng Jews in 1613.

Cibot, S. J., Pierre-Martial (1727-1780, French); no. 419, v. 2, p. 899. no. 52, *Parallèlle des moeurs et usages des Chinois avec les moeurs et usages décrits, au livre d'Esther;* no 53, *Mémoire sur les Juifs de la Chine,* Pékin, 1770.

Domenge, S. J., Jean (1666-1735, French), no. 231, v. 1, p. 499-500. Reference to his visit to the Kaifeng Jews in 1722. "On a de qui... six *Lettres* sur les Juifs de K'ai-fong-fou, à la Bibliothèque de l'Ecole Sainte Geneviève. (Sommervogel, t. III, col. 126.)"

Gaubil, S. J., Antoine (1689-1759, French); no. 314, v. 2, p. 684-685. Reference to his visit to the Kaifeng Jews in 1723, when he sent the translation with notes of four inscriptions in the synagogue to the P. du Halde.

Gozani, S. J., Jean Paul (1647-1732, Italian); v. 1, p. 470 471. Reference to his visit to the Kaifeng Jews in 1704; letter containing his report is dated November 5.

Kögler, S. J., Ignace (1680-1746, German); no. 297, v. 2, p. 649. Reference to his publications on the Chinese Jews.

Ricci, S. J., Matthieu (1552-1610, Italian); no. 9, v. 2, App., Addenda et Corrigenda, p. 9*, to be supplemented in v. 1, p. 30, line 3. Reference to the conversation with the Jew Ngai from Kaifeng.

In all instances extensive references to Catholic sources have been given. These are indispensable for the study of the early history of the Jews in China.

156a   Polo, Marco: *Marco Polo il Millione*. Prima edizione,
       integrale a cura di Luigi Foscalo Benedetto.   Comitato
       Geografico Italiano.   Publicazione N. 3.   Florence,
       1928.   (Leo S. Olschki).
       p. 17, fn. 23, f. Jews in Tiflis.
       p. 70.   Nayan; cf. also fn. 81.

156b Polo, Marco: *The Book of Ser Marco Polo the Venetian*,
       concerning the kingdoms and marvels of the East.—
       Transl. and edited, with notes, by Colonel Sir Henry
       Yule.—3rd ed. rev. throughout in the light of recent
       discoveries by Henri Cordier.   London, 1903. v. 2.

       p. 343-344.   Enmity of the Jews towards the Christians
       who had supported Nayan in his rebellion against his
       nephew Kublai Khan.

       p. 346-347, fn. 3.   Record of the Jewish community
       in Kaifeng.

156c Polo, Marco: *Le livre de Marco Polo*.   Transl. by
       A. J. H. Charignon. Peking, 1926. (A. Nachbaur).
       v. 2, ch. 79, p. 27-28.   Des honneurs que le Grand
           Khan accorde aux fêtes des Chrétiens, Juifs, Mus-
           sulmans et Buddhistes.

157   Powell, *Rev*. R.: "*Chinese Jews.*" (*China's Millions*.
       March, 1903.)

       The essence of this article was reprinted in the "Notes
       and Queries" of the *T'oung Pao*, série 2, v. 4, May,
       1903, p. 174-175.   "In June, 1900, some Jewish gentle-
       men in Shanghai wrote to Mr. Powell in K'aifengeg Fu,
       asktng for information regarding their brethren in that
       city."   Powell furnished them with the required data

about the community, which at that time consisted of some 140 people who were in greatly straitened circumstances.

158   Prévost, Georges: *Les inscriptions sémitiques de Loyang,* conservées au Musée Gouvernemental de Pékin. Peking, 1926. (Imprimerie des Lazaristes) 31 p.

This "contribution to the study on the Jewish question in China" was printed for private circulation; at present it is entirely out of print.

Kindly lent by the Imprimerie des Lazaristes de Pékin

The pamphlet contains a photograph, and also a black-and-white reproduction, of three Hebrew stone inscriptions written in the Palmyrian style, found in Loyang. The latter is, by the courtesy of the *Imprimerie des Lazaristes de Pékin*, shown in the above illustration. The inscriptions have been translated and amply commented upon. In ths conclusion the author conjectures that the incriptions might date back to the Han dynasty, presumably to the 2nd century A. D. He thinks that possibly Syrian-Jewish merchants slipped into China, when from Palmyr, then the capital of the kingdom of Kushanas (貴霜國) annual embassies were sent with tributes to China.

Cf. also "Inscriptions hébraïques"; (title no. 223).

Cor   159   Price, Julius J.: "Jews in China." *(The Monist,* 1916.)

160   Purchas, Samuel: *Hakluytus Posthumus or Purchas his pilgrimes,* Glasgow.

v. 8, 1905; p. 584. "Country of Sin."

v. 12, 1906; p. 467-468. Early report on the Jews in Kaifeng and Hangchow.

Cf. Benjamin of Tudela (title no 15).

161   Ricci, S. J., Matteo: *Opere storiche del P. Matteo Ricci S. I.* Edite a cura del Comitato per le Onoranze Nazionali con prolegomeni note e tavole dal P. Pietro Tacchi-Venturi S.I. 2 vols. Macerata, 1911-1913. Vol. I, „I commentarj della China"; vol. II, "Le lettere dalla Cina."

v. I, p. 86-88. "Mohammedans, Hebrews and Christians in the Celestial Empire."

v. I, p. 468-473. "The Conversation of Ricci with the Israelite *Ngai.* The Hebrews in China. — Further information about the Hebrews of Kaifeng. — Attempts to trace (the origin) of the Christians and Hebrews of Kaifeng prove useless."

v. II, p. 290-293. Letter No. 35 addressed to the General of the Jesuits, Claudio Acquaviva, dated: Peking, July 26, 1605. This letter reports on the visit of the Jew *Ngai* and was written about a month after the event.

From this first foreign source on Chinese Jews many subsequent authors have copied, with or without acknowledgment. The original Italian text concerning the subject has been given in full in Appendix I.

162a Richards, L. (夏之時): *Géographie de l'Empire de Chine.* Shanghai, 1905, (T'usewei Press)

162b Richards, L, (夏之時): *Comprehensive geography of the Chinese Empire and dependencies.* Translated into English, revised and enlarged by M. Kenelly, *S. J.* (甘浠樹), Shanghai, 1908. (T'usewei Press. p. 60, 363. 383, and 472.)

Cor 163 Sacy, Silvestre de — : "Notice d'un manuscrit du Pentateuque, conservé dans la synagogue des Juifs de Cai-fong-fou."*(Notices et extraits des manuscrits de la Bibliothèque du Roi,* Paris, 1799, v. 4, p. 592-625.)

Cor 164 Sacy, Silvestre de — : "Notice d'un manuscrit syriaque écrit à la Chine, contenant une portion de la version syriaque de l'Ancien Testament des Cantiques, et diverses prières." *(Notices et extraits des manuscrits de la Bibliothèque du Roi,* Paris, 1831, v. 12, p. 277-286.)

Cf. letter by Gaubil in *Lettres édifiantes* (title no. 230).

Sk 165 Самойлов, Вл.: Бледнолицые черти в Китае (из линыьх впечателний). Варшава, Варшавская эстетическая тип., 1911. 56 стр. С иллюстрациями.

Samoilov, VI: *Palefaced devils in China (from personal impressions).* Warsaw, 1911. (Warsaw Esthetic Printing Press) 56 p.

The book contains a section on the Chinese Jews.

166 Sassoon, David S. D.: "Inscriptions in the Synagogue in Kai-fung-foo." *(Jewish Quarterly Review,* Philadelphia. New series, 11:2. October, 1920. p. 127-144; with 4 facsimiles)

p. 127. "The following article is in connexion with the important document (Codex Sassoon, No. 456) which has lately come to me as a gift from....Mr. Reuben D.E. J. Abraham of Shanghai....President of the Society for the Rescue of the Chinese Jews...."

p. 131. "The English translation....was done by Mr. Charles Budd of the Tung Wen Kwan Translation Office, Shanghai...."

The authenticity of the MS is testified to by the Jesuit visitor, Philippus Grimaldi, and is dated Peking, November 8, 1705. The document "has seventeen inscriptions, ten horizontal and seven vertical". (p. 129.) The author of the article has compared the inscriptions of his document with those of Father Jérôme Tobar, *S. J.,* in his book *Inscriptions juives de K'ai-fong-fou* (see title, no. 188). Sassoon further gives the translation of the inscriptions by Budd. He then draws parallels to Hebrew quotations and attempts to evolve "The Principles of Faith of the Chinese Jews". (p. 136.)

p. 142-144. "A Hebrew letter to the Jews of Kai-fung-foo." The final section contains a facsimile and translation of a Hebrew letter written by Isaac Faraj ben Reuben Jacob of Shanghai to the Jewish community of

Kaifeng. "The document (Codex Sassoon 54) was given to Sassoon 'by the late Mr. S. M. Moses in 1908 ."

167 Schereschewsky, Samuel Isaac Joseph (施約瑟 Shih Yüeh-se) 1831-1906.

a. Muller, James Arthur: *Apostle of China. Samuel Isaac Joseph Schereschewsky, 1831-1906.* New York — Milwaukee, 1937.

Bishop Schereschewsky was born of Jewish parentage at Tauroggen, Russian Lithuania, in 1831. His father's family was of the Ashkenazic branch of Jewry. On the maternal side he was of Sephardic extraction, his mother being of a Spanish Jewish family. It was the intention of his relatives that he become a Rabbi.

In 1854 Schereschewsky went to America, and definitely accepted Christianity in 1855. Four years later he went to China as a missionary. In 1875 he acquired American citizenship. During the same year he was elected Bishop of China (Episcopal Church, Anglican Communion). He accepted this office after his re-election in 1876. In 1879, St. John's College (now St. John's University) at Shanghai was opened upon his initiative.

Schereschewsky was paralyzed by a sunstroke in 1881. He remained an invalid for the rest of his life, but he continued his translation of the Bible into Chinese, for which he is best known. Schereschewsky could speak 13 languages and read 20. Among them were Hebrew, in which he had had early training, and Chinese. He mastered Chinese fully, being familiar with the classical Wen-li, Mandarin and the Shanghai dialect, having at his command between 9,000 and 10,000 Chinese characters.

[89]

Schereschewsky also went to Kaifeng. Instigated by the visit of three Kaifeng Jews to Peking in March, 1867, the various Protestant missionaries urged him to investigate the conditions of the Kaifeng Jewish community. This he did in the middle of 1867. The trip took him fifteen days. After a stay about twenty-five days in that city he was driven out by a mob. He reported that some 200 or 300 Jewish families were left there, a fair proportion of them in good circumstances. They had entirely lost their religion and had "idols in their houses, and ancestral tablets." Schereschewsky further related that the Jews intermarried with the local population and were scarcely distinguishable from them. "In features, dress, habits, religion, they are essentially Chinese." The Jews were no longer able to read their own Scriptures, and Blodget, from whose report this passage is drawn, concludes: "It is not known that they (the Jews) have ever had any religious works in the Chinese language."

b. Martin: "Schereschewsky's Pentateuch." (*The Chinese Recorder*, Shanghai. 30:6. June, 1899. p. 287-289.)

Appreciation of the Pentateuch translation from Hebrew into Chinese.

c. Graves, *Rt. Rev.* F. R.: "In memoriam: Bishop Schereschewsky." (*The Chinese Recorder*, Shanghai. 37:11. November, 1906. p. 615-617.)

This obituary was translated by B. Truxler, *S. J.*, "Note sur les traductions de Schereschewsky." (*Digest of the Synodal Commission*, Peking. v. 8, 1935. p. 343-345.

Shu   168   Scherzer, Karl von — :   *Die Juden in China.*   Vienna,
            1901.   (Gesellschaft für Sammlung und Conservirung
            von Kunst und historischen Denkmälern des Judenthums.
            Jahresbericht 4.)

      *169   Schindler, B.: „Bericht über die Juden in China."
            (Die Erde, February, 1914.)

Cor   170   Schwab, Moïse: *Itinéraire juif d'Espagne en Chine au
            IXe siecle.* Paris, 1891.   (Ch. Delagrave.)   19 p.
            Extract from the *Revue de Géographie,* Institut Géo-
            graphique de Paris.
            See also letter by the author addressed to the director of
            the *Revue de Géographie,* Paris, dated April 30, 1892.
            The letter was published in the *T'oung Pao,* v. 3, August.
            1892, p. 316-317; and in the *Revue de Géographie.* (Cf,
            also article by J. de Goeje, title no. 79.)

Fi   171   Semmedo, Père Alvaro: *Imperio de la China, i cultura
            evangelica en él.*   Madrid, 1642.   p. 196.

      172   Shen Yen-ping and Shen Tse-min (transl.):   *New collection
            of Jewish short stories.*   Shanghai, 1933 (or earlier).
            (Commercial Press.)
            Stories by Perez, Rabinowitsch, Ash, and Vendroff.
            沈雁冰, 沈澤民譯: 新猶太小說集. 上海 (商務印書館.)

      173   Sheng Kung-pu (translator):   "Some facts concerning the
            Israelites of Kaifeng."   *(Revue Catholique,* Shang-
            hai).
                  20:1; January, 1931; p. 14-20;
                  20:3; March, 1931; p. 141-143;
                  21:1; January, 1932; p. 16-25;
                  21:2, February, 1932; p. 75-82.
            The article is based upon the correspondence of the PP.
            Gozani, Domenge and Gaubil; see *Lettres édifiantes* title
            no. 230).

沈公布 譯： 關於開封一賜樂業之吉光片羽. (聖教雜誌. 上海 民國二十年至二十一年.)

174 Shryock, John K.: *The origin and development of the state cult of Confucius.* New York—London, [1932] p. 131. "....the Jews probably came during the ninth century."

Cor 175 Sionnet, *Abbé: Essai sur les Juifs de la Chine et sur l'influence qu'ils ont eue sur la littérature de ce vasie empire avant l'ère chrétienne.* Paris, 1837. 24 p. (Merlin.)

Cor 176 Sionnet, *Abbé:* "Epoque de l'entrée des Juifs en Chine; preuves qu'ils y portent le Pentateuque au 6e siècle avant notre ère." *(Ann. de Phil. chrét.,* 2e série. XIV.)

177 Скачков, П. Е.: Библиография Китая. (Систе-матический указатель книг и журнальных статей о Китае на русском языке. 1730-1930. Москва-Ленинград, 1932 г. Государственное Социально-Экономическое издательство.)

Skahkov, P. E.: *Bibliography on China (1730-1930),* Moscow—Leningrad, 1932. (Commun. Academy, Inst. for Scientific Research on China.)
Titles no. 3199, p. 218; no. 5202, p. 369; no. 5507. p. 370; no. 5540, p. 372; no. 6582a, p. 445.

178 [Smith, George — and W. H. Medhurst]: *A narrative of a mission of inquiry to the Jewish Synagogue of K'aifung fu, on behalf of the London Society for promoting Christianity among the Jews.* Shanghai, 1851; with Hebrew facsimiles. 94 p.

A summary of the book is also given in *The Chinese Repository,* Victoria, Hongkong. 20:7. July, 1851. Art. 7. p. 436-466.

Bishop Smith of Victoria in conjunction with the Rev. Dr. W. H. Medhurst "planned the scheme of dispatching two trustworthy Chinese to Honan, to learn all they could of the Jews." The names of the two emissaries were K'iu T'ien-sang and Tsiang Yung-chi.

"This interesting account is written by two Chinese who were sent from Shanghai in November last (1850) to the cap tal of Honan to learn what is the present condition and numbers of the Jewish community residing there, and to induce some of them to visit Shanghai. The narrative is preceded by an introduction of the Bishop of Victoria, from which we learn that the undertaking was set on foot by the Committee of the Society in London for promoting Christianity among the Jews, to whom funds had been left by Miss Cook for the purpose of prosecuting such an inquiry."

Shu 179 Solomon, Elijah: *Jews in China and India.* Baltimore, 1900. (Jewish Comment Publishing Co.)

Reprinted from the *Jewish Comment* of October 5, 12, 19 and 26. 1900.

180 [Sopher, Arthur — and Edward Isaac Ezra]: *Chinese Jews.* Printed by *The China Press*, Shanghai, 1926. [V] +79 pp.; with 18 illustrations and a map.

This booklet was issued to propagate the aims of the Society for the Rescue of Chinese Jews. It contains an article on the Chinese Jews by E. I. Ezra which was first published in the *East of Asia Magazine* (see title no. 60a), including the ten original illustrations (p. 1-46). Sopher has contributed a preface of five pages and an appendix (p. 47-76). In the preface he points out similarities between the Chinese and Jews, implying early relationships

[93]

between them.   The appendix supplements Ezra's article. Eight new illustrations have been added, among which are photographs of members and groups of the Kaifeng Jewish community, the site of the synagogue, the "Jewish Colony Lane", and the laver formerly used in the synagogue.   The pamphlet concludes with a chronological table and a plea for support on the part of the Society for the Rescue of Chinese Jews.

Sopher's appendix contains some useful information con-cerning the whereabouts of some of the manuscripts and utensils of the synagogue.   On his map he claims the existence of former Jewish colonies in Canton (Kwangtung), Ningpo and Hangchow (Chekiang), Kaifeng (Honan), Sian (Shensi), and Peking (Hopei).   Moreover, he reports briefly on the alleged discovery by Lehmann (p. 50):—

> "………in 1899 a colony of ahout five hundred Jews was discovered in Tangchwang, a hundred miles south-west of Kaifeng-fu, by Col. Lehmann, of the German army then stationed at Tsingtao. He reported that the men were engaged generally in the silk trade, and were, on the whole, well-to-do."

This statement, however, has never been corroborated or substantiated,

Referring to various efforts to rescue the Kaifeng commu-nity, the unsuccessful attempt by Schereschewsky is men-tioned (p. 62):—

> "………Somewhat after the middle of the last century, Bishop Schereschewsky……induced twelve of the more promis-ing youths of the colony to come to Peking, where he tried to give them a liberal education, including the study of Hebrew. Unfortunately, the life away from home did not satisfy them, and one by one they travelled back."

Not mentioned elsewhere is a mission of inquiry, organized by the Society for the Rescue of Chinese Jews in 1924 (p. 64-65):—

"A representative of the Society, Mr. Wong (David Levy), a Sinkiang (Chinese Turkestan) Jew, was sent ....to Kaifengfu to get more intimate details than could be obtained by a foreigner."

"....... ..investigation showed, there were but 99 Jews left in Kaifengfu, most of them very poor, only a few families being well-to-do. The plan of the synagogue represents a plot of ground about 480ft. by 240ft."

181 Spengler, Oswald: *Der Untergang des Abendlandes.* München, 1927. (First publ., 1923.) v. 2.

p. 318. „....im Osten sind sie (die Juden) schon im 2. Jahrhundert in China nachzuweisen. Im Norden trat später das Chazarenreich mit der Hauptstadt Astrachan zum Judentum über. Von dort aus sind Mongolen jüdischer Religion bis ins Innere Deutschlands gedrungen und 955 mit den Ungarn auf dem Lechfeld geschlagen worden", p. 390. „Das kleinste Ghetto ist ein wenn auch noch so armseliges Stück Grosstadt, und seine Bewohner zerfallen wie die des erstarrten Indien und China in Kasten—die Rabbiner sind die Brahmanen und Mandarinen des Ghetto—und die Masse der Kuli mit einer zivilisierten, kalten, weit überlegenen Intelligenz und einem rücksichtslosen Geschäftssinn."

182 Stein, *Sir* M[arc] Aurel: *Ancient Khotan:* A detailed report of archaeological explorations in Chinese Turkestan. Oxford, 1907. 2 vols.

Vol I, ch. X, section ii p. 306-309; vol. II, plate CXIX.
Vol I. "An early Judaeo-Persian document from Khotan in the Stein Collection, with other early Persian documents."
Vol. II. "Judaeo-Persian document, brought from Dandan-Uiliq."

[95]

The author recovered a Judaeo-Persian MS from Dandan-Uiliq in Chinese Turkestan. According to Professor Margoliouth's translation and notes, this "much mutilated fragment of a letter written by a Persian-speaking Jew" referred mainly to certain business affairs. As far as can be ascertained from the text, the letter must have been written in 718 A. D. The historical facts and the microscopical analysis of the paper by Professor J. Wiesner confirm the age of the document.

Vol. I. Appendix C., edited by D. S. Margoliouth: "The Judaeo.Persian Document from Dandan-Uiliq." p. 570-574.

The text, the modern Hebrew transliteration and English translation of the document are given. Margoliouth gives briefly the related philological and historical data and claims that the document is older than any Judaeo-Persian and even Persian document as yet known. Notes explain further details.

183 Storfer, A. J.: "Jews in China." *(Magazine Digest,* Toronto, Ontario. 18:6. June, 1939. p. 105-108. Condensed from the *Basler National-Zeitung,* Basle, Switzerland.)

General historical account of the Kaifeng Jewish community. Reprinted also in *The China Digest,* Shanghai, 55: 598. January, 1940. p. 60-63.

184 Stoss, Alfred (Korvetten-Kapitän a. D.): *Der Kampf zwischen Juda und Japan.* Japan als Vorkämpfer freier Volkswirtschaft. Ludendorffs Verlag, München, 1934. 51 p.

The author, a retired commander in the German navy, alleges that the Jews promote capitalism and communism and that they have attempted to fight Japan and to help

China, where they supposedly have been trying to get
control of the Kuomintang.   Anti-semitic pamphlet.
亞路夫電德，亞特斯 猶太與日本之戰， 北京，新民會，中央指導部.
Chinese translation of the above title, published by the
headquarters of the Hsin Min Hui, Peking, with a preface
by a Japanese Brigadier-General (尺 甫 根 木 博).

185   Streit, Robert—and Johannes Dindinger: *Bibliotheca
       Missionum.*   (Veröffentlichungen   des   Internationalen
       Instituts für Missionswissenschaftliche Forschung.)
Münster, 1916, v. 1; title no. 1029, p. 498.
Aachen, 1929, v. 5; title no. 2110, p. 736.
Aachen, 1931, v, 7; titles no. 2854, p. 211; no. 2878, 5,
    p. 216; no. 3490, p. 357, no. 3526, 3. p, 369.

186   T'ao Hsi-sheng: "The lending at high interest and ex-
       action of women, children and domestic animals on the
       part of the inhabitants of the Western regions of China
       and of the Jews under the Yüan dynasty." (*Shih Huo*,
       Shanghai. 1:7, March 1, 1935. p. 54-55.)
       陶希聖: 元代西域及猶太人的高利貸與頭口搜索. (食貨, 上海.
       第一卷第七期, 54-55頁)

The "Western regions" (*Hsi-yü* 西域) correspond to the
present Chinese Turkestan.   The period under discussion
is the last decade of the 13th century.

The author uses wrongly the term *Kan-t'o* 幹脫 , instead
of its correct form *Wo-t'o* 斡脫 .   The article suffers
from the lack of proper historical documentation, and
wrongly applies the name of *Wo-t'o* to Jews. (Cf. *Introduction.*)

Cor   187   Terrien de Lacouperie, A.E.J.B. de — : "On the entrance
       of the Jews into China during the first century of our
       era." (*Babylonian and Oriental Record.* 5:6. June,
       1891. p. 131-134.)

188 Tobar, *S.J.*, Jérôme: *Inscriptions juives de K`ai-fong-fou.* Shanghai, 1st ed., 1900; 2nd rev. ed., 1912. (Variétés sinologiques no. 17.—La Mission Catholique.) VI + 112 p.; with 1 wood-cut and 7 photo-lithographic reproductions.

The volume contains the Chinese text and the French translation of the three inscriptions dated 1489, 1512 and 1663 in the Kaifeng synagogue. Rubbings of these inscriptions have likewise been reproduced. A fourth illegible inscription, made in 1779, the author has not attempted to decipher, due to its illegibility.

The book consists of eleven articles. Their contents which go far beyond the mere translation of the inscriptions; represent a careful study of the history of the Kaifeng Jewish community. The table of contents reads as follows: —

Art. I. Description de la synagogue.—Art. II. Inscriptions horizontales, *p'ien* 扁. —Art. III. Inscriptions verticales, *toei-lien* 對聯 —Art. IV. Des travaux antérieurs sur les inscriptions lapidaires.—Art. V-VII. Inscriptions de 1489, 1512, 1663.—Art. VIII. De l'entrée des Juifs en Chine.— Art. IX. Le Pentateuque de K`ai-fong.—Art. X. Autres livres sacrés conservés dans la synagogue.—Art. XI. Résumé des inscriptions.—Conclusion.

Cf. also the review by P. Pelliot in the *Bulletin de l'Ecole Francaise d'Extrême-Orient*, Hanoi. v.1, 1901, p. 263-264.

189a Torrance, *Rev.* Thomas: *The history, customs and religion of the* Ch'iang. An aboriginal people of West China. 青衣羌 . (American Bible Society, Chengtu; printed by The Shanghai Mercury, Ltd.) Shanghai, 1920. 36 p. with 11 illustrations.

189b Torrance, *Rev.* Thomas: "The religion of the Ch'iang." (*Journal of the North-China Branch of the Royal Asiatic Society*, Shanghai. v. 54, 1923. p. 150-167.)

189c Torrance, *Rev.* Thomas: "The basic spiritual conceptions of the religion of the Chiang." (*Journal of the West China Border Research Society*, Chengtu, Szechwan prov. v. 6, 1933/34. p. 31-48; with 7 plates.)

Lecture delivered to the West China Border Research Society, May 12, 1934.

189d Torrance, *Rev.* Thomas: *China's first missionaries—Ancient Israelites.* London, 1937. (Thynne & Co., Ltd.) 125 p.; with 27 plates.

189e Torrance, *Rev.* Thomas: "The survival of Old Testament religious customs among the Chiang people of West China." (*Journal of the Transactions of the Victoria Institute*, London; v. 71, 1939, p. 100-116.)
Lecture delivered before the society on March 20th, 1939. The author, one of the pioneer missionaries of West China, in his earlier writings believed the Ch'iangs "to be of Semitic stock", but now he is convinced that they are "truly descendants of ancient Israel". The purpose of his book, *China's first missionaries*, is "to describe the customs and religious observances of a colony of people descended from Israelitish settlers who came to the Western borderland of China several hundreds of years before the time of Christ". In this connection he also mentions a paper read before the British Association in 1860 by Dr. McGowan. "Dr. McGowan ...... stated he found evidence of the existence of a numerous colony of Jews in the City of Chintu (Chengtu) about a century before the

Birth of Christ, and that in all probability some of them had made their way to the mountainous regions lying between China and Burmah." (p. 8.)

Deducting from the appearance and the religious rites of the *Chiang-Min* (羌民) and *Baelan-Min* (白闌民), the author believes to have traced in them descendants of "ancient Israelites." According to the author's description most of these people live in Szechwan, west of the Min river, in the districts of Wenchuan, Lifan, Monghsien and Tiehchi. The author claims that formerly the territory inhabited by these people stretched from Kansu in the North to Yünnan in the South. The book furnishes, however, no convincing proof.

189f B., [*S.J.*] C.: "Un tribu juive au Thibet." (*Bulletin Catholique de Pékin*, Peking. 26:307. March, 1929. p. 142-143.)

Reviewing note on Torrance's: *China's first missionaries— Ancient Israelites.* Cf. title no. 189d.

189g B., [*S.J.*] C.: "Les Juifs en Chine." (*Bulletin Catholique de Pékin*, Peking. 26:309. May, 1939. p. 271-273.)

This note deals likewise with the book by Torrance, followed by an editorial note on the Loyang stone inscriptions; cf. titles no. 189d and 158.

The work by Torrance was reviewed in the "Literary Supplement" of the London *Times*. An extract of this review was reprinted in the *Chinese Recorder*, Shanghai, 69:3; March, 1938; p. 136.

190 Trebitsch-Lincoln, Ignatius Timothy; *alias Abbot* Chao Kung (照空):

    a. Lincoln, I.T.T.: *Revelations of an international spy.* New York, 1916. V + 323 p., with 16 illustrations. (Robert McBride & Company.)

b. Trebitsch-Lincoln, I [gnaz] T.: *Der grösste Aben-teurer des 20. Jahrhunderts!?* Die Wahrheit über mein Leben. Wien, (1931). (Amalthea Verlag.) 290 p., with 18 illustrations and a map.

Trebitch-Lincoln, Ignatius Timothy: *Autobiography of an adventurer.* Transl. from the German by E. Burns. London, 1931. (Stein.) New York, 1932. (Holt.) 291 p.

English translation of *Der grösste Abenteurer.*

c. Chao Kung; *Dawn or doom of humanity.* Shanghai, 1937. (Shanghai Times.)

d. Chao Kung (Trebitsch-Lincoln), various articles: In *The China Weekly Review*, Shanghai:

Hunter, E.: "Trebitsch Lincoln, ex-British parlia-mentarian, international spy, becomes Buddhist monk." (57:3. June 20, 1931. p. 97-98 and 115.)

"Growing occidental interest in oriental Buddhism." (57:9. August 1, 1931. p. 361.)

The article contains data on the life of T.L. and his photograph.

Brown, Constantine: "White nations bicker while Black Dragons plot world overthrow." (74:7. October 19, 1935. p. 234)

The article contains data on the life of T.L. who is allegedly connected with the Black Dragon Society of Japan.

"Abbot 'Chao Kung' in new role—heads Japan 'Truth League'." (83:1. December 4, 1937. p. 1-2.)

Report on the pro-Japanese activities of T.L. in Shanghai as head of the "Truth League". Cf. also *Newsweek*, New York, of October 25, 1937.

In *The China Weekly Chronicle*, Peiping:

"Trebitsch Lincoln in libel suit—Shanghai Russian paper defendant." (6:21/160. November 24, 1935. p. 32.)

"Loss of lawsuit by Trebitsch Lincoln." (6:25/164. December 22, 1935. p. 31.)

Trebitsch Lincoln (Chao Kung) had brought libel action of $10,000 against a Russian newspaper, the Shanghai *Zaria*, beause he had been accused in its columns of being a spy for Abyssinia and of purchasing arms for that government. The defendants were, however, found not guilty and the claim for damages was dismissed by the court.

"Chao Kung planning monastery in China." (*Trans-Pacific*, Tokyo. 21:11. August 3, 1933.)

"Again Chao Kung." (*Time*, New York. 35:1. January 1, 1940. p. 19, with photograph of T.L.)

The article contains a brief but comprehensive biography of T.L. The following data have been taken partly from this article.

Ignatius Timothy Trebitsch-Lincoln, *alias Abbot* Chao Kung: Born at Paks near Budapest in 1878 as a Hungarian Jew, he added *Lincoln* to his name in admiration for the great reformer. He went to England, became a Presbyterian missionary, then an Anglican curate, subse-

quently a Quaker as secretary to the Quaker B. Seebohm
Rowntree. Before the first World War he was elected
as British Liberal M.P. for Darlington (1906). He "was
accused in a secret session of Parliament of being a spy.
Later it was rumoured he had spied for both the Allies and
Germany. He made his way to the United States, was
extradited to England, where he was convicted of forgery,
imprisoned until the war's end. Then he went to Germany,
helped in the abortive Kapp *Putsch* of 1920."

After further adventures he went to China, "where for a
time he seemed to be close to the late Warlord Wu
Pei-fu." In 1931, he became a Buddhist monk, adopting
the name of Chao Kung. He collected some European
followers and spent his time intermittently in China and
Japan. His Japanese connections date to 1935 or earlier.
At the end of 1937, he acted as head of the "Truth
League" in Shanghai under Japanese auspices.

During the last days of 1939 he "called upon the govern-
ments of Great Britain, France, Germany, and Russia to
resign simultaneously as prelude to a peace conference.
Otherwise, he predicted, 'the Tibetan Buddhist supreme
masters, without prejudice, pre-direction or favor, will un-
chain forces and powers whose very existence is unknown
to you and against whose operations you are consequently
helpless.' " (For further particulars cf. also *The Peking
Chronicle*, Peking. January 4 and 10, 1939; April 18,
1939; September 2, 1939; January 4, 1940.)

191 Trigautius, Nicolaus (Trigault, Nicholas): *De Christiana
expeditione apud Sinas suscepta ab Societate Jesu.* Ex
P. Matthaei Ricii eiusdem societatis comentariis libri V.
Roma, 1615.

Book 1, p. 118-120. First report on the Jews in Kaifeng. This work contains a rather free translation of the memoirs of Ricci; (see title no. 161). Several editions of the work by Trigault have been published and it has been translated into German, Spanish and Italian.

192 Tung Fen, Hsi Chen and Ch'en Ku (trsl.): *David Pinski's tales.* Shanghai, 1933 (or earlier). (Commercial Press.)

冬芬, 希真, 陳瑕: 賓士奇集. 上海. (商務印書館.)

193 Виноградов, (Иеромонах) Алексей: История Библии на Востоке. 1889.

Vinogradov, *Hieromonach* Alexei: *The history of the Bible in the East.* 1889.

The author assumed that the Jews had come to China before the time of Moses.

194 [Wei I-heng: *The Jewish community of Kaifeng.* Kaifeng, (Honan Chung Hua Shêng Kung Hui.)]

The work was announced in May, 1936, but its publication was delayed because of the present hostilities.

魏亦亨. 開封猶太教. 開封. 民國二十五年五月. 河南中華聖公會刊.

195 Wei Wei-chen: "General conditions of the Jews in Kaifeng." *(The China Church Year Book 1921.* 6th issue, Shanghai, 1921 p. 89-90.) (The China Continuation Committee.)

魏維貞: 河南猶太人之概況. 上海. 民國十年 (中華基督教年鑑 第六期, 89-90 頁.)

Cor 196 Weissenberg, S.: „Anthropologische Untersuchungen an zentralasiatischen Juden." *(Deutsche Rundschau für Geographie und Statistik.* v. 32, 1909-1910, p. 89.)

"Observations faites par le Dr. S. Weissenberg en Palestine sur les Juifs venus de l'Asie Centrale, principalement de Boukhara. Le voyage du Dr. W. était payé par le fonds Rudolf Virchow."

Cor 197 Weissenberg, S.: ,,Die zentralasiatischen Juden in anthropologischer Beziehung." (Mitteilungen der Anthropologischen Gesellschaft, Wien. v. 43, 1913.)
Verzeichnis der Anthropologischen Gesellschaft, (1870-1919), 1920, in the Sitzungsberichte, p. 25.

198a White, Rt. Rev. William C.: "Chinese Jews." (Asia, New York. 36:1. January, 1936. p. 54-61; with 4 p. of illustrations.)

Popular account of the subject. The article was reprinted in the North China Star, Tientsin, on June 1, 1936, p. 11; and on June 2, p. 11-12.

198b К.,С.: Китайские Евреи, (Вестник Китая, Тяньцзин. 1:1. Март 1936 г. стр. 12-14.)
K., S.: "Chinese Hebrews." (Vestnik Kitaia, Tientsin. 1:1. March, 1936. p. 12-14.; with 5 illustrations.)

Extract from the above article.

199 Whyte, Bishop Wm. C.: "The Jews of Kaifengfu, in Honan." (In: China Mission Year Book. 4th issue. Shanghai, 1913. Christian Literature Society for China. p. 162-165.)

p. 163. "Of (the) ...... three stones the first and the third are still to be found, the second having disappeared, though there are still rubbings of it extant. The lettering on the third stone, which has only in recent years been dug up after being lost in the soil, is practically illegible." The two stones were placed under the custody of Bishop

Whyte in an agreement with the head Jew "until a synagogue should again be built and should require them." The Anglican Mission also acquired the site of the former synagogue.

p. 164-165. "The leading Jew has been helping us to trace the articles formerly used in the synagogue, and we have been successful in acquiring several, and have been able to trace others ......"

"In a letter written from Kaifeng, November 5th, 1704, Father Gozani, S.J., mentions a pair of large stone lotus-carved flowerpots, and we have obtained one of these and part of another. A marble balustrade of the synagogue has, for over fifty years, been used in the Confucian Temple, while two large stone lions are outside one of the Buddhist Temples. A small black marble slab, used in the synagogue as a gong to call the worshippers to service, has come into our hands, together with some other things. Large iron incense urns have been scrapped and sold to a blacksmith, while other smaller urns have been sold to pawnshops and so far have not come to light. Green tiles that once roofed in the synagogue now cover the leading Mohammedan mosque, though we hear that about two thousand more lie buried on the original site. Some forty or more wooden tablets have entirely disappeared, the ark that contained the Emperor's tablet is said to be in a nearby mosque, and the gilt ark of exquisite workmanship that once contained the rolls of Hebrew Scriptures was sold to an offical and taken to no one knows where. Over the sale of this latter a bitter feud sprang up between the two leading families, which resulted in bloodshed on both sides, and the descendants of one of these families are now in exile for fear of their lives "

"The rolls of Scripture were of sheepskin parchment, but none are now to be found. Some were sold to foreigners from time to time, some were actually cut up by one of the Jews to line his winter garments, and the remainder were cozened out of them by a Taoist priest. This Taoist must have known of the interest Europeans attached to these parchments, and of their probable money value. Having got into touch with the Jews he suggested that parchment would soon go bad if not aired from time to time, and so one day the precious rolls were spread out in the sun under the supervision of the Taoist. After a few hours the parchments had disappeared, and the Taoist said it must have been the strong wind, which was blowing at the time, which had whisked them away. However the man disappeared, and it was said that some time after a Taoist priest in Shanghai was offering Hebrew Scripture rolls for sale."

The author has remarked about the members of the Jewish community that "in their mode of life and conduct they are exactly like their ...... neighbours, and in their features it is hard to detect any differences from ordinary Chinese."

200 Wieger, *S.J.*, Léon: *Textes historiques de la China depuis l'origine. jusqu'en 1912.* 2nd ed. Hsienhsien. 1923. v. 2.

p. 1507. The massacre in Canton during the years 878/879 included 120,000 Mohammedans, Jews, Christians and Parsees, in addition to the indigenous population. Wieger claims that the above number is accurate, because the population figures were known from the registers for the head tax.

[107]

p. 1623-1624. During their early history the Jews were called Chu-hu-tê 朱 乎 得 by the Mohammedans.

Cf. also the review of the *Textes historiques* by Ed. Chavannes in the *T'oung Pao*. Ser. 2, no. 5, 1904. p. 482-483. According to Chavannes the traditional view that the Jews came to China during the Chou or Han dynasties is extremely vague. Accurate facts are available only for the Sung dynasty (960-1126), when Jews came from India with tributes for the Chinese court. They came by sea and not by land through Central Asia.

201 Wilhelm, Richard: ,,Die Juden in China.'' (*Der Morgen*, Berlin. 2:1. April, 1926. p. 3-12.)

The author rejects the early theories of etymological connections between Hebrew and Chinese which had been made by enthusiastic missionaries, largely for theological reasons.

The author voices the opinion that the first Jews entered China at the time of the destruction of Jerusalem (70 A. D.) and summarizes the threefold wave of Jewish settlement in China: (1) the Jewish community in Kaifeng; (2) the Bagdad Jews in Hongkong and Shanghai; (3) modern Jewish merchants and scholars.

The author also mentions that nothing has remained of the early Jewish communities in Nanking, Hangchow and other places.

202 Williams, S. Wells: *The controversy among the Protestant missionaries on the proper translation of the words God ond Spirit into Chinese.* Andover, 1878. (Warren F. Draper.)

From the *Bibliotheca Sacra* for 1878. 35:140, p. 768-773. The author mentions that the Kaifeng Jews use the

terms *Tao* 道. *T'ien* 天, and *Hao T'ien* 昊天 for "God".
He objects to Legge's contention that *Shang-ti* 上帝 or
Ti 帝 are the best renderings of *elohim*.

203 Williams, S. Wells: *The Middle Kingdom*. v. 2.
  London, 1st ed., 1861, p. 287-289, rev. ed. 1883, p.
  271-273.

The volume contains a brief account of the history of the
Jews in China. "They probably entered China through
the north-western route, and there is no good reason for
rejecting their own date, during the Han dynasty. Within
the last three centuries all have lived in Kaifung . . . . . .
wherever they may have lived in earlier days." (p. 271.)
The author mentions the report by the Jesuit Gozani and
gives an account of the visits to Kaifeng by Dr. Martin
and Bishop Schereschewsky.

204 Winterbotham, W.: *Historical, geographical, and philosophical view of the Chinese empire*. London, 1795.
  p. 358-362, "Jews and Mahometans."

The information contained in this section is based on the
report by Gozani.

205a Wolff, *Rev.* Joseph: *Researches and missionary labors*.
  2 vols. London, 1835.

205b Wolff, *Rev.* Joseph: *Mission to Bokhara*. London,
  1846.

205c Wolff, *Rev.* Joseph: *Travels and adventures*. London,
  1861.

The author, a converted Jew, became an Anglican mission-
ary to Oriental Jews. His works contain references to
Chinese Jews. Some of his findings are reproduced in
A.H. Godbey, *The lost tribes* (cf. title no. 78).

p. 371. "Wolff found a report that some ōf the Khiva
Jews had emigrated to Kamtschatka; *(Travels and
adventures.* II, 152, 379.) again he found these Khiva
Jews were Turkomans who mingled a Hebrew slogan or
two with their Turkoman war-cries, and intermarried with
Moslem Turkomans *(Mission to Bokhara,* p. 380.). And
Khiva was founded by a Jewish Persian Prince ......
(400-420 A.D.) ...... It was a proselyted commingling
that settled at Khiva. The Turkoman and Mongol tides
centuries later overwhelmed this Persian Judaism. The
Jewish brigands in the mountains about the ancient capital
of Parthia in Benjamin of Tudela's time, 1173 A.D., were
probably Judaized Turkomans. He was told they were
in league with the Turk against Persia. Wolff was told
that the Samarkand and Bokhara Jews had been expelled
by Jagatai, successor of Genghis Khan, who had favored
the Jews; many of them emigrated to China."

p. 372. ".... the statement of Dr. Wolff that Genghis
Khan had a corps of Jewish troops; some today claim him
as a Jew."

Mö 206 Wright, T.: *Israel in China.* London, 1842.

207 Wu Shu-t'ien: *The Song of Songs.* Shanghai, 1930;
with 8 illustr., 130 p. (English text with Chinese
translation.) Followed by an essay by Chou Tso-jen:
"Comparison between the Bible and Chinese literature." 60 p.
吳曙天：雅歌．一周作人：聖書與中國文學．上海，1930.
（北新書局．）

208a Wylie, Alexander: "Israelites in China." *(The Chinese
and Japanese Repository.* London. 1:1 July, 1863.
p. 13-22; and 1:2. August, 1863, p. 43-52.)

This article was also reprinted in the author's "Researches" (see title no. 208b).

208b Wylie, Alexander: *Chinese researches.* Shanghai, 1897. Pt. 2, p. 1-23. "Israelites in China."

This article is based on the conjecture that the *Hsienchiao* 祆教 mentioned in the Chinese annals of the middle ages, referred to Jews. Meanwhile the followers of this sect have been identified as fire-worshippers or Parsees.

Cor 208c Wylie, A.: *Recherches sur l'existence des Juifs en Chine depuis les temps les plus reculés jusqu'à nos jours.* Mémoire traduit de l'anglais par M. l'abbé Th. Blanc, et annoté par M. G. Pauthier. (Extrait des *Annales de Philosophie chrétienne.* Nos. 50 et 51, février et mars 1864.) 33 p.

French translation of the article "Israelites in China."

209 Yakobs, Roeh Hayim: *Hithgaluth Hayehudim Hasinim.* Me'eth Royeh Hayim Yakobs, me'turgam min halashon ha'anglith al yedei ha-mehaber, Yaffo, (5685) 1925; Yerushalaim, (5687) 1927. (in Hebrew).

Jacobs, Roeh Hayim: *The discovery of the Chinese Jews.* Transl. from the English by the author. Jaffa. 1925; Jerusalem, 1927.

210 Yamaguchi, Iwao: "The Jews and the Chinese," (*Shina.* Tokyo, 9:3. February 1, 1918. p. 19-21.)
山內嵓：猶太人與支那人．(支那，東京．大正七年．第九卷第三號第十九至二十一頁．)
The article is of general nature, comparing the Jews with the Chinese.

[111]

211 Yŭ Kan: "The migration movement of the Jews in
     Russia." *(The Eastern Miscellany,* Shanghai. 25:
     11. June 10, 1928. p. 3-5.)

The article deals with the Jewish colonization movement
in Russia between 1925 and 1928, when the Jews were
moved from urban districts into the country.
育幹:俄國猶太人的移殖運動.(東方雜誌,上海 第廿
五卷第十一號,民國十七年六月十日,第三至五頁.)

212 Yü Sung-hua: "The Jews and the Zionist movement."
     (The Eastern Miscellany, Shanghai. 24:17. Sep-
     tember 10, 1927. p. 21-28,)

The article deals with the Zionist movement in Palestine
during the years 1908 to 1926.
兪頌華:猶太人與猶太復與運動.(東方雜誌,上海.第
廿四卷第十七號,民國十六年九月十日;第廿一至
廿八頁.)

213 Yü Sung-hua: "The Arabs and the Jewish national
     movement in Palestine." *(The Eastern Miscellany,*
     Shanghai. 25:8. April 25, 1928. p. 27-39.)

The article deals with Zionism, with the Jewish Arab
relations, and with the British policy towards the Jews.
兪頌華: 巴力斯坦地方亞剌伯人與猶太人的民族運
動.(東方雜誌,上海.第廿五卷第八號;民國十七年
四月廿五日;第廿七至三十九頁.)

214 Yüan Ting-an: *Sketch of the Jewish religion.* Shanghai,
     1935. (Commercial Press.) 97 p.

The booklet is divided into six chapters dealing with the
history, foundation, development, comparison with other
religions, and scriptures of the Jewish religion.
袁定安:猶太教概論,上海.民國二十四年.(商務印書
館.)

215 Yule, *Sir* Henry: *Cathay and the way thither.*
Being a collection of medieval notices of China transl.
and ed. by Sir Henry Yule.— New ed. rev. throughout
by Henri Cordier. London (Hakluyt Society).

a   Andrew of Perugia (*O. F. M.*): "Letter from An-
     drew Bishop of Zayton in Manzi or Southern
     China, 1326." v. 3. 1914; p. 74.
     "Of the Jews. . . . there are indeed no converts."

b   Rashiduddin: "Cathay under the Mongols." Ex-
     tracted from Rashiduddin. "Introductory notice."
     v. 3, 1914. p. 108-110.
     A Jewish statesman in Mongol service.
     "Fazl-Ullah Rashid, otherwise Rashid-ud-din, . . .
     was born at Hamadan about A.D. 1247. His
     enemies, in the latter part of his life, called him
     a Jew both by birth and religion . . . . He was a
     physician by profession, and, in that capacity ap-
     parently, passed a considerable part of his life at
     the court of Abaka Khan and his immediate suc-
     cessors."   In 1298 Rashid was "named Wazir
     of the Persian empire in conjunction with Saad-ud-
     din."   With changing success Rashid held this
     position up to 1318, when he was killed together
     with his son at the instigation of his enemies.

     Marignolli, John de —:   "Recollections of travel
     in the East, by John de Marignolli, Papal Legate
     to the Court of the Great Khan, and afterwards
     Bishop of Bisignano." v. 3, 1914. p. 215. Disputa-
     tions with Jews; cf. also fn 1 on p. 215.
     Marignolli lived from 1303 to 1377.

d Ibn Batuta: "The travels of Ibn Batuta in China "
v.4, 1916; p 130.

"... we entered the second city (or Khansa; *i.e.*
Hangchow) by a gate called the Jews' Gate. This
town was inhabited by Jews, Christians, and by
those Turks who worship the sun; they are very
numerous."

e Goës, Benedict: "The journey of Benedict Goes
from Agra to Cathay." "Introductory notice."
v.4, 1916; p 175.

Report by a Mohammedan merchant at the end of
the 16th century. Allegedly he went as ambassador of the king of Kashgar to Kambalu (situated
near the present Peking) and saw there *Mussauites*
(i.e. Jews, for Moses in the tongue of these people
is called Mussau)."

The facts concerning Andrew of Perugia (title no. 215a)
and Goes (title no 215e) are also to be found in the book
by Frances Markley Roberts: *Western travellers to
China.* Shanghai, 1932; on p. 22 and 44 respectively.

216 "Attempt, An—to reorganize the Chinese Jews of
Kaifeng." (*The Chinese Recorder*, Shanghai. 50:
11. November, 1919, p. 780-782.)

In May, 1919, the Rev. J.J. Blackstone and other workers
of the Canadian Anglican Mission held a series of meetings
for the Chinese Jews with the purpose:

(1) of making them mutually acquainted and of organiz-
ing them;

(2) of making them acquained with their own history;

(3)   of making them acquainted with the religion of their forefathers and the Scriptures;

(4)   of making them realize their connections with their co-religionists throughout the world; and

(5)   of teaching them that Jesus Christ was a Jew, and that he came to save the world.

JE   217   *Cat. of Burrow Library.*   Chinese scrolls in possession of Judge Sulzberger, Philadelphia, Pa., and of Lenox Library, New York.

218   "Chine, La - a ses Juifs, mais elle les absorbe." (In: *A travers le monde*, Paris, 1912, v. 12, p. 231.)

219   "Chinese, The - Jew." (*Asia*, New York. 34:12. December, 1934. p. 712.)
Picture of a Chinese Jew from Kaifeng; no name of the photographer.

Sk   220   "Евреи в Китае." (Прав. Обозр. 18:8; 1864. стр. 348-351, Прилож к. "Гакармелю" 1869, 38-40, 43 and 45; Вестн. Русск. Евр., 1871; 32, 36, 37; Сиоч, но. 8, 1861; но. 37, 1862.)
"Hebrews in China."

Cor   221   "Etablissement des Juifs à la Chine." - Mémoire du Marquis de Fortia d'Urban inséré pp. 51/59 de la *Relation d'Eldad le Danite* . . . par E. Carmoly.   Paris, 1838.

Cor   222   "Fac-similes of the Hebrew manuscripts, obtained at the Jewish Synagogue in K'ae-Fung-Foo." Shanghai: Printed at the London Missionary Society's Press, 1851.

223   "Inscriptions, Les — hébraiques du Musée de l'Université du Gouvernment chinois à Pékin." (*Le Bulletin Catholique de Pékin*, Peking. 11:134. October, 1924 p. 407-410.

[115]

The article contains a photograph of the inscriptions on the stones found in Loyang; cf. Prévost (title no. 158).

224 "Itinéraire des marchands juifs et russes qui se rencontrent dans les parages de la mer Caspienne." (*Revue du Monde Musulman*, Paris. June, 1910. p. 273-274.)

Sk 225 "Иудейство в Китае." (Китаиский Благовестник. 1911, 5, стр. 3-4.)

"Judaism in China." (*Kitaisky Blogovestnik.* v. 5, 1911. p. 3-4.)

226 "Jews and Christians in China." (*The China Review* Hongkong. v. 13, ⌊1884 (?)⌋, p. 361.)

"Bell of Antermony found a few Jews and Mahometans at Peking in 1720, whom he supposed to have entered China about A.D. 1100 in company with the Western Tartars."

•227 ("Jews in China.") (In: *Hebrew Year Book*, St. Petersbourg. 1901. p. 381-391.)
(Еврейский Ежегоднйк, Ст. Петербург, 1901. стр. 381-391.)

Cor 228 "Juden, Die — in China." (*Ausland*, no.8, 1858.)

JE 229 "Letter in Hebrew from Jews of London to Jews of China in 1760." (Brit. Mus. MS, Add. No. 29868.)

This letter is reproduced in Cordier's *Bibliotheca Sinica*, vol. 2, col. 1353-1354; (see title no. 49).

230 *Lettres édifiantes et curieuses*, Paris.

a) Gaubil, Antoine: "Découverte d'un manuscrit en caractères estranghelo." - *Panthéon litteraire*, v. 4, p. 58-59.

The reference is contained in a letter addressed to *Monsieur* de L'Isle of August 12, 1752. The MS referred to contains in part a Syriac version of the Old Testament, of songs and of various prayers. It is supposed to date from the time of Chinghis Khan. The MS was acquired by Sylvestre de Sacy and was eventually sent to France. On the last page it contains explanatory notes by the two Jesuits Marie Antoine de Moyria de Mailla and Antoine Gaubil, both dated June 23, 1727.

b) Gozani, Jean Paul: "Lettre du Père Jean-Paul Gozani, Miss. de la Cie. de Jesus, au Père Joseph Suarez, de la même Cie. Traduite du Portugais." (A Cai-fum-fou, capitale de la province de Honan à la Chine, le 5 novembre 1704.)

Lettres édifiantes, anc. éd., VII., p. 1; Merigot. XVIII. p. 31-38. *Pant. litt.*, III, p. 149. - Trad, en allemand dans le *Welt-Blatt*, IV, no. 89.

Remarques sur la lettre du P. Gozani: *Let. éd.,* anc. éd., VII, p. 29; Merigot, XVIII. p. 48-55; *Pant. litt.*, III, p. 153-154.-Voir l'épitre du P. Ch. le Gobien en tête du VIIe Rec. des *Let. edifiantes.*

Mö   c) Gozani: "Lettre sur les juifs à Kai-fong-fou, 1701." *Lettres edifiantes,* nouv. éd., XXVII. 1832. p. 266-287.

Cor   d) "Mémoire sur les Juifs établis en Chine." *Let éd.,* anc. éd., XXXI, p. 296 et seq.; éd. de Mérigot. XXIV, p. 56-100, *Panthéon litt.*, IV, p. 140-150.

[117]

"Les lettres qu'ils [les PP. Gaubil et Domenge]
écrivirent à ce suject [les Ms. hébreux de K'ai-
foung-fou] contenoient des particularités importantes;
& les savans qui en avoient eu quelque connaissance,
regrettoient qu'elles ne fussent pas publiées. Ce fut
le motif qui engagea le savant abbé Brottier . . . à
en donner l'extrait dans une dissertation sur les Juifs,
qui se trouve dans le troisième volume de sa belle
édition de Tacite, publiée en 1771. Un nouvel extrait des mêmes lettres a été donné depuis au public
dans le trente-unième volume du Recueil des Lettres
édifiantes: ce n'est presque que la traduction de celui
qui se trouve dans l'édition de Tacite de 1771.
Quoiqu'il ait été publié sous le nom du P. Patouil-
let, il est l'ouvrage de l'abbé Brottier, ainsi qu'il
l'observe dans sa seconde édition de Tacite, publiée
en l'année 1776 (Tome V, p. 303), & dans laquelle
il a supprimé la dissertation sur les Juifs de la Chine.
L'identité de la dissertation latine & du mémoire
françois, est d'ailleurs assez justifiée par la confor-
mité des réflexions critiques qu'on trouve dans l'une
et dans l'autre, ce qui n'empêche pas que l'on ne
rencontre dans le dernier quelques détails plus circon-
stanciés." (S. de Sacy, Notice d'un Ms. du Pentateuque, *Not. et Ext.*, IV, pp. 593/4.)

The report was presumably written in 1770. It is
based upon the letters written on the subject by
Gozani, Domenge and Gaubil. It represents an
extensive summary of all the information available at
the time of writing.

Cor 231 *MS. British Museum, add. 29868.* Cf. *Revue de
l'Extrême-Orient,* I, No. 1, 1882, pp.116 117:

"L'une de ces pièces est une lettre en hébreu adressée en 1760 aux juifs de Chine par les juifs de Londres; voici la copie de la lettre en anglais qui l'accompagne, donnée aussi dans le recueil en question:

"Sir,

My good friend Mr. David Salomons having several times acquainted me with the knowledge you have acquired of the Chinese Language, their Manners, and the interior parts of that vast Empire. I was persuaded no Person could so well take the charge of informing me of the particulars I desired; I therefore beg'd he would recommend me to you, and I hope you will oblige me in aiding to discover the following matters, and forwarding the inclosed papers in the best manner for that purpose.

The Royal Society and other Persons have been inform'd by several Jesuit missionaries and others, that in several of the Northern and Western Provinces of the Chinese Empire there are People who profess the Jewish Religion or somewhat like or dependent upon it, and particulary that there are some at Pekin, but that there are more in the Province of Honan, and particularly at Caifengfu; now our curiosity leads us to get some knowledge of these people, and particularly of their manner of living, writing and customs. Anything whereof that you shall be willing to communicate to me I shall receive with thankfullness; and in order thereto, and that you may meet with the easier access among these people, some of our Priests and Scribes have wrote to them in Hebrew a copy of which you [sic] have wrote in English for your perusal, this letter I desire you would forward them

[119]

with all care and precaution, and endeavour to get an answer. I think it prudent that you should be cautious that this design should not be known to the Papists, and particularly to the Jesuits, lest they should endeavour to hinder our discoveries; for 'tis possible, were such a thing to prove true, that the British Interest might be strengthened in China, and some new branches of commerce open'd to the honourable Company, all which I ardently wish to promote. Should your affairs not permit you to attend this matter, you will oblige me greatly, in recommending it to some Person you may think properly qualified to execute it, and any expence you may be at, not exceeding Fifty Pounds sterling I shall repay with thanks. I am with great regard,

   Sir,

     Your very obliged servant.''

Cf. also titles no. 4a and 229.

Cor 232 "On Jews in China." (*The North-China Herald*, Shanghai. no. 25. January 18, 1851; cf. also no. 55. August 16, 1851.)

  233 Religion The — of the Israelites and Mohammedans in China." (*Moslem Affairs*, Tokyo. 1:3, November 16, 1938. p. 53-66.)

   Brief historical summary.

   支那に於ける一賜樂業(猶太)教, 回教 (回教事情 東京. 1:3.)

  234 "Remarkable, A — attack." (*The Peiping Chronicle*, Peiping. October 10, 1937; reprinted from *The Japan Chronicle*, Tokyo.)

   Alleged activities of British and French Jews in favour of the Chinese government against Japan.

235   *Secret plans, The — of the Jews in the whole world.*
      Tientsin, 1927. (Chung Hua Min Kuo Sheng Tao Hui)
      世界秘密猶太人之陰謀.天津,民國十六年(中華民國
      聖道會.)

236   "Ten Lost Tribes, The — " (*The Chinese Recorder*,
      Shanghai. 16:1. January-February, 1885. p. 47-48.)
      In the "Critical Notes" it is mentioned that some writers
      believed that the Jews in China were descendants of the
      Ten Lost Tribes.

SUPPLEMENT

237   Hauser, Ernest O.: *Shanghai: city for sale.* New
      York, 1940. (Harcourt, Brace & Co. - Authorized
      edition for China publ. by The Chinese-American
      Publishing Company, Inc., Shanghai.) p. 273-280, the
      Sassoon family.

      In the 12th century the Sassoon family settled under the
      name of Ibn Shoshan in Toledo, then under the rule of
      the Moors. In the 15th century the family was driven
      out of Spain and went into exile in Bagdad. New per-
      secutions forced them to leave that city. The family
      marched through Persia to India, and in 1832 settled in
      Bombay. David Sassoon (+1864), the head of the
      family, became a British subject and took up business
      connections in China.· In 1931, Sir Ellice Victor Sas-
      soon transferred his fortune to Shanghai for investment.

238   Havret, S.J., Henri: *La stèle chrétienne de Si-ngan-
      fou.* IIème partie.*Histoire du monument.* Shanghai,
      1897. (Variétés sinologiques no. 12. Imprimerie de
      la Mission Catholique.) p. 297.

      The book contains particulars about the Jewish sino-
      logues, Isaac Jacob Schmidt and Charles Frédéric

Neumann, who had discredited the authenticity of the Christian stele at Sian.

239 Mendelssohn, Sidney: *The Jews of Asia, especially in the sixteenth and seventeenth centuries.* London-New York, 1920. (Kegan Paul - Dutton & Co.) Ch. IX, p. 133-163.

The author has summarized the findings from foreign sources. According to his view the Jews entered China in 845 A.D. A passage from the work by Basnage is quoted in the chapter on China. It has been reproduced in this bibliography; (cf. title no. 14).

240 Miller, G.E. (Pseudonym: *Diplomat*) : *Shanghai, the paradise of adventurers.* New York, 1937. (Orsay Publishing House Inc.)

p. 47-49, 53-54, 60, 268-269: Sir Ellice Victor Sassoon.

p. 153-162, 271: Opium trade of the Ezra brothers.

p. 203-218, 270: I.T. Trebitsch-Lincoln (Chao Kung).

241 Sassoon, *Sir* Ellice Victor : "Sir Ellice Victor Sassoon." (*Time,* Chicago. 35: 7. February 12, 1940. p. 61.)

242 "Jews." (North Manchurian Special Investigation Bureau.) Published in Manchuria after 1932.
猶太人. (北 滿 洲 特 務 機 關 調 查.)

243 Franck, Harry A.: *Wandering in Northern China.* New York - London, 1923. (The Century Co.)

p. 83, 93-94, and 93. Observations concerning Russian Jewish immigrants in Manchuria.

p. 334-336, with 1 illustration. The author reports on the findings of his visit to Kaifeng. He states that "some doubt whether there are a hundred individuals left: the present head of the clan put the number at 'one or two hundred . " The author admits that the

Jews have practically been assimilated by the Chinese
population through intermarriage and oblivion of their
own traditions.   In this connection he mentions: "Several portions of Hebrew scriptures have been found on
the streets for sale, evidently as mere curios."   "All
those I saw looked less Jewish than do some of the
Chinese."

244   Chou Wei-t'ung: "The Kaifeng Jews." (*Light in Darkness*, Peking. 11:6. June, 1940. p.365-366;) with two
illustrations

The author visited the Kaifeng community together with
the Rev. Hu (古 牧 師). He took some pictures of which
two are reproduced on the front cover of the magazine.
1) Chao Tzu-fang 趙 子 方 the present head of the Chao
family; 2) the lotus stone basin, in the possession of the
local Canadian Episcopal Mission, which is now used as a
baptismal vessel.

周維同: 在之開封的猶太人. (暗中之光. 北京. 第十一卷
第六期第三六五至三六六頁.)

245   White, *Rev.* H.W. (Pai Hsiu-sheng); Chou Wei-t'ung
(transl.): "Historical lecture on the arrival of the Jews
in China." (*Light in Darkness*, Peking. 11;6. June
1940. p. 366-368.)

This brief article is mainly based on the report by W.A.
P. Martin.

白秀生著, 周維同譯: 猶太人到中國來的歷史講演.
(暗中之光. 北京. 第十一卷第六期第三六六至三六八
頁)

246   Mailla, *S.J.*, Joseph-François-Marie-Anne de Moyriac
de - : *Histoire générale de la Chine.* v. 13, *Description générale de la Chine ou tableau actuel de cet*

[123]

empire; rédigée par M. L'Abbé Grosier, Chanoine de
S. Louis du Louvre. Paris, 1758. Ch. 7, p. 610-617.
"Juifs établis à la Chine."

The contents of this chapter are based upon the letter by
Gozani. Cf. also Grosier, title no.82. Mailla mentions
also that the Jesuits Figueredo and Herdtricht (Enri-
quez) had had contacts with the Kaifeng Jewish community (p.614).

247 Wieger, *S. J.*, Léon: *Chinois parlé; manuel.* 4e éd. refon-
due. Sienhsien, 1936.

p.179. "Les Chinois, comme les Juifs, désignent par les
mêmes appellatifs, les degrés qui sont à la même hauteur
sur l'arbre commun, frères et cousins germains, neveux et
cousins issus de germains."

248 Boone, W.J.: "Defense of an essay on the proper rendering of the words Elohim and θεος into the Chinese
language." (Continuation) (*The Chinese Repository*,
Canton. 19:11. November, 1850. p.468, note B.)

,.. . . We have also a Tablet giving an account of the
spread of the *King kiáu* (Illustrious religion) in China,
written by *King Tsing* in the second year of *Kien-chung*
(A.D. 781). Now to explain the character *Hien*, or
Yáu 祆 , it is from *hsi* 示 and from *t'ien* 天 and is the
god (*Shin*) of Heaven, whose religion arose in Palestine."

249 [Morrison; *Rev.* Robert: *Morrison's journal.*] (*The
Chinese Repository*, Canton. v.1, 1832; p.44.)

Quoted from the review of the work by Eusebius REN-
AUDOT, *Ancient account of India and China, by two
Mohammedan travellers*, etc., London, 1733:—

"The most recent testimony which we have on this
subject (the Chinese Jews) is contained in Morrison's

Journal, written in the interior of China, from which we give the following passage. 'October 10th, 1818. - Had a conversation with a Mohammedan gentleman, who informed me, that at Kae-fung Fu in the province of Honan, there are a few families denominated the *Teaou-kin-keaou*, or'the sect that plucks the sinew,' from all the meat which they eat. They have a Le-pae-sze, or house of worship; and observe the eigth day as a Sabbath."

250 Van den Brandt, *C.M.*, Joseph: *Catalogue des princi-paux ouvrages sortis des presses des Lazaristes à Pékin de 1864 à 1930*. Pékin, 1933. (Imprimerie des Laza-ristes.) (Cf. also titles. no. 158 and 223.)

p. 57, title no. 279. - " . . . . La découverte de trois fragments d'inscriptions, à Loyang au Honan, est heu-reuse, d'autant plus que ce sont, croyons-nous, les premières inscriptions lapidaires qu'on possède. L'auteur pour sa part a essayé d'en donner la traduction et d'en établir l'époque appoximative, et ainsi donne sa contribution à l'étude de la question juive en Chine.

A propos de ces inscriptions, le conservateur du musée nous racontait qu en realité quatre fragments avaient été trcuvés à Loyang, mais qu'on en avait égaré un lors de leur transport, à Pékin. Le porte-faix, ne comprenant pas l'utilité de ces pierres cassées, aura trouvé le moyen de se débarasser d'une, certainement pas de la plus légère, sans se douter que cette perte pouvait laisser des regrets."

251 Various notes from *The Chinese Repository*, Canton.

a) "Jews in Thibet." (2:5. Sept., 1833. p. 237-238.) According to this note some Jewish shawl manu-facturers from Tibet attended the Leipzig fair in

[125]

1833. Presumably the Rev. Joseph Wolff was responsible for the reproduction of this note from other sources.

b) "The Lost Ten Tribes of Israel." (2:9. Jan., 1834. p. 428.)

Anonymous contribution, apparently made in reply to the above statement. The author refutes the authenticity of that information, partly on personal grounds.

c) "Notices of the Catholic religion in China, in a letter from the Rt. Rev. Joseph Rizzolati, vicar apostolic of Hu-kwang." (15:1. Jan., 1846. p. 43-44.)

This letter was addressed to the Very Rev. Joseph d'Alexandrie, General of the Franciscans, and dated from Nov. 25th, 1842. "Having been read at a meeting of the Society for the Propagation of the Faith, held in St. Patrick's church, Syndey, (it) was afterward published."

The letter contained a passage concerning the Jews. It mentioned that they were called "Hwui-hwui Ku-kiáu" 回回古教 and that they lived scattered in various places in China.

252 Shimitsu, Yasuzo: "Miscellaneous notes on Chinese studies." (Shi-so, Tokyo, special China edition. no 86. July, 1929. p.174-175 [p.596-597]. "Kaifeng and the Israelites.")

清水安三: 支那學雜記. (思想, 特輯支那號, 東京. 第八十六號, 昭和四年七月, 174-175 (596-597)(頁). 開封四樂桀人.)

The author raises briefly the question of the date and route of entry of the Jews into China. The note is based on European sources.

253 Asch, Scholom [A Hsü]; T'ang Hsü-chih (transl): *The God of Vengeance.* Shanghai, 1936. (Commercial Press.) IV + 95 p.

Translation of a play.

阿背著, 唐旭之 譯: 復仇神. 上海, 中華民國二十五年. （商務印書館.) IV + 95 頁.

254 Browne, L. [Pu La-en]; Ni Hsiu-chang (transl.): *The story of the Jews.* Shanghai, 1939. (Commercial Press.) 354 p. (Cf. also title no. 27.)

Translation of a popular history of the Jews.

布拉恩著. 倪秀章 譯: 猶太民國旗史. 上海, 中華民國二十八年. （商務印書館.) 354 頁.

255 Weng Chung-ma: "Jewish refugees in Shanghai." (*West Wind Supplement*, Shanghai. no. 21. May 16, 1940. p. 398-401.)

Reflections on some personal contacts with Jewish refugees.

翁仲馬: 猶太難民在上海. （西風副刊. 上海. 第二十一期. 廿九年五月 十六日. 第三九八至四〇一 頁.)

*256 Teng Shao-yin: *Commentary on the "Analects" of the Jewish religion.* Peking, 1922. 2 vols.

The compiler has not been able to secure a copy of this work. Hence, it is impossible to give any further information on it. The term "Analects" 論語 was apparently borrowed from Confucian terminology.—From other publications by the same author it appears that he was a native of Szechwan and advocated a synchretic religion, embracing Buddhism, Taoism, Confucianism, Mohammedanism, Christianity, and Judaism. The philosophical ideas represented a kind of degenerate Taoism.

鄧紹雲: 猶太教論語微冒. 北京. 民國十一年. 兩册.

257 Wu Han: "Social organization of the Yüan dynasty."
(*The Social Science*, National Tsing Hua University,
Peiping. 1:3. April, 1936. p. 616.

The author wrongly identifies the *Wo-t'o* 斡脫 as Jews.
Cf. *Introduction* and title no. 34.

吳晗: 元代之社會. (社會科學. 國立清華大學 北平. 民國二十五年
四月. 第一卷第三期, 616 頁.

258 Zi, *S.J.*, Joseph [Hsü Tsung-tse]: *Evangelisatio Sinarum*
Shanghai, 1938. (Société de la Revue catholique.
Ch. 1, p. 1-63. "The Jews of Kaifeng."

On pages 1-16 the author summarizes briefly the history
of the Kaifeng Jews, basing his facts mainly on foreign
sources. This section is supplemented by a reprint of the
article by Shen Kùng-pu (沈公布), "Some facts concerning
the Israelites of Kaifeng." (關於開封 - 賜樂業之吉光片羽.)
(p. 17-47.—Cf. title no. 173). In three further supplements
the Chinese stone inscriptions of 1489 (p. 48-52), of 1512
(p. 53-55) and of 1663 (p. 56-63) are reproduced.

徐宗澤: 中國天主教傳教史概論. 上海, 民國二十七年. (聖教雜誌社.)
第一章, 1—63頁. 開封猶太教.

APPENDIX I (to title no. 161).

RICCI, *OPERE STORICHE* (TACCHI-VENTURI)

Volume Primo: I Commentarj della Cina.

p. 86-87 (p. 86, line 32).—*Maomettani, ebrei e cristiani nell' Impero di Mezzo.* Ritrovassimo parimente in questo regno, come di poi si dirà, Giudei che vivono nella legge antica di Mosè, ma· sono puoche famiglie, e non sappiamo avere sinagoga in altra parte che nella metropoli della provincia di Honan, detta Chaifum fu e in quella di Cechiano, detta Hanceu fu. In essa guardano con grande veneratione il Pentateuco di Mosè in lettera hebraica, scritto in carta pecora, senza punti, al modo antico irrolati. De gli altri libri del Testamento Vecchio non habbiamo anco saputo quanti ne habbino. Conservano la cerimonia della circoncisione et si astengono dal mangiar porco e d'ogn. carne con nervi conforme al loro antico rito.

Puochi anni sono sapessimo di certo che vi forno anco christiani specialmente in queste provincie settentrionali sotto il nome di adoratori della croce, e fiorivano tantoi in numero di famiglie, lettere et armi che, sessanta anni fa, i Cinesi vennero ad avere cattiva sospitione di essi, mossa forse dagli Maomettani che in ogni parte sono nostri inimici. Per il che li solsero prendere, e così si nascosero tutti facendosi alcuni Turchi e Giudei e la maggior parte gentili, e le loro chiese furono fatte tempi de idoli, et i suoi discendenti, ancorchè molti conservino il costume di far la croce nelle cosi che mangiano e bevono, restorno con tanta paura che non vogliono confessare esser loro posteri, e nessuno vi è, nè tra loro nè di altri, che sappino dare nessuna causa del fare queste croci; ma nella loro

[129]

figura chiaramente dimostrano esser figliuoli di gente
forastiera nella Cina.

A tutti questi forastieri chiamono i Cinesi *hoethoei*,
del qual nome non potessimo sapere l'origine..............ai
Giudei chiamono *hoethoei che togliono i nervi della carne
che mangiano*.............

p. 463—469. *Abboccamento del Ricci coll'israelita Ngai.
Gli Ebrei nella Cina.*

Venne questo libro anco alle mani di un giudeo di
natione e di professione, della provincia e metropoli di
Honan, di cognome *Ngai*, che haveva già conseguito il grado
di licentiato nelle lettere della Cina, e venne questo stesso
anno a Pacchino all'essame di dottori. E avendo letto in
questo libro che noi non eramo della legge de'Saraceni,
come moltissimi che stanno nella Cina, nè adoravamo
altra cosa che li re del cielo, si persuadette che eramo
della sua legge mosaica, e entrò nella casa de'padri con
molta allegrezza, dicendo esser della nostra legge. Et era
la sua figura assai diversa della cina nel naso, negli occhi
e tutto il viso.

Il p. Matteo lo menò subito alla cappella, dove stava
nell'altare, per esser la festa di s. Giovanni Battista, novamente posta una bella ancona della Madonna, che d'un
lato aveva il Bambino Giesù, e dall'altro s. Giovanni
Battista che l'adorava inginocchioni.

Il giudeo, che veniva con quella imaginatione di aver
ritrovato gente della sua legge, non dubitò niente esser
quella la imagine di Rebecca, con suoi figliuoli Iacob e
Esaù; e così gli fece imantenente riverentia, dicendo: "Io

non voglio adorare imagini, ma voglio riverire questi che
furno origine della mia generatione e prosapia." E perchè
anco stavano d'ambe le bande della cappella i quattro
Evangelisti, domandò il giudeo se erano quelli degli dodici
figliuoli di quello che stava nell'altare. Il padre, pensando
che parlasse de'dodici Apostoli, gli rispose che si, e lo
menò nella sua camera per essaminarlo più e saper che
huomo era questo. E venne puoco a puoco a sapere esser
giudeo, se bene egli non si nominava, nè sapeva il nome di
giudeo, ma solo di israelita.   Gli mostrorno la Bibbia di
Plantino in ebreo, e subito riconobbe la sua lettera, se bene
non la sapeva leggere.

Da questo seppero i nostri nella metropoli di Honan,
detta Caifun, esservi dieci o dodici famiglie di Giudei con
una sinagoga molto bella, che novamente era stata ristaurata
da loro con spesa di diecimilia ducati, nella quale tenevano
il Pentateuco di Mosè, scritto in carta pecorina, irrolato
con cinque ruoli con molta veneratione. E stavano qui di
cinquecento o seicento anni in qua; e che nella metropoli
di Cechiano, detta Hanceo, stavano molto più famiglie della
loro legge con sinagoga, et [in] altra parti, ma senza
sinagoga, per andarsene loro puoco a puoco spengendo. E
per quanto loro non mangiano carne di porco, i Cinesi
fanno puoca distintione da loro ai Saraceni della legge di
Maometto, se bene questi Giudei sentono male di quella
setta e la aborriscono.

p. 469-473 (p. 470, line 33).—*Vestigj di un'antica
cristianità in K'aifong.*

Ai Saraceni chiamava quest'uomo, e così diceva esser
chiamati fra Giudei, *sanchiao*, che vuol dire di tre leggi,
per quello che tengono di giudei, de' christiani è di gentili.

[131]

Ma gli Cinesi distinguono, como sapessimo dipoi, queste tre leggi per altri nomi; cioè, ai Saraceni chiamavano "huomini che non mangiano porco", ai Giudei "huomini che non mangiano nervi", perchè guardano questi sin adesso la legge vecchia di tagliare di tutti gli animali che mangiano i nervi. et ai descendenti di christiani "huomini che non mangiano animali di ugna rotonda" perchè mangiando e Mori e Giudei e tutta la Cina carne di cavallo, mulo et altri simili giumenti, loro per il costume della patria non la mangiano.

Ulteriori ragguagli sopra gli Ebrei di K'aifong.

Contava questo giudeo molte historie del Testamento Vecchio come di Abram, di Iuditta, di Mardocheo, di Hester et altre; se bene nel suono delli propri nomi era assai diverso, e puo essere che il suo era piu proprio e vicino all' hebreo. E cos a Gerusalemme chiamava Hierusoloim, et al Messia, che diceva egli aver da venire, chiamava Moscia. Disse ai padri che in Caifun vi erano molti che sapevano hebraico, e che tra questi vi era un suo fratello, e che egli da piccolo si era dato alle lettere della Cina; e così non aveva imparato le lettere hebree. E dava a intendere che, per seguir le cose de letterati della Cina, era stato cacciato fuora della sinagoga dallo archisinagogo, che là è presidente di essi, et andava mezzo scomunicato, e facilmente avrebbe lasciato questa legge se avesse potuto ottenere il grado di dottore, come fanno anco tutti i Saraceni che, potendo ottenere il grado di dottore, non hanno più paura del loro *Mollà* e lasciano la legge.

Con questa nova restorno i nostri molto contenti, parendo che questi nepoti di christiani facilmente ritornerebbono alla loro avita religione.

*Provvedimenti per rintracciare i cristiani e gli Ebrei di
K'ai fong riusciti inutili.*

Per questo tre anni dipoi il p. Matteo mandò a quella i
città un nostro fratello cinese a inquirere che reliquie vii
erano tra questi di christianità e vedere anco che lettera
e che imagini usavano, insieme con un letterato di quella
terra, che in Pacchino aveva riceuto il santo battesimo.
Ma là gli fu fatto più accoglienza da'Giudei che dagli
adoratori della croce, i quali non volevano confessare al
fratello esser descendenti di quelli, o per paura che fusse
venuto a inquirere questo per fargli qualche male, o perché
questi figliuoli vogliono esser tenuti per Cinesi e si disprez-
zano di venire da gente forastiera, che fra ogni natione
e puoco onore, e fra Cinesi è cosa ignominiosa; e così
non potette sapere altro che quello che di sopra si è detto.

Fece scrivere il principio et il fine dei libri hebraici,
che tenevano i Giudei nella sinagoga, et erano l'istesse lettere che del nostro Pentateuco, ma senza punti, secondo
l'antico costume, sotto le lettere.

Aveva il p. Matteo scritta una lettera al'archisinagogo
in lettera cinese, nella quale gli diceva aver seco in Pacchino tutti i libri del Testamento Vecchio et anco il Novo
delle cose del Messia già venuto al mondo; ma lui rispose
al fratello che il Messia aveva da venire da qui a diecimila
anni. E, perché avevano loro avuto molto grande e buona
fama del padre, gli mandorno a dire che, se voleva lasciar
di mangiar carne di porco et andare a star con loro, lo
farebbono là loro archisinagogo.

Vennero dopo questo a Pacchino tre altri giudei di
quella terra sì disposti a farsi christiani, che, se potevano
stare alcuni giorno di più, facilmente avrebbono riceuto il

[133]

santo battesimo. Et uno di questi era nepote, figliuoli di
un fratello del licentiato *Ngai*, ai quali i padri fecero grande
festa, dichiarandogli molte cose della loro legge, che nè
loro nè i loro maestri sapevano, e che il Messia era venuto
et la sua imagine era quella che havevano visto nella nostra
chiesa, la quale tutti tre adororno inginocchiati, come se
fussero christiani, e portorno seco la *Dottrina christiana* et
altri libri delle nostre cose fatti in lettera cinese.

Stavano questi tre molto dolorosi der vedere che la
loro setta si giva spengendo per nessuno sapere le loro lettere
e che si avevano da fare o gentili o saraceni come i christiani che anticamente stavano in quella città. E dicevano
che era già morto l'archisinagogo vecchio che sapeva qualche cosa, e gli era succeduto per heredità un suo fi-
gliuolo giovane, che non sapeva niente delle cose della loro
legge, e che era cosa che pareva molto male in un tempio
molto ben fatto, che loro avevano, non vi esser nessuna
imagine, e ne' loro oratorij, anco non poner niente nelle loro
case; che se e nel tempio e nelle loro case avessero l'imagine del Salvatore, avrebbe fatto grande divotione a
tutti. E sopratutto questo si doleva delle obbligationi che
l'archisinagogo gli poneva, come di non mangiare niente di
carne che non fosse di animale ammazzato per sua mano,
dicendo che quivi a Pacchino, se avessero voluto guardar
questo, sarebbono morti di fame; e come anco quello di
circoncidere i fanciulli otto giorni doppo de nati, che pareva
alle loro mogli et ai loro parenti gentili cosa molto crudele;
e concludevano che, se fossero da' nostri assolti di queste
cerimonie, seguirebbono la nostra legge, facendo puoca
difficoltà in mangiare carne di porco.

Per questo si risolse il p. Matteo nella prima buona
occasione e commodità che vi fosse mandar là un padre,

che stando là per sempre, potesse puoco a puoco scoprire le reliquie che vi fossero della christianità e procurare di convertire anco questi giudei. E non lo potette subito esseguire, per essere in questi tempi uno governatore di quella città, che non era affettionato, anzi era averso, alle cose della christianità.

Volume Secundo: Le lettere dalla Cina.

p. 286. no. 35. Pechino, 26 luglio 1605. Al P. Claudio Acquaviva Prep. Gen. S. I. a Roma.

p. 289-292. *(3) Famiglie discendenti da antichi christiani nella provincia di Honan.*

Puochi giorni sono venessimo a sapere per cosa certa che dentro delle Cina, vi fu da cinquecento anni in qua buon numero de christiani, e che ancora ve ne resta grande vestigio in molti luoghi. Gli anni passati scrissi a V. P. che avevamo scoperta una chritianità in terre soggette alla Cina, ma fuori degli grandi muri settentrionali. dove sin ora per mancamento di puochi scuti per fare questa giornata, non habbiamo mandato nessuno ad investigare quanti sono e donde vennero. Adesso sapessimo che nel mezzo della Cina, lengi da qui mezzo mese, et altre tanto di Nanchino, nella provincia di Honan, e nella metropoli che si chiama Caifun fu, vi sono cinque o sei familie da christiani, ma già spento quasi tutto quel puoco che vi era di christianità, per avere già parecchi anni che della chiesa fecere tempio di un idolo, che si chiama Çuanguam. Quello che ci impeditte a saperlo sin hora fu non si nominare loro per nome de christiani, ma per gente di *Terza;* pare nome del regno donde vennero alla Cina, e dalla lege de *xezu* che vuol dire della lettera di dieci, che nella lettera cina è una croce perfetta, di questo modo +;

[135]

perchè nella figura e fisonomia del viso e in non adorar
idoli erano simili ai Mori e Giudei; solo erano diversi, che
mangiavano carne di porco ed ogni carne, facendoli sopra di
essa una croce con la mano.

Sapessimo questo per mezzo di un giudeo di legge,
natione e figura, che i giorni passati mi venne a visitare per
la fama che aveva udita e per un libro stampato
de' molti che si fecero delle nostre cose; dal quale
intendendo che non eravamo mori nè gentili, pensò egli che
eravamo della sua legge. E' quest'huomo di cognome
Ngai della provincia di Honan, habitatore della metropoli; suo padre hebbe tre figliuoli; e gli sediede alle lettere
della Cina e si graduò in licentiato; e già di sessanta anni,
venne quest'anno a chiedere offitio, che gli fu dato in una,
schuola nella città di Ianceo. Gli altri duoi fratelli
attesero alle lettere hebree, e sono, pare, tra loro rabini,
dicendo che nella sua terra vi era una sinagoga grande,
dove spesero dieci milia scuti, e che sette o otto familie vi
erano della sua legge.

Venne a casa nella ottava di san Giovanni Battista,
et avevamo posta nell'altare un'imagine grande e bella della
Madonna con il bambino Giesù d'una parte e dall'
altra di san Giovan Battista. Non sapeva quest'huomo il
nome di giudeo, ma solamente si chiamava israelita. E
vedendo questa imagine, pensò che erano i due fanciulli
Iacob e Esau, e così disse: "Sebene io non adoro imagini,
voglio fare riverentia a questi miei primi avi"; e così si
abassò e fece riverentia; e parlando egli nel principio che
il capo della sua setta hebbe dodeci figluoli, pensai io
che era christiano e che parlava de dodici apostoli. Alfine
ritrovai non essere christiano, ma non molto averso della
christianità, perchè, mi diceva egli, non potersi guardare

la sua legge nella Cina per causa della circoncisione,
purificatione, carne de porco et altre cose che impedivano
il comercio con gli altri, specialmente quei che volevano
andare in magistrati, e ci dava a intendere che *factus erat
extra synagogam* e non sapeva molte cose, sebene contava
molte istorie del Testamento Vecchio, delle dodici tribù
di Moisè sino alla istoria di Aman e Mardocheo, ch'egli
chiamava Amaan e Mardocai, e diceva che suoi fratelli
sapevano tutto che sta ne' libri della sua legge, e penso
che vi hanno anco altri libri superstitiosi.

Disse che tenevano per traditione che quando il re
Tamorlano conquistò tutta la Persia, conquistò anco la Cine
e vennero con esso molti mori, christiani e giudei, averà
già ottocento anni, e che i mori forno quei che più
prevalsero, e così i christiani e giudei restorno puochi;
ma che nella terra di Honan vi erano di tutte le tre sette,
ma la christiana quasi extinta; ma che tra loro vi erano molta
letterati e magistrati grandi. Tra gli altri vi è adesso vivoi
un *scianciu* di Nanchino che si chiama *Ciammennan*, molt.
nostro amico, quando quivi stetti, e l'anno passato, venendo
a Pachino, mi venne a visitare e mi fece molte carezze, e
la fa bene con i padri di Nanchino, e diceva che questi non
vogliono confessare l'esser descesi da forastieri, cosa di
puoco onore nella Cina. Questo *Ciammennan*, nella fisonomia, pare huomo di nostra terra.

Il giorno seguente il giudeo meno a nostra casa un
della sua terra di cognome *Cian*, che diceva esser descen-
dente de' christiani, che anco aveva a procurare offitio e
l'ottenne nella provincia di Xens presso a quei christiani
antiqui fuora della mura, che sono soggetti a lui per questo
nove offitio. Con questo facessimo molta amicitia e mostrò
grande voglia di intendere pienamente le cose della nostra

[137]

legge e tornare alla legge de suoi antepassati, ma in sei giorni si fu di Pachino, e stette sempre occupatissimo, oltre l'impedimento che teneva della poligamia; e così lasciai, sino conchiuder questo in altro tempo. Con tutto mi promesse di fare agni diligentia ne' duoi luoghi, cioè in sua terra et in quella dove tiene il suo offitio, per sapere quanto vi resta anco di christianità e, quello che più desidero, di che lettera usano, se della suriana o, quello che più probabile pare, della greca, mosso a questo per una campanella che, dieci anni sono, viddi nelle mani di un cina, antiquissima con croci e con lettere greche, che, pare, era venuta di quella terra di Honan.

Aspettiamo adesso il p. Visitatore, che ha da venire a visitare queste case, e non ha dubbio che subito si mandarà a sapere quanto vi è di buono in quelle parti, e spero in Dio che con questo si apra anco più larga questa porta della christianità nella Cina.

p. 293. *(4) La Cina è il famoso Cataio di Marco Polo. Invia due copie del Catechismo per mostrarle al papa.*

Di qui entendessimo che molto manco adesso è dubbio che la Cina è il Catayo di Marco Polo veneto, e che non e falso quello che egli dice nel Cataio esservi christiani, perchè in suo tempo ve ne sarebbono molti. Mi fece anco questo giudeo considerare, se quello che signoreggiò la Cina cinquecento anni fa fu il Tamorlano, sì nominato tra di noi; perciochè, quello che entrò nella Cina sappiamo che fu figluolo di quello che conquistò la Persia, e sebene il padre non conquistò la Cina, tutto si attribue a sua padre.

APPENDIX II (to title no. 108; cf. also titles no. 92 and 145).

THE OFFICIAL HISTORY OF THE YÜAN DYNASTY. 欽定元史

Chapter 33; second year of the reign of Yüan Ming-tsung (1329).

".... The merchants among the Christians, Jews and Mohammedans shall be taxed as before...."

卷三十三; 元明宗天曆二年 (1329):—

...也里可溫朮忽合失蠻爲商者乃舊制納稅. ...

Chapter 40; sixth year of the reign of Chih Yüan (1340) *

"...... In the same month (July) foreigners were prohibited from marrying their (widowed) paternal aunts (wifes of their fathers' younger brothers)...."

卷四十; 元順帝至元六年 (1340):—

.........是月禁月人勿妻其叔母..........

Chapter 43; fourteenth year of the reign of Yüan Shun-ti (1354):—

"..A Erh-hui, the Prime Minister (the Right-hand Counsellor), attacked Luchou. He summoned the skilful archers of Ninghsia and the wealthy Mohammedans and Jews from various places to the capital to join the army...."

卷四十三; 元順帝至正十四年(1354):—.

...阿兒灰爲右丞討廬州蔡寧夏善射者及各處回回朮忽殷富者赴京師從軍....

---

* B. Laufer referred apparently to the above passage in his article: "A Chinese-Hebrew manuscript", p. 190-191; (cf. title no. 108):—
"In 1340 the levirate was interdicted to Mohammedans and Jews (the levirate was an abomination in the eyes of the Chinese, and under the Manchu dynasty was prohibited on pain of death.)"
Unfortunately the author did not indicate the sources of his information.

APPENDIX III (to title no. 92).

HUNG CHÜN: *"A SURVEY ON THE VARI-
OUS RELIGIOUS SECTS DURING THE YÜAN
DYNASTY"* (LEAVES 1 - 3.)

The two characters, *Wo-t'o* 斡 脫 found in the *Ching-
shih Ta-chien* 經 世 大 典 mean "Jewish religion". If we
examine the sound of these two characters, they really should
be *Yu-t'e* 攸 特. Concerning (the sound of both) the first
characters, *yu* 攸 is preferable to *wo* 斡; concerning (the
sound of both) the second characters, *t'o* 脫 is preferable
to *t'e* 特. Some people use the three characters *Ju-te-ya*
如 德 亞 which refers to the geographical location of the
people in question. *Ju-te* 如 德 is the same as *Yu-t'e* 攸特.
Since the fall of the Jewish kingdom 猶 太 國, its population has dispersed in all directions. Today most of the
merchants in the various European countries are Jews.
Large numbers of people of Jewish race live in Persia and
Bokhara. I have heard some Westerners say that in Kai-
fong, Honan, there are also Jews to be found, whom the
Chinese mistakenly class together with Mohammedans. In
Kaifeng, there is a Jewish monument (碑), the inscription
of which is appended below. Their occupation consists
chiefly in the slaughtering of cattle. Their religious principles are vague and obscure. Their high and hooked
noses have remained unchanged as a prominent feature. Of
the three Western religions, the oldest is the Jewish, from
which Catholicism and Islam have originated. The Ten
Commandments which survive even to-day, were given by
God on Mount Sinai to Moses, the Father of the Jewish
religion. The belief in one God, and the practice of rest-
ing one day in seven, are Jewish traditions. Their written

[140]

language runs horizontally from right to left, like that of
the Turks. Those Westerners who believe in the Jewish
religion must learn Hebrew, as the Bible (Old Testament)
is written in that language. In my visits to foreign
churches, those who accompanied me, informed me that
the religious rites are very strict; e. g., the failure to doff
a hat is a sign of disrespect. Smilingly I repl′ed that
Jesus himself was an Aaiatic with black hair and eyes,
similar to myself. If he knew that I, an Asiatic, am visiting
him, he would make haste to welcome me, and would
not stickle over European customs. Of what importance
is it not to doff one's hat?

洪鈞: 元世各教名考. 1-3 頁.

經世大典之斡脫卯猶太教審定字音當云攸特首
字今譯爲勝次字大典譯音爲勝或稱如德亞則言其地
如德亦攸特也自猶太失國戶口四散今歐羅巴諸國貿
遷有無多猶太人波斯布哈爾等地種族甚夥聞諸西人
今中國河南開封仍有猶太人華人不知但以回回統之
地有猶太碑（碑文附後）其人多業屠牛本教理致茫
昧若遺惟鼻高而鉤厥形未變案西土三教猶太最古天
主天方二教皆濫觴於此今世所傳耶穌十戒爲古時寧
西登西奈山受諸天帝者摩西即猶太教之宗主也專奉
天地七日一安息皆猶太之說其文字旁行自右而左與
突厥同西人奉教者必習猶太文以耶穌經典用本國文
字也鈞嘗遊西國教堂從者謂堂中嚴禮節不免冠謂不
敬笑應之曰耶穌即亞細亞人髮睛色黑與我貌同彼如
有靈聞亞細亞人來且倒屣之不暇必不以歐洲之禮苛
我不免冠奚害焉

[141]

AUTHOR, PERSON AND SUBJECT INDEX

A Hsü; see *Asch, Sholom* 阿胥

Abraham, David Ezekiel; 4a

Abraham. Reuben D.E.J.; 166

Abu Zaid, see *Hasan ibn Yazid, Abu Zaid, al Sirafi*

Acquaviva, *S.J.* (General), Claudio; 161

Adam; 9

Adler. Elkan N.; *1, 2,* 4a, 142

Adler, Marcus Nathan; *3, 4a-c, 28b,* 109, 112

Ai T'ien, see *Ngai T'ien* 艾田

Alechem, Sholom; *117*

Aleni, *S.J.,* Jul'us (It.); 63, *155* 艾儒略 思及

Alexander, J.; *5*

Andree, Richard; 6

Andrew of Perugia, *O.F.M.*, (Bishop of Zayton); *215a*

Annaud, A.S.; *7*

Anti-Semitism; 36, 184, 234, 235

Anwhei; 28a

Arnauld, *Grand-Rabbi of Strasbourg* Aaron; 16

Asch, Sholom, [also spelled *Ash, Sholem*]; *172,* 253 阿胥

B , *S.J.,* C.; *189f-g*

Bacher, W.; *123*

Bainbridge, Oliver; *8a-b*

Balfour, Frederic Henry; *9*

Ball, James Dyer; *10, 11*

Barrow John W.; 12

Bartoli, *S.J.,* Daniello; *13*

Basnage, Jacob Christian; *14,* 239

Bell of Antermony; 226

Benjamin of Tudela, *Rabbi*; *15,* 25, 26, *43,* 49, 50, 160,
205 本雅民

Lung Ta-chün; *118* 龍大均

Ma Li-se (French); 119 瑪利瑟

MacGillivray, *Rev.* D.; *120a-b*

McGowan; 189e

McLeod, *Rev.* N.; *121a-c*

Mailla, *S.J.*, Joseph-François-Marie-Anne de Moyria de—; 82, 230a, *246* 馮秉正 端友

Maizel, Lev; *98b* Майзель, Лев

Manchuria; *127, 132,* 242, 243

Mann, Erika and Klaus; *122*

Manuscripts, Hebrew; see also *Facsimiles, Kaifeng, Letters to Kaifeng community* and *Literature, Chinese*

British Museum MS, Add. No. 29868; 4a, 10, *229, 231*

Pelliot fragment, *17, 18*, 78, 136

Pentateuch; 10, *12*, 16, 67, 76, 90, 131a-b, 142, 144, *163, 164, 176*, 188, 199, 217, *222*, 230a and d, 243

Stein fragment; *18*, 78, *123*, 136, *182*

Register of the Kaifeng community; *108*

Margoliouth, D.S.; 78, *123, 182*

Marignolli, John de—(Bishop of Bisignano); *215c*

Marriage; 148, 167a, 243

Martin, *Rev.* W.A.P.; 9, *124-126, 167b*, 203 丁韙良

Maurus; *96*

Medhurst, *Rev.* W.H.; 74c, 131, 142, *178*

Mémoire sur les Juifs (1770); 30, *40*, 49, *230d*

Mémoires concernant les Chinois; 40, *41*

Menahem, M. Ben; *127*

Menashe ben Israel; *128*

Mendelssohn, Sidney; 14, *239*

Michaelis, Johann David; *129*

Miller, G.E.; *240*

Milne, *Rev.* William C.; *130, 131a-b*

Mills, Dennis J.; 4a

Mishkowsky, Noiah (Noach); *132*

Möllendorff, O.F. von—; *133*

Möllendorff, P.G. von—; *133-135*

Mongolia, see also *Chenghis Khan,Jagatai, Kublai Khan*;
    11, 78, 86a-d, 132, 145, 181 205, 215b-c, 257

Montan, Benoit Arian (Montanus, Benedictus Arianus); 15

Morrison, *Rev.* Robert; *249* 馬禮遜

Moses; 86a-d, 193

Moses, S.M.; *166*

Moule, *Rev.* A.C.; 108, *136*

Mowrer, Edgar Ansel; *137*

Müller, F.W.K.; *138*

Münsterberg, Oskar; *139*

Muller, James Arthur; *167a*

Murr, Christoph Gottlieb von—; *101b, 140, 141*

Mussauites; *215e*

Nanking; 201

Nayan; 156a-b

Neubauer, Adolf; 1, *142*

Neumann, Charles Frédéric; 238

Ngai T'ien; 13, 108, 150, 155, 161 艾田

Ni Hsiu-chang; 27, *254* 倪秀章

Nieto, David; 4a

Ningpo; 130, 180

Nomenclature; 28a, 134, 143, 145, 160, 200, 208a-c,
    251c

Notices biographiques et bibliographiques; 40, *155*

Noyé, *O.F.M.*, Edmond (Fr.); 116, *143* 賚

Folklore Studies

Published by the Museum of Oriental Ethnology
The Catholic University of Peking

Reprint from Vol. V., 1946

THE EARLY JEWS IN CHINA: A SUPPLEMENTARY
BIBLIOGRAPHY

by

Rudolf Löwenthal 羅文達
Yenching University

THE CATHOLIC UNIVERSITY OF PEKING

THE EARLY JEWS IN CHINA: A SUPPLEMENTARY BIBLIOGRAPHY

by

Rudolf Löwenthal 羅 文 逵

Yenching University

PREFACE

The first group of Jewish immigrants in China — with the possible exception of a few unidentified individuals — presumably arrived during the 9th or the 10th century by the Arabic sea route at the Chinese south coast in the company of and influenced by the energetic Mohammedan traders. Both, Jews and Mohammedans, had their origin in Persia or India and they used New Persian as their medium. This language was then the *lingua franca* of the Far East as well as of the Near East, which has now been replaced by English.

Subsequently the Jews were asked by the Sung emperor to come to Kaifeng, Honan province, then the capital of the country. There they offered tribute of foreign fabrics, probably cotton cloth. Dr. Ch'i Ssu-ho 齊 思 和 of Yenching University suggests that they were invited because of their knowledge in the manufacture of such cloth and the dyeing or printing of coloured patterns. A number of reasons speak for the accuracy of this surmise, but we do not possess any documentary proof for it. The wide international contacts of the Chinese during the Sung and Yüan periods were severely curtailed under the more self-sufficient Ming rule, as a reaction against foreign domination. This low tide of foreign intercourse left the Jewish minority stranded like a fossil species when the waters recede. Owing to these unfavourable outward circumstances they gradually died out or were absorbed by their Chinese hosts and their Mohammedan neighbours, the latter to whom they were intimately related. Their contacts with their co-religionists abroad were almost completely interrupted, so that they lost their tradition altogether. In Kaifeng vestiges of these early immigrants have remained until our days, but all traces have been obliterated in places like Canton, Ningpo, Ch'üan-chou, etc., where there had formerly existed settlements.

Among the variegated foreign minorities in China, the early Chinese Jews represent a particularly picturesque group. Another small

353

group entered China in the wake of the British during the second half of the past century from Bagdad and the Iraq. Two more substantial waves of immigrants reached China during the 20th century. The first influx took place in the North after the Russian Revolution of 1917. Some 11,000 Russian and Baltic Jews went to Harbin and other places in Manchuria and from there migrated mainly to Tientsin, Shanghai, and Tsingtao, when the Japanese occupied Manchuria in 1931/32. A new impetus to Jewish immigration was given, when Germany initiated a large-scale persecution of the Jews in Europe. Since 1933 they began to arrive in Shanghai; the peak of their influx was reached between 1936 and 1940, when the persecutions were at their worst and the doors were barred to them in the rest of the world. In 1940, the Japanese, who were then in control of that city, throttled the entry of these refugees altogether in Shanghai as well as in the north, where a few individuals had arrived. Altogether some 20,000 or 25,000 Jews from Germany, Austria and, to a lesser extent, from other European countries sought shelter in China during that period. Many of these refugees had hoped to go on eventually to the United States, to South America, or to other parts of the world. Owing to the outbreak of the Pacific War many of them were stranded and their problem remains as yet unsolved.

In the interest of uniformity, only the first phase of the Jewish immigration has been dealt with in this bibliography; *i.e.*, the history of the early Perso-Indian Jews who came to China during the Sung dynasty. It represents a supplement to "The Jews in China, an annotated bibliography", which appeared in *The Chinese Social & Political Science Review*, Peiping, vol.24, no.2, July/September, 1940, pp.119-261.

The *Appendices* contain: (1) The English translation of the letter by Diaz (1619) ; (2) the French text from the *Description de la Ville de Peking* by de l'Isle and Pingré (1765) ; (3) the Italian text and the English translation of the letter by Longobardi (1610) ; (4) the German text of the report of Francis Xavier (1546) by Schurhammer; (5) the English text of the work by Semedo (originally written in Portuguese, 1640) ; and (6) the English translation of the report on the Kaifeng Jews by Ricci (1605).

Here the compiler expresses his gratitude to his numerous unnamed Chinese and foreign friends who, throughout these years, on many occasions supplied him with references and information pertinent to the topic.

[164]

Aleni, Giulio (Jules; *Ai Ju-lüeh* (*Ssu-chi*) 艾 儒 畧 (思 及) ; Italian
Jesuit, 1582-1649, arrived in China in 1613)

Li Ma-tou hsing-shih 利 瑪 竇 行 實 (The Life of Father Matteo
Ricci. Peking, 1620. Also to be found under the title of *Ta-hsi Li
hsien-sheng hsing-chi* 大 西 利 先 生 行 跡 . Reprinted in 1919
by the Catholic University of Peking and edited by Ying Lien-chih
英 歛 之·

On fol. 5 it contains a description of the visit of the Jew Ai 艾 to Ricci.

The Rev. P. Henri Bernard, S.J., drew the attention of the compiler to the fact
that Aleni, who arrived in China in 1613, at that time could not possibly have visited
Kaifeng. This erroneous information was given by Semedo and later repeated by
Pfister. For Aleni's itinerary cf. J. Dehergne, S.J.: "Le premier voyage missionnaire
d'est en ouest dans la Chine des Ming (1620)." Bull. de l'Univ. l'Auro. Shanghai,
series III, v. III, no. 3, 1942, pp. 618-642. At the earliest Aleni could have gone to
Kaifeng in 1621/22, if he went at all.

Andreas de Perusia (Franciscan Bishop) :

("Letter to his Superior at the Convent of Perusia, dated Zayton
(Ch'üan-chou 泉 州 , Fukien prov.), January, 1326." In: *Sinica
Franciscana*, v.I, Florence, 1929, p. 376. (Cf. *Introductio*, p. 1.)

5. "Sane in isto vasto imperio sunt gentes de omni natione quae sub coelo est,
et de omni septa. Et conceditur omnibus et singulis vivere secundum septam suam.
Est enim haec opinio apud eos, seu potius error, quod uniusquisque in sua septa
salvatur. Et nos predicare possumus libere et secure; sed de iudeis et saracenis nemo
convertitur; de ydolatris battizantur quam plurimi, sed battizati [multi ex baptisatis]
non recte incedunt per viam christianitatis [sicut decet]."

As a matter of fact, in this vast empire are living many people of every nation
under the sky and of all sects. As a group and as individuals they are allowed to
live according to their tradition. They hold, namely, the view, although a rather
erroneous one, that everybody will be saved within his [own; tr.] sect. And we can
freely and unmolested preach, but none of the Jews and Saracens [Mohammedans; tr.]
is converted. Very many of the idolaters are baptized, however they [many of them]
do not properly walk on the path of Christianity [, as it behoves].

[Argens, Jean Baptiste (marquis) d':]

*Lettres chinoises; ou correspondance philosophique, historique &
critique, entre un Chinois voyageur & ses correspondans à la Chine,
en Moscovie & au Japon.* Nouvelle édition augmentée de nouvelles
lettres & de quantité de remarques. 6 vols. A La Haye 1755.
(Chez Pierre Paupie.)

The first edition of this work of fiction appeared in 5 vols. in 1739, its German
translation in Berlin in 1768. The author, a protégé of Frederick the Great, probably
inspired the Prussian king to write his Relation de Phihihu, émissaire de l'empereur
de la Chine en Europe.

Vol. IV, p. 309, lettre CXVI: Sioeu-Tcheou, à Yn-Che-Chan & vol. VI, p. 67,
lettre CXLIX: I-Tuly, à Yn-Che-Chan contain brief references concerning the Kaifeng
Jews, based on Jesuit sources.

Bernard, Henri (S.J.):

"Notes on the introduction of the natural sciences into the Chinese Empire." *The Yenching Journal of Social Studies*, Peiping, 3:2, Aug., 1941, 239.

"The missionaries found in this interest of K'ang-hsi in medicine an occasion for introducing another celebrity of the 'Grand Siècle' of whom Fontenelle has also written an eulogy, the converted Jew Moïse Charas (1618-1698)." fn. 78. Biography in the Journal de Pharmacie, v. 26, 1840, pp. 229-240.

Borea Regoli, Giorgi:

"Gli Ebrei Cinesi." *Il Marco Polo*, Shanghai, 3:10, Jan., 1942 (A. XX), 50-63; with two facsimiles of plans of the synagogue by the Jesuit father Brotier.

The author, who himself visited the Kaifeng community, gives a rather confused and incoherent narrative of the history of the Jews, of their synagogue, and of their scriptures. His facts are based on the writings of Semedo, Brotier, Domenge, Ricci, Martin, etc.

Brerewood, [Edward] (1565-1615):

"Master Brerewoods Enquiries of the Religions professed in the World: Of Christians, Mahumetans, Jewes and Idolaters: with other Philosophicall speculations, and divers Annotations added." — In: *Hakluytus Posthumus or Purchas His Pilgrimes* ... by Samuel Purchas, v.I, Glasgow, 1905, p. 326.

Four editions of Brerewood's work appeared between 1614 and 1674 and it was translated into Latin, German, and French. The author refutes the assumption, based on mistaken etymological derivations, that the Tartars are descendants of the Ten Lost Tribes.

* Brotier, Gabriel (*French Jesuit*):

"Antiquités chinoises, in-folio. Contient des Let. du P. de Mailla, du P. de Chavagnâc, sur les Juifs de Kai-foung-fou, etc." Extraits faits par le p. Brotier de divers Mémoires sur la Chine.

Ms. de L'Ecole Ste-Geneviève, S.J. — La Bibliothèque de. L'Ecole Sainte-Geneviève, de la Compagnie des Jésus, rue Lhomond, à Paris, comprenait une serie de pièces manuscrites relatives à la Chine du plus grand interet; ces ms. qui étaient en grande parti compris parmi les papiers de Brotier, disperses a la vente de Langlès, ont ete relies en 34 volumes de formats divers. (Cf. Cordier B.S., II, 1048, no. 21.)

* — "2 lettres du P. de Mailla; autres du P. Domenge; mémoires du même; 3 lettres du P. Gaubil, mémoires du meme; et autres lettres et mémoires sur les Juifs de la Chine, sur la chronologie chinoise, sur l'astronomie, avec fig., le tout autographe et sorti de la plume des savants missionnaires de cet empire, de 1723 à 1728.".

* — "Diverses lettres et mémoires du P. Gollet, à l'appui de son système sur les anciens livres chinois touchant la venue du Messie."

* — "Pro expositione figurae Sephiroticae Kabalae Hebraeorum et generatim demonstrandâ mirâ conformitate primaevae Sinarum sapientiae hieroglyphicae, cum antiquiore et sincerâ Hebraeorum Kabalâ, ab ipsis mundi primordiis, per sanctos patriarchas et prophetas successive propagatâ." In-fol. de 11 pag., sur pap. de Chine. — Avec notes en chinois et fig.

Manuscrits provenans du P. Brotier, contenus en 6 cartons, nos. 6, 7, et 23, en possession des PP. de la Cie. de Jésus dans la Rue Lhomond, l'Ecole Ste. Geneviève. (Cf. Cordier, B.S., II, 1046-47.

Brown, David A.:

("Chinese Jews.") *The American Hebrew and Jewish Tribune,* Jan. March, 1933.

Reprinted in the work by W. C. White, Chinese Jews, Toronto, 1942, I, 149-164, "Through the eyes of an American Jew." — Dr. Brown, who visited the Kaifeng community in Nov., 1932, was a guest of Bishop White.

Budge, (Sir) E.A. Wallis:

The monks of Kûblâi Khân emperor of China or the history of the life and travels of Rabban Sawma, envoy and plenipotentiary of the Mongol Khans to the kings of Europe, and Markôs who as Mâr Yahbh-Allâhâ III became Patriarch of the Nestorian Church in Asia. Transl. from the Syriac. London, 1928. (The Religious Tract Society.) pp. 1-3 & 63.

The work contains a complete English translation of the Syriac history of the two Nestorian Uigur monks, Bar Sâwmâ (Pa Sao-ma 挹 掃 馬 of Khan Balik (Peking) and Markôs (Mark; Ma Ku-ssu 馬 古 思) of Kawshang. The Syriac text of the history represents an abridged translation from the Persian original, written by Rabban Sâwmâ, one of the two monks. He was apparently an eyewitness of many of the events in the Patriarch's life which he describes, and he probably wrote in the first half of the 14th century. But the author of the Syriac version is unknown.

(p. 1) "According to the Ecclesiastical Chronicle of Bar Hebraeus * (ed. Abbeloos and Lamy, tome iii, col. 451) two monks of Uighûr origin, were sent from China 'by the command of the great Mongol king Kûblâi Khân and ordered to go and worship in Jerusalem.' (fn. 1) It is not clear (p. 2) whether the word I translated by 'command' (pukdânâ) is to be understood here as a mere permit to travel westwards from Pekin, or as an Imperial Edict ordering the monks to go to Jerusalem. But it is well known that the Mongol Khans wished to gain possession of Jerusalem and there can be no (p. 3) doubt that the two monks were sent to the West as propagandists, and to obtain the help of the Christian kings of Eastern Europe. The ease with which they travelled shows that they were emissaries of Kûblâi Khân, and that they were armed with proofs of his authority.

"Bar Hebraeus * goes on to say that the Uighur monks arrived in Kurdistan, but were unable to proceed further west because fighting was going on and all the roads were blocked.....But he tells us nothing about Yahbh-Allâhâ's fellow-monk, or what became of him, and, as Bar Hebraeus died in 1286 his Chronicle does not contain any account of the Patriarchate of Yahbh-Allâhâ, which lasted until 1317."

* Gregory Bar Hebraeus, Abu Al-Faraj Ibn Harun, Jacobite Syrian historian, physician, and theologian; born at Maiatia, Asiatic Turkey, 1226; died at Maragha, Persia, 1286. His father Aaron, a Jewish physician, embraced Christianity. (Cf. Jewish Encycl., 3rd ed., VI, 91.)

pp. 1-2, fn. 1. "It is nowhere stated in the Syriac text of the narrative translated in this volume that Bar Sâwmâ and Mark were sent to worship in Jerusalem by Kûblâi Khân, the Kakhan, but this fact does not invalidate the assertion of Bar Hebraeus' that they were. Bar Hebraeus lived in Mârâghâh, which the Mongols had made one of their capitals, and his position in the city gave him the opportunity of learning what the plans and aspirations of the Mongols were. And though he was a Jacobite, he was well acquainted with the politics of the Nestorian Church. Moreover, he knew, as did every other instructed Christian and Jew and Armenian, that all the Khakans, from Chingiz downwards, and all the Îl-Khans, had wanted to wrest Jerusalem from the Saracens, and that it was the dream of Kûblâi Khân to get possession of the Holy City before he died.... (p. 2) It seems to me a fact that Kûblâi Khân wanted information about the state of affairs in Jerusalem, and that he felt he was more likely to get it from a couple of monks, whose ostensible object was to pray at the Holy Places for the salvation of their souls, than from envoys who were great officers of State. The monks, being Christians, would be received without suspicion by the Christian communities in Syria and Palestine. And they would learn from them whether there was a possibility that any of the Christian kings of Eastern Europe would assist the Mongols with armed forces if they marched on Jerusalem."

p. 63. "Some of Arghôn's predecessors had wished to invade Syria and Palestine and capture Jerusalem, but they had never, for various reasons, been able to do so. Arghôn had the same wish, but he realized that he would never be able to capture Jerusalem unless he could obtain the help of the Western kings, and he therefore asked the Patriarch to find him a suitable ambassador to carry letters to the kings of Byzantium, Italy, France, and England. Yahbh-Allâhâ knew well that there was only one man who was fit to undertake this difficult task, namely, Rabban Sâwmâ, and without more ado he ordered him to prepare for the journey to the West." (1288/89.)

p. 106. "Mangu, the fourth Kakhan (1251), treated the Christians as he treated the Muslims, Jews, Buddhists, and followers of Lamaism, that is to say, he favoured no one religion."

(In 1281, Yahbh-Allâhâ was elected Catholicus and Patriarch of the East (d. 1317) and Rabban Sâwmâ, Visitor-General of the Eastern (i.e. Nestorian) Turks (d. 1294).)

Chang Hsiang-wen 張 相 文 :
   "*Ta-liang fang pei-chi* 大 梁 訪 碑 記 ." (A report on the visit to the Ta-liang [Kaifeng, Honan prov.] stele.) In: *Ti-hsüeh tsa-chih* 地 學 雜 誌 , 1:2, Hsüan-t'ung 2nd year, 2nd moon (1910) ; reprinted in Nov., 1920, fol. 6a-10a.

The stone inscriptions of 1489 and 1512 are reproduced on fol. 8a-10a. The article (without the inscriptions) is also contained in Chang's collected works, Nan-yüan ts'ung-kao 南 園 叢 稿 , chüan 4, Travels, fol. 8a-9a.

— translated by Wang Lien-tsu 王 聯 祖 , with introduction and notes by Rudolf Löwenthal 羅 文 達 :
   "An early Chinese source on the Kaifeng Jewish community." *Folklore Studies*, Peiping, v. 4, 1945, pp. 327-331.

English translation of the above title. Chang Hsiang-wen was the first Chinese to investigate the history of the Chinese Jews on the spot.

Chao Nien-tsu 趙 念 祖 , see *Finn, James*: *"Consular Correspondence."*

* Chao Ying-ch'eng (*tzu*: Hang-chang) 趙 映 乘 字 涵 章 : *Chieh-nan-t'u* 刧 難 圖 . 30 ts'e. Fukien prov., about 1650.

Illustrations of the sufferings of the Fukien population from bandits; mentioned in the Fu-chien t'ung-chih 福 建 通 志 , ed. 1737, 32, 33b. This work is presumably lost.

* — *Sheng-ching chi-pien* 聖 經 記 變 (The History of the Holy Scriptures.) Kaifeng, before 1663.

Mentioned in the stone inscription of 1663. (Cf. White, Chin. Jews, II, 66, and Tobar, Inscr. juives, 79.)

* — *Ssu-chu t'ang chi i* 四 竹 堂 紀 異 . 240 *chüan*. (Uncertain, whether published or not.)

Mentioned in the K'ai-feng-fu chih fu-lu ming-chia shu-mu 開 封 府 志 附 錄 名 家 書 目 , ed 1695, 38, 14b, and in the Hsiang-fu chih 詳 符 志 , ed. 1739, 22, 5a.

* Chao Ying-tou 趙 映 斗 :

Ming-tao-hsü 明 道 序 (Introduction to. the Understanding of the Doctrine), in 10 chapters. Kaifeng, before 1663.

Mentioned in the stone inscription of 1663. (Cf. White, Chin. Jews, II, 66, and Tobar, Inscr. juives, 79.)

* Chavannes, Ed[ouard]:

("The Jews in China." *Revue de Synthèse historique*, Dec., 1900, p. 296.

Cf. Cordier, B.S., IV, 3136.

* Chavée:

"Sur la morphologie des syllabes chinoises comparées à celles des langues ariennes et sémitiques." *Bul. Soc. Anthrop.*, 1862, pp. 346-352.

Cf. Cordier, B.S., III, 1722.

Ch'en Chi-t'ung 陳 季 同 , see *Tcheng Ki-tong*

Ch'en Tseng-hui 陳 增 輝 :

Yu-t'ai-jen hua-hua k'ao 猶 太 人 華 化 考 (The assimilation of the Chinese Jews). Peiping, 1946. (M.A.-thesis, Yenching University.)

* Cheyne, T.K.:

"The Land of Sinim in Isaiah." *Babylonian & Oriental Record*, 1:11, Sept., 1887, 182.

Cf. Cordier, B.S., III, 1919.

Chiang Jung-chi 蔣 榮 甚 see *Smith, George: The Jews at K'ae-fung foo.*

Ch'iu T'ien-sheng 邱 天 生, see *Smith, George: The Jews at K'ae-fung foo.*

Cordier, Henri: ....

"Narrative of recent events in Tongking:" *Jl. of the North China Branch, R.A.S.,* Shanghai, N.S. IX, 1874, 127.

"Father de Rhodes in his History of Tongking* gives also some very interesting particulars about the Jewish impostor Xaca, Xechia or Thicca." *Tunchinensis historiae, lib. I, cap. xvii.

The work of Alexandre de Rhodes: **Historia Regni Tunchinensis,** Lugduni, 1651, Liber primus, caput XVII, pag. 46-51, "Altera superstitionum secta", contains on p. 46 a passage on Xaca. Apparently Cordier misunderstood the Latin text. Father de Rhodes wrote that Xaca was "aequalis ... aeuo Salomonis" (a contemporary of Solomon). Otherwise, there is not the slightest indication that this Indian princeling, whom de Rhodes depicts as a depraved character, had any connection with the Jews.

— "Origine des Chinois. Théories étrangères." *T'oung Pao,* Série II, v. 16, 1915, pp. 575-603.

"Forme le Chapitre I d'une Histoire générale de la Chine." The author enumerates the theories of early sinologues, who claimed that countries like Babylon, Elam, and Egypt were older than China and that the Chinese actually originated from Egypt. Particularly in connection with Egypt, Semitic tribes were supposed to be linked up with China. (1) Huet, Bishop of Avranches, in his work, **Histoire du commerce des anciens,** 1716, ch. X, pp. 40-42, claimed that India and China were Egyptian colonies (p. 584). (2) Abbé Barthélemy and de Guignes, **Mémoire dans lequel on prouve que les Chinois sont une colonie égyptienne,** Paris, 1759, pp. 36-38 (pp. 585-586).

— "Le passage d'Isaie (XLIX, 12): 'Voici, ils viendront de loin; voici, ceux-ci viendront d'Aquilon, et de la mer, et ceux-là du pays des Siniens." In: *Bibl. Sin.,* 2nd ed. Paris, 1906-07, III, 1918-19.

Cordier thought it possible, if not likely that the "Land of Sinim" referred to China.

Couling, Samuel:

The Encyclopaedia Sinica. Shanghai, 1917, p. 49a.

The T'ai-p'ing rebels "also issued part of the Old Testament."

Crow, Carl:

Handbook for China. 5th ed., rev. throughout. Hongkong-Shanghai-Singapore, 1933. (Kelly & Walsh.) pp. 245-247.

A second-hand account of the Jews in Kaifeng from unquoted sources. The author accepts the view that the Jewish settlement took place soon after 34 A.D. in consequence of the Babylonian persecution. He claims that in 1870 the community numbered 200 persons belonging to seven clans.

Darmesteter, J.:

"La flèche de Nemrod en Perse et en Chine." *Journal Asiatique,* 8ème série, tome 5, Febr.-Ap., 1885, 220-228.

The author claims that legend was originally Chinese and reached the Jews and Mohammedans by way of Persia. (Cf. also Cordier, B.S., III, 1873.)

Davis, John Francis:

The Chinese: A general description of the Empire of China and its inhabitants. London, 1836, I, 16-17.

Extract from the letter by Father Gozani of Nov. 5, 1704.

Delisle, see *l'Isle de: Description de la Ville de Peking.*

* Dennys, N.B.:

The Folk-lore of China, and its affinities with that of the Aryan and Semitic Races. London-Hongkong, 1876. ("China Mail" office, Trübner.)

Cf. Cordier, B.S., III, 1872.

Diaz, Emmanuel, surnommé l'ancien (Li Ma-no (Hai-yu) 李瑪諾 (海嶽); Portug. Jesuit, 1559-1639, arrived in China in 1601):

"Relatione dell'anno 1619, Macao: 7. XII. 1619." In: *Relatione delle cose piu notabili scritte ne gli anni 1619, 1620 et 1621 della Cina.* Roma 1629.

For the English translation of the text see **Appendix I.** Through the courtesy of the Rev. P. Henri Bernard, S. J., the compiler was furnished with a French rendering of the original text taken from the very rare Italian work.

Duvigneau, A.B. (*C.M.*):

Saint Thomas a-t-il porté l'Evangile jusqu'en Chine? Peiping, 1936. (Extrait du *Bulletin catholique de Pékin,* Juin-Octobre 1936.) Part III, pp. 18-37. "Y avait-il des Juifs en Chine?"

The author rejects the following assumptions: (1) that St. Thomas the Apostle had come to China; (2) that the Jews had entered China during the Chou period (1122-255 B.C.), corresponding to the epoch of King Solomon (1082-975 B.C.); and (4) that China is meant by the term **Sinim** in Isaiah, 49, 12.

Edkins, Joseph (*Rev.*):

"Connection of the Chinese and Hebrew." *The Chinese Recorder,* Shanghai, Jan., 1871, to April, 1872; 3:8, 203-205; 3:11, 323-326; 4:1, 23-26; 4:2, 48-51; 4:3, 74-77; 4:4, 102-105; 4:5, 123-126; 4:7, 182-186; 4:8, 215-217; 4:9, 245-247; 4:10, 279-280; 4:11, 287-291.

The whole essay consists of nine instalments, of which the last one remained incomplete, presumably, because the magazine suspended publication for two years in May, 1872.

Cf. also the article by P. G. von M[öllendorff]: "Mr. Edkins and comparative philology." Chin. Rec., 4: 10, March, 1872, 253-257; and Edkins' reply: "A reply to P. von M's paper in the March number of the Recorder." 4:11, May, 1872, 326-329.

According to Edkins, "the Hebrew and the ancient Chinese were probably dialects of a still more venerable mother speech which was truly antediluvian and began with Adam." Möllendorff rightly pointed out some of the inconsistencies of this theory.

* — "The Hebrew Bible in China." *The Far East,* I, 1906, 84-87.

Cf. Cordier, B.S., IV, 3133.

— "Die kanonischen Bücher der Hebräer in China." *Der Ferne Osten,* Shanghai, 1906, III, 1905/06, 91-95.

German translation of the above title. Report on the Hebrew Scriptures of the Kaifeng Jews.

— "The Land of Sinim." *The Chinese Recorder,* Shanghai, 19:10, Oct., 1888, 479-481.

Attempt to clear up the meaning of the word Sinim in Isaiah 49, 12, and etymological digressions.

— "On the three words 'I Hi Wei,' in the Tau Te King." *The Chinese Recorder,* Shanghai, 17:8, Aug., 1886, 306-309.

The author rejects the opinion that the three syllables, I 夷, Hsi 希, and Wei 微, denote "Jehovah" and that Lao-tzu "knew the holy Hebrew name and the doctrine of the Trinity from Jewish sources." Edkins argues for the Babylonian origin of this trinity.

— "Wine and wine making. Chinese process and nomenclature. Hebrew words. Bible translation." *The Chinese Recorder,* Shanghai, 19:12, Dec., 1888, 577-583.

The Hebrew transciptions together with their Chinese equivalents are given.

Ellis, Henry (*third commissioner of the Amherst Embassy*):
Journal of the proceedings of the late embassy to China. 1st ed., London, 1817, 282-283; 2nd ed., 1818, I, 427.

The Rev. Robert Morrison, who joined the embassy as interpreter, inquired from a Mohammedan about the Jews, but received little information. A few details about the report by Gozani (1704) have likewise been given.

* Fang Hao 方豪:
Chung wai wen hua chiao t'ung shih lun ts'ung 中外文化交通史論叢. Chungking, (?). Ap., 1944.

In two sections the author gives attention to Chinese Pews. The most interesting are certain data relating to Chao Yin-tou 趙映斗 who served as magistrate in K'unming and I-liang (Yünnan) in 1663-67, and Li Kuang-tso 李光座 who became imperial examiner in Yünnan in 1660.

Attention to this title was drawn through the kindness of Prof. L Carrington Goodrich, Columbia University, New York. At the time of publication of this bibliography the compiler was unable to consult this book locally.

Farissol, (*Rabbi*) Abraham Ben Mordecai; also known as Peritsol or Peritzol (Italian-Jewish scholar and geographer, born at Avignon, France, 1451, died in 1525 or 1526):
Iggheret orechot olam. (Small treatise of the world routes.) Ferrara 1524 or 1525.

According to the Jew. Encycl., this work was written in Ferrara, 1524, according to Cordier, in 1525. It appeared first in Hebrew in Venice, 1587. Thomas Hyde translated it into Latin: **Tractatus itinerum mundi,** Oxford, 1691.

" ... la seule allusion ... a la Chine et peut-être à Cambalu se trouve dans le chap. XXVIII." (Cordier, B.S., III, 2060; cf. also the Jew. Encycl., 3rd ed., V, 344.

* Feist, S.:

Stammeskunde der Juden. Leipzig, 1925. pp. 51-62, with 2 illustr.

The chapter on the Jews in China is based on Ezra's article, "Chinese Jews", which appeared in 1902 in the East of Asia Magazine, 1:4, 278-296.

Finn, James —, Temple H. Layton, and Chao Nien-tsu 趙念祖 :
"Consular correspondence (1849-1851)." Reprinted in W.C. White, *Chinese Jews,* Toronto, 1942, I, 76-91.

(1) The efforts of Finn, then British Consul at Jerusalem, to get further elucidations on the Kaifeng Jews. In 1844, a year after the publication of his book, **The Jews in China,** he contacted T.H. Layton, who later on, furnished him with additional information (76-79).

(2) Four letters of Layton, then British Consul at Amoy, to J. Finn. (79-85).

(3) English translation of the Chinese letter written by Chao Nien-tsu, a Kaifeng Jew, to T. H. Layton (85-91).

Fishberg, Maurice:

The Jews. London, 1911. (The Walter Scott Publ. Co., Ltd.) "Chinese Jews." pp. 134-137.

Brief summary of the Kaifeng community, based on the reports by Laufer, Andree, Martin, and others. The figures 97-99 on p. 137 represent three poorly reproduced photographs, two individual protraits to be found elsewhere and a family portrait not generally known.

Franke, Otto:

Geschichte des chinesischen Reiches. Berlin-Leipzig, II, 1936; III, 1937. (Walter de Gruyter & Co.)

II, 500 & 550 (Note in III, 420-421; cf. also III, 358-359). According to Arabic sources Jews lived side by side with Arabs and Persians in Khanfu (Canton) during the second half of the 9th century.

II, 510. Reference to the Canton massacre of 879.

— "Leibniz und China." In: *Aus Kultur und Geschichte Chinas.*
Vorträge und Abhandlungen aus den Jahren 1902-1942. Peking,
1945.

"Dieser Aufsatz ist ein etwas erweiterter Vortrag, der am 22. März 1927 im
'Hauptverband Chinesischer Studenten' gehalten wurde. — Der darin verarbeitete, zum
grössten Teile noch ungedruckte Briefwechsel zwischen Leibniz und den Jesuiten-
Missionaren ist mir von der Leibniz-Kommission der Preussischen Akademie der
Wissenschaften zur Verfügung gestellt worden."

p. 323. "[Leibniz] hat gehört, dass es in China jüdische Gemeinden gibt, und
will wissen, welche hebräische Schrift sie haben."

Fréret, Nicolas (1688-1749) ; Virgile Pinot (ed.) :

*Documents inédits relatifs à la connaissance de la Chine en France
de 1685 à 1740.* Paris, 1942. (Geuthner.)

On pp. 47, 51-52, 66, 69, 89-90, 111, 129, 148-149, 171-172, & 178, Fréret in his
letters critically analyzes the Jesuit attempts to coördinate the Chinese and the
Biblical chronologies. — On p. 118 he draws a parallel between the Confucianists and
the Spinozists.

* Friedrich der Grosse (*king of Prussia*) :

Oeuvres. Berlin, 1852 and later. "Relation de Phihihu, émissaire
de l'empereur de la Chine en Europe." (1760.)

In the third letter Phihihu reports to the emperor of China about his conversation
with a Portuguese on the Catholic church, morals, and Judaism. Quoted by Ursula
Aurich in her dissertation: **China im Spiegel der deutschen Literatur des 18. Jahrhunderts.** Berlin. 1935. (**Germanische Studien,** Heft 169; Verlag Dr. Emil Ebering.)
p. 111.

Probably Frederick the Great was inspired by the **Lettres chinoises** of his
protégé, the Marquis d'Argens, to write this political satire during the closing years
of the Seven Years' War.

Gaubil, Antoine (Sun Chang-te 孫 璋 德 or Sung Chün-yung (Ch'i-ying)
宋 君 榮 (奇 英); French Jesuit, 1689-1759, arr. in China in
1722) :

"Situation de Ho-lin [Karakorum] en Tartarie, manuscrit inédit
du Père A. Gaubil, S.J., publié avec une introduction et des notes
par Henri Cordier." *T'oung Pao,* IV, 1893.

p. 33. Three Ms. volumes of Father Gaubil are kept in L'Ecole Ste. Geneviève,
S.J., à Paris, rue Lhomond.

p. 34. Vol. II. **Histoire et Géographie,** no. 7. Juifs de Cai-fong-fou, Capitale
du Honan. 4 feuillets in-folio.

Commence recto folio 1: Dans le temps que la dynastie de Tcheou regnoit en
Chine, les Juifs de Perse, Et du Corassan venoient dans cet Empire, Et ils y
avoient des Sépultures, et des Endroits destinés à honorer leurs parents morts.

Finit verso folio 3: Si je puis jamais aller à Caifonfou passer quelques jours
je tacheray de tirer d'eux ce qu'on peut raisonnablement en attendre. Peking,
ce 4 7bre 1725.

[174]

Verso folio 4: Pour le R.P. J. Du Halde de la Comp. de Jésus. A Paris.

p. 35. Vol. III. Lettres, no. 4. Juifs de Cai-fon-fou en Chine (Reçeue le 15 Octobre 1724). Commence: Le P. Ricci découvrit le ler les Juifs en Chine. 4 feuillets. A Pekin, ce 18 août 1723.

p. 37. A Canton, ce 12 9bre 1722 (Reçeue le 25e Janv. 1724). Au R. P. Etienne Souciet, S. J. pp. 38-39.

p. 38. Je ne vois pas qu'on fasse aucune (p. 39) attention au mémoire que Ve Re me donna sur les Juifs, et sur le reste; si je n'étois venu icy pour souffir et pour expier mes péchés, je serois un peu interdit et embasse...

Cf. also Cordier, B.S., II, 1050. — In contrast to Gaubil's Chinese name by Cordier, Sun Chang-te, A. Pfister in his Notes biogr. et bibliogr. gives Sung Chün-yung.

Giles, Herbert Allen:

> *Adversaria Sinica.* Shanghai 1914. (Kelly & Walsh, Ltd.) pp. 55-57, with 1 plate. "Moses."

Giles gives three Chinese parallels to the Bible story of the discovery of Moses in a basket. (Exodus ch. 2, vv, 5, 6, 10.) These, he claims, "seem to suggest some knowledge of the story of Moses" in China.

> — *A glossary of reference on subjects connected with the Far East.* 3rd ed., Shanghai, 1900, p. 138.

Brief note on the Kaifeng Jews.

> — *An introduction to the history of Chinése pictorial art.* London, 1918. (Between pp. 112 & 113.)

Reference to the Jewish community in connection with Kaifeng, "the capital of China under the Five Dynasties, A.D. 907-960, and again under the Sung dynasty, 960-1260."

Goodrich, L[uther] Carrington:

> *A short history of the Chinese people.* New York-London, 1943. (Harper & Brothers Publishers.)

pp. 121 & 130. Reference to the massacre at Canton (879) of 120,000 foreigners, incl. Jews. — pp. 130 & 147. Mention of Chinese-Jewish trade relations during the Sung and Yüan dynasties.

Gozani, Jean-Paul (Lo Pao-lu 駱 保 祿; It. Jesuit from Piedmont, 1647-1732, arr. in China in 1694):

> "Juedenschul zu Caifumfù in Honan in dem Reich Sina nennet GOTT Thien. verehrt den Confutium und die Voreltern &tc." *Welt-Bott*, v. IV, no. 89, pp. 37-40.

German translation of Gozani's letter about the Chinese Jews, dated Nov. 5, 1704. (Courtesy of the Rev. P. Jos. de Lapparent, S.J., Directeur du Bureau Sinologique, Zikawei.) — For an English extract see also: **Davis, John Francis: The Chinese.**

[175]

Graves, R[osewell] H[obart] (*Rev.*):

"Bible Reptiles," *The Chinese Recorder*, Shanghai, 23:4, Ap., 1892, 158-162.

The Hebrew, Greek, and Chinese equivalents of the terms, together with the biblical references regarding the reptiles are given.

Grousset, Rene:

L'empire des steppes. Paris, 1939. (Payot.)

p. 449. "...Le roi d'Arghoun est uni d'amitié avec monseigneur le Patriarche (Yahbh-Allâhâ; comp.). Il a le désir de s'emparer de la Syrie et demande votre aide pour delivrer Jérusalem."

Arghon sent in 1287 Rabban Çauma to Rome to get the help of the Pope and of other European princes.

* Guignes, de:

"Mémoire dans lequel, après avoir examiné l'origine des lettres Phéniciennes, Hébraiques, &c., on essaye d'établir que le caractère épistolique, hiéroglyphique & symbolique des Egyptiens se retrouve dans les caractères des Chinois, & que la nation Chinoise est une colonie Egyptienne." **Rec. de l'Académie des Inscriptions & Belles-Lettres,** Mém., XXIX, 1764, pp. 1-26 avec 3 tables de caractères.

Cf. Cordier, B.S., III, 1735.

Haenisch, Erich:

Steuergerechtsame der chinesischen Klöster unter der Mongolen-herrschaft. Leipzig, 1940. pp. 38-39.

Reference to the Mongol decree dating from 1320, regulating the taxation of minorities, incl. the **Chu-hu** 竹忽 (Jews).

Hammer-Purgstall, Joseph (*Baron*) von (1774-1856):

Geschichte der Ilchane, das ist der Mongolen in Persien. 2 vols. Darmstadt, 1842.

This marginal item has been included because it contains a few references about the Mongol-Jewish relations in Persia. These contribute to the better understanding of the condition of Chinese Jews during the Yüan dynasty.

I, 184. (During the capture of Haleb by the Mongols in 1261.) "Das Schwert wüthete durch fünf Tage, von Sonntag bis Freitag, bis Hulagu's Befehl dem Morden Einhalt that; nur sechs Gebäude waren durch besondere Sicherheitsbriefe von der allgemeinen Plünderung ausgenommen, nämlich vier Häuser der Prälaten, das Kloster der Ssofi und die Synagoge der Juden, aber weder die griechische noch die syrische Kirche."

II, 241. (During the funeral of Oldschaitu Chodabende in 1316.) "Acht Tage lang dauerte die Trauer, nach deren Gesetzen die Wehklagende blau gekleidet auf der blossen Erde sassen; die Minarete und die Kanzeln waren mit blauem Filz überzogen. Diese mongolische Trauerordnung vereint die Gebräuche der alten Perser und der Juden des Mittelalters und der neuesten Zeit. Die blaue Farbe kommt schon im Schahname als die der Trauerkleider vor; veilchenblau war die Trauerfarbe des byzantinischen Hofes, welche die der Trauerordnung Napoleons für den Kaiser und die Prinzen von Geblüt erneut hat, und die Juden begehen noch heute die Todtenklage auf dem Boden sitzend mit Geheule, welchem das irländische Howl antiphoniert."

II, 260. Many references regarding Reschideddin, who was killed in 1318 at the age of 80, a Jew, as was wrongly believed by the author and other historians of his time.

Seaad or Saad, a Jewish physician, became Vezir in 1289 and was killed in 1291.

Hartwell, C. (*Rev.*):

"Terms for Bible wines in Chinese." *The Chinese Recorder*, Shanghai, 19:10, Oct., 1888, 458-464.

The Hebrew transcriptions and their Chinese equivalents with notes are given.

Havret, Henri (*S.J.*), see *T'ien-hsia ti-i shang-hsin-jen* 天下第一傷心人

Hogg, C.F. (*Rev.*):

"Mahommedanism." *The Chinese Recorder*, Shanghai, 23:2, Feb., 1892, 61.

"Chu-hu 觑虎, Chu-hu-te ssu 觑乎德寺、 A Jewish synagogue. Yahudi, a Jew; Jahud, Jews, Ar. Juhud, Juhudi; Pers."

* Horne, T.H.:

Int. to the Crit. Study and knowl. of the Holy Scriptures, 9th ed., 1846, III, Geographical Index, p. 653.

"Sinim, a land very distant from Palestine. From the context of Isa. XLIX. 12, it appears to have been situated towards the south or east. Some expositors have supposed it to be Pelusium or Syene; but these are only cities, and not sufficiently remote. It were better (says Gesenius) to understand it of an eastern country, perhaps China; of the name of which the Hebrews may have heard, as well as of Scythia and India."

Cf. Cordier, B.S., III, 1918.

* Hsieh T'ai-tsan 謝泰贊:

The Creation. The real situation of Eden and The Origin of the Chinese. By Tse Tsan Tai 女聖謝泰贊. With Portrait, Map, and Tables. Hongkong, 1914. (Kelly & Walsh.) in-8, 5 ff. n. ch.-pp. 35-5 ff. n. ch.

* — *China in Time of The Deluge.* — Origin of the Crustaceans of Tai Hu Lake of China. — A Reply to Notes of the Royal Asiatic Society ... Engl. Ed. Publ. by Kelly & Walsh ... 1914. — Chin. Ed. (Containing Proofs of the Deluge.) Publ. by Tsun Wan Yat Pa, Hongkong, 1917. — Reprinted from "The Shanghai Times" dated 4th July, 1918, in-8, 2 p.

* — *Proofs of the Deluge and a Reply to Alfred H. Crook ...* Engl. Ed.

Publ. by Kelly & Walsh ... 1914. — Chin. Ed. (Containing Proofs of the Deluge.) Publ. by Tsun Wan Yat Po, Hongkong, 1917. —

Reprinted from "The South China Morning Post", dated 12th November, 1917, in-8, pp. 8.

Cf. Cordier, B.S., V, 3469-3470.

I Heng 亦 亨 :

"Shih-chi 史 蹟*."* (Relics.) In: *K'ai-feng Chung-hua Sheng-kung-hui san-i tso t'ang* 開 封 中 華 聖 公 會 三 一 座 堂 , *tz'u-yang shih-t'ung-chi nien-k'an* 自 養 十 週 年 紀 念 刊, Kaifeng, Dec., 1935, p. 28.

The author, formerly secretary to the Anglican Bishop W. C. White, reports briefly on the Jewish steles and some utensils of the former synagogue. He mentions that by an optical delusion, on the vessel which is now used for baptisms the carvings viewed from close range, form lotus flowers, but seen from the distance, each four petals resemble the face of the Buddha.

Ibn-Khordadbeh (about 820-912/3); C. Barbier de Maynard (transl.): "Le livre des routes et des provinces par Ibn-Khordadbeh, publié, traduit et annoté par C. Barbier de Maynard."' *Journal Asiatique,* Mai-Juin 1865, p. 512. "Itinéraire des marchands juifs, dits Radanites."

p. 513. "Ils s'embarquent sur la mer orientale (la mer Rouge) et se rendent de Kolzoum à El Djar et à Djeddah; puis ils vont dans le Sind, l'Inde et la Chine."

This section has been rendered in English by Henri Pirenne, **Mohammed and Charlemagne**, London, 1939, p. 258. Transl. by Bernard Miall from the French of the 10th ed., Paris-Brussels.

According to Barbier (p. 513, fn. 2 from p. 512.), "Le surnom (**Radanites**) donné ici à des marchands me paraît devoir son origine aux trois cantons de Radan, dans la partie orientale du Sawad... Cette forme est expliquée de la même manière par Soyouthy, dans son Dictionnaire des surnoms ethniques."

Barbier, p. 231. "Sawad (portion cultivée de la Mésopotamie). Les rois de Perse l'avaient surnommé le Coeur de l'Irak "dil iranschehr".

Cf. also N. Slousch, Itinéraire des marchands juifs.

* Justi, Johann Heinrich Gottlieb:

Vergleichung der europäischen mit den asiatischen und anderen vermeintlich barbarischen Regierungen. Berlin, Stettin und Leipzig 1762.

"Anhänger der Lehre des Konfuzius, des Laotse und Fo, selbst Juden und Jesuiten wohnen friedlich nebeneinander." /

Quoted by Ursula Aurich in her dissertation: **China im Spiegel der deutschen Literatur des 18. Jahrhunderts**. Berlin 1935. p. 67.

Kafarov, Piotr Ivanovitch, see *Palladius*

Kawamura, Kyōdō 川 村 狂 堂:

猶 太 敎 の 一 文 献. ("A literary document on the Jews.")
Shoko 舊 香, Dairen, 1:4, July, 1929, p. 2 (26).

Description of a manuscript containing horizontal and vertical tablet inscriptions
of the Kaifeng synagogue. The Ms. is contained in the library of the South Manchurian Railway, Dairen, Coll. Ros. Its authenticity is certified by Fr. Grimaldi, S.J.,
on April 8, 1705 on the Ms. The article contains two reduced facsimiles.

Kircherus, Athanasius (S.J., 1601-80):

*China Monumentis qua Sacris qua Profanis nec non variis Naturae
& Artis spectaculis Aliarumque rerum memorabilium Argumentis
illustrata,* Auspiciis Leopoldi Primi. Amstelodami, apud Joannem
Janssonium Anno M DC LX VII.

p. 31. Description of the "Regnum Tan cin (id est Judaea)" according to the
Chinese geographers of the "Han & Guei" periods.

p. 48. R. Abraham Pizol's reference to the "Regnum Thebeth" in Hebrew with
Latin translation.

p. 58. The Hebrew text with the Latin translation from Benjamin of Tudela
about the bishops of the Church of St. Thomas, who also came to the Far East. They
were of Syrian and Chaldean origin.

Laimbeckhoven, Gottfried-Xaver (Nan Huai-jen (O-te) 南 懷 仁 (叟 德),

Msgr., S.J., 1707-87, arr. in China in 1738):

"Dritter Brief R.P. Godefridi Laimbeckhoven, Missionarii des
Ges. Jesu in Ch., aus der Oesterr. Provinz, an seine Anverwandte
zu Wien in Oesterreich. — Geschrieben zu U-tschang-fu in der
Provinz Hu-quam, dem 3. Christmonats. 1739." *Weltbotte,* Wien,
30. Teil. 1755, No. 592, p. 124a.

"Man findet auch, besonders in der Landschafft Ho-nan, einige Juden, welche,
wann und mit was Gelegenheit sie in dieses Kayserthum eingeschlichen seyen, kan
man mit keiner Gewissheit sagen. Glaublich ist, dass einige nach dem End der
Babylonischen Gefangenschafft sich daher verloffen, von welchem die heutige Chinesische Juden, die zwar die Schrifft im Hebräischer Sprach, aber von der Geburt und
Tod Christi gar keine Nachricht haben, scheinen abgestammet zu seyn."

One also finds some Jews, particularly in Honan province. It is not known for
certain when and how they slipped into this empire. It is credible that a few strayed
into this country after the Babylonian captivity. The present Chinese Jews, who know
the Scripture in Hebrew, but have no information at all of the birth and death of
Christ, are apparently descended from these. (Dated: Wu-ch'ang-fu 武 昌 府, Hu-
kuang 湖 廣 prov., now Hupei prov., Dec. 3, 1739.)

Latourette, Kenneth Scott:

The Chinese, their history and culture. New York, 1934.

I, 204. "In the ninth century we hear of Nestorian Christians, Jews, Moslems,
and Persians in Canton — all of them obviously from the West."

210. "Jews there were in China of the T'ang but probably few in number and all merchants. The Jewish community in Honan which disappeared only in our own day was of much later origin."

251. "A colony of Jews which has been finally absorbed into the surrounding population only in our own day built a synagogue at Kaifeng."

Laufer, Berthold:

"A Chinese-Hebrew manuscript, a new source for the history of the Chinese Jews." *The American Journal of Semitic Languages and Literatures*, 46:3, April, 1930, 189-197; reprinted in the *Folklore Studies*, Peiping, IV, 1945, 319-326.

Layton, Temple H., see *Finn, James: "Consular Correspondence."*

Leibniz, Gottfried Wilhelm (Frh.) v. (1646-1716); see *Franke Otto: "Leibniz und China."* and *Merkel, Franz Rudolf: G.W. von Leibniz und die China-Mission.*

Li Jung-fang 李 榮 芳:

(*Sinim, Isa. 49, 12.*) Ms. notes 8 pp., a copy of which is in the possession of the compiler.

Lecture delivered in Chinese before the School of Religion of Yenching University, Peiping, in 1931. — The author concludes that Sinim is not identical with China, but must be a place in Asia Minor.

Lin Ch'uan-chia 林 傳 甲:

Ho-nan ti-li chih 河 南 地 理 志. (Peiping) 1932. Ch. 33, pp. 64-65. *Yu-t'ai-chiao* 猶 太 敎.

A brief and somewhat inaccurate account of the Kaifeng community without any indication of sources. The author introduces among the seven clan-names the name of Ma 馬, instead of Li 李. He also mentions that the Jews imported **hua-wen-pu** 花 紋 布 or "cloth with decorative patterns" into China (cf. Shih Ching-hsün, **Ho-nan ti-chih**).

l'Isle, de (or Delisle; d. 1768) — and Pingré:

Description de la Ville de Peking. Paris, 1765, 29-30.

Allegedly a copy of the Hebrew Bible was preserved in the "Fang-king-tchan" (**Fang-ching-ch'ang** 番 經 廠), where all the foreign classics were stored. The Jesuit Fathers, Bouvet and Gaubil, went to this place, but could not find the copy, although this tradition was kept among the Kaifeng Jews. For the full French text cf. **Appendix II.**

Liu Chih 劉 智, *tzu* Chieh-nien 介 廉, *hao* I-chai 一 齋:

T'ien-fang chih-sheng shih-lu nien-p'u 天 方 至 聖 實 錄 年 譜 2 vols. Nanking, 1st ed. 1775, 2nd. ed. 1778, 3rd ed. 1782. Publ.

[180]

by Yüan Kuo-tso 袁 國 祚 . The ed. consulted dates Nanking, 1872, *chüan* 1, section *fan-li* 凡 例 , fol. 90b.

This section of the biography of Mohammed consists of a translation from the Arabic, Chih-sheng-lu 至 聖 錄 , prepared by Liu Chih between 1661 and 1664, when he was about 60 years of age.

The author mentioned the Chu-hu-te 朱 乎 得 (Jews) together with other religious sects.

For the bibliographical data the compiler is indebted to Prof. Teng Chih-ch'eng 鄧 之 城 of Yenching University.

Liu Lung-Kuang 柳 龍 光 :

"Kuan yü K'ai-feng ti Yu-t'ai-jen ti ch'uan-shuo 關 于 開 封 的 猶 太 人 的 傳 說 (The myth of the Jews in Kaifeng.)" *The Kabun Osaka Mainichi* 華 文 大 阪 每 日 , 4 :56, Febr. 15, 1941, 23-24.

The information contained in this article is largely extracted from the Guide to Kaifeng 開封案內 , written by a Japanese, who visited that city twenty years previously. (The compiler was unable to trace this Guide.)

According to the tradition among the local Jews about 200 of them bearing six different surnames have survived. Most of them are living in the Chiao-ching Hu-t'ung 敎 經 胡 同 , or the "Street of the Religion with Holy Scriptures". The Jews are now usually called Ch'ing Hui-hui 青 回 回 , or "Blue Mohammedans" (they formerly wore blue turbans during their religious services; comp.).

The Jewish men, although not the women, intermarried with the Chinese. Hence, the author claims, they remained a white-coloured race with highbridged noses and deepset eyes. This statement appears, however, entirely unwarranted.

In addition to the popular appellation, T'iao-chin-chiao 挑 筋 敎 , or "the sect which extracts the sinews", he has substituted the Chinese characters by those of a similar sound, T'iao-ching-chiao 挑 景 敎 , or "the sect which does not accept Christianity". The author implies that this name was chosen in order to distinguish the Jews from the Nestorians. This latter term is quite likely a typical Chinese word-play of the original informant, Shih 石 , to please his Japanese visitor. In any case, the term is not mentioned elsewhere.

Stone lions, now placed at the Nan-men ta-chieh 南 門 大 街 and at the Tung-kuan Shih-fang-yüan 東 關 什 方 院 , likewise belong to the early period of the Jewish settlement. A stele dating from the Yüan period (1280-1367) was sold several decades ago to a Shanghai curio dealer; two others have been preserved in the local Canadian Episcopal Mission.

Löwenthal, Rudolf 羅 文 達 :

("The Jews in China.") *Fu Jen* 輔 仁 *Magazine*, Peiping-Techny, Ill., 1941 or 1942, with two photos.

A brief summary of the history of the Jews in China. The article was sent to the U.S. shortly before the outbreak of the Pacific War, but, so far, no copy of the issue concerned has been received locally.

— "The Jews in China, an annotated bibliography." *The Chinese Social & Political Science Review*, Peiping, 24 :2, July/Sept. 1940, 119-261, with 1 facsimile. — Also reprinted for private circulation.

Reviewed by K(azuo) Enoki 榎 一 雄 in The Tôyô Gahukô 東 洋 學 報 , Tokyo, 28: 3, Aug., 1943, 140-143.

— "The nomenclature of Jews in China." *Collectanea Commissionis Synodalis in Sinis*, Peking, 17:5/12, May-Dec., 1944, 354-370.

Owing to the Pacific War only some ten copies of the issue in question were actually preserved. Hence, the MS. of a considerably enlarged revision is now with the Monumenta Serica of the Catholic University, Peiping, where it is supposed to appear in vol. XI, fasc. 2, 1946.

This article deals with the four following topics: (1) the Chinese biblical names contained in the four Jewish stone inscriptions of 1489, 1512, 1663, and 1679 at Kaifeng with their Mohammedan, Nestorian, Catholic, and Protestant equivalents; (2) the Jewish theological titles borrowed from the Mohammedans and contained in the four stone inscriptions; (3) the Jewish surnames in the four stone inscriptions; and (4) the Chinese designations for Jews, Judea, Hebrew, etc.

— "A Taoist interpretation of the Old Testament." *Collectanea*, 14:12, Dec., 1941, 1183-1186.

Description of a fantastic work by Teng Shao-yün 鄧 紹 雯 , Yu-t'ai-chiao 猶 太 敎 , an outline of the Old Testament in 6 vols., lithographed on 360 folios, published under the auspices of the Pei-ching shih-chieh tsung-chiao ta-t'ung-hui 北 京 世 界 宗 敎 大 同 會 in the collection Chieh-k'ai pao-yin 揭 開 寶 印 (altogether 23 vols.), incl. also Buddhism, Confucianism, Islam, and Christianity. The author, an impostor, evolved a kind of synchretic Taoist philosophy. (Cf. title no. 256 of the previous bibliography.)

Longobardi, Nicolo (Lung Hua-min (Ching-hua) 龍 華 民 (精 華); It. Jesuit, 1559-1654, arr. in China in 1597) :

"Letter to his general, Claudio Acquaviva, in Rome, dated Shao-chou 韶 州 , Kwangtung prov., Nov. 23, 1610." In: *Opere Storiche del P. Matteo Ricci S.I.* Macerata, 1913, II, 493.

Postscript: "Help to be given to the Jews of China in order to draw them to Christianity." For the Italian text and the Engl. transl. see Appendix III.

* Lowrie, Walter M(acon) (*Rev.*; Lou Li-hua (婁 理 華):

The Land of Sinim or an Exposition of Isaiah XLIX, 12 together with a brief account of the Jews and Christians in China. 2nd ed. Philadelphia, 1850. 147 pp. (William S. Martien.) pp. 30-33. "The Jews in China."

This work had first appeared in The Chinese Repository, XIII, 1844. (Cf. old bibliogr. title no. 116) "It was published in this country (America) in the year 1845 without the Knowledge or the name of the Author." (Advt.)

Cf. Cordier, B.S., II, 768-769.

Martin, W.A.P. (*Rev.*) :

The awakening of China. New York, 1907. (Doubleday, Page & Co.)

The pp. 43-44 contain a brief summary of the author's earlier reports on the Kaifeng Jews.

Mason, Isaac:

List of Chinese-Moslem terms. Shanghai, rev. ed. 1928. (The Society of Friends of the Moslems in China; first publ. in 1919.) p. 4.

Terms for Israel, Jews, Judaism, and Judea; of these the following are not mentioned elsewhere: I-ssu-la 以 思 啦 (Israel); Chu-hu-tai-jen 朱 乎 代 人 (Jews); Yu-na-ni 有 那 泥 (Judea); erh-shih chih-jen 二 氏 之 人 (Jews and Christians).

* **[Masson, Philippe:]**

Dissertation Critique, où l'on tâche de faire voir, par quelques exemples, l'utilité qu'on peut retirer de la Langue *Chinoise* pour l'intelligence de divers mots & passages difficiles de l'Ancien Testament. (Art. III, *Histoire critique de la République des Lettres tant Ancienne que Moderne.* Tome II. A Utrecht, Ches Guillaume à Poolsum, M DCC XIII, in-12, pages 96 à 153.)

Cet article est anonyme.

* — Dissertation Critique sur la Langue *Chinoise,* où l'on fait voir, autant qu'il est possible, les divers rapports de cette Langue avec l'Hebraisque; adressée à Mr. Reland, Professeur en Langues Orientales dans l'Université d'Utrecht. (Art. II, *Ibid.,* Tome III. A Amsterdam. Chez Jaques Desbordes. M DCC XIII, in-12, pages 29 à 106.)

Signée: Philippe MASSON. A Vliet ce 25. de Mars 1713.

* — Nouvelle Dissertation Critique, où l'on fait voir, par de nouveaux Exemples, l'usage de la Langue *Chinoise* pour l'intelligence de quelques endroits du Texte Hebreu de l'Ancien Testament. Par M. Ph. M. (Art. II, *Ibid.,* Tome IV, *Ibid.,* M DCC XIII, in-12, pages 29 a 69.

A Berlin, le 20. Mai 1713.

* — Eclaircissemens au sujet de la Dissertation qui fait le second Article du Tome precedent, adressez à l'Auteur de cette Histoire Critique. (Art. IV, *Ibid.,* Tome IV, *Ibid.,* in-12, pages 85 à 93.)

De Masson. — A Utrecht ce 9. septembre 1713. — Addition à son article precedent. (Cf. Cordier, B.S., III, 1578-1579.)

* **Matsumoto, Bunzaburō 松 本 文 三 郎:**

("The Kaifeng Jews.")

This item is mentioned in the article by T. Mikami, "Report on the actual conditions of the Kaifeng Jews", but without bibliographical reference. Because of the present lack of facilities the compiler has been unable to trace it.

Merkel, Franz Rudolf:

G.W. von Leibniz und die China-Mission. Eine Untersuchung über die Anfänge der protestantischen Missionsbewegung. Leipzig, 1920 (J.C. Hinrichs'sche Buchhandlung.) pp. 83-84 & 174-176.

p. 83. Leibniz "erhoffte selbst für die Geschichte des biblischen Kanons von dort her [China] neue Aufschlüsse. Denn da er von (p. 84) einer sehr frühen Einwanderung der Juden nach China (fn. 1) Kunde erhalten hatte, vermutete er, dass sich dortselbst ältere hebräische Handschriften finden könnten, die bei einer textkritischen Ausgabe des Alten Testaments von Nutzen wären (fn. 2)."

p. 84, fn. 1. "Vgl. darüber H. Hermann, **Chinesische Geschichte,** S. 56, und die hier in Anm. 1 angeführte Literatur."

fn. 2. "Schon am 1. Januar 1700 schreibt Leibniz an P. Verjus: Je crois d'avoir prié le R. P. Gobien de s'informer en écrivant à la Chine si on ne peut voir le vieux testament des juifs de la Chine pour le comparer avec le texte Hebreu de l'Europe. Car suivant le P. Semedo relation de la Chine (1 part. chap. 30) et ce qve dit Mons. Bernier sur les lettres de de (sic!) vostre compagnie (voyage de Cachemire p. 140 de l'edition de la Haye, 1672), on y pourrait trouer les lumieres, puisqv'il paroist qve depuis longtemps ces juifs de la Chine n ont aucune communication avec ceux d'Europe et qv'ainsi on trouueroit peut estre chez eux des livres ou passages qve les juifs de l'Europe peuuent avoir changés ou supprimes en haine des Chrestiens. Il seroit important de faire copier au moins leur commencement de la Genese, pour voir si leur Genealogie des patriarqves s'accorde peut estre avec les 70, ou aumoins avec le texte des Samaritains. Und im Brief an Bouvet vom 13. Dezember 1707 lesen wir: 'Je vous envoye maintenant les Qvestions sur les Juifs de la Chine, qve viennent de M. Jablonski tres savant en Hebreu, qvi nous a donné, il y a qvelqves années une fort bonne edition de la Bible Hebraiqve. Il suppose sur des relations imprimées, qv'il y a des Juifs habitues dans la Chine depuis fort longtemps. En ce cas il est important d'approfondir leur doctrine et leur rites.' Schon vorher (1705?) hatte er in einem Brief an denselben geschrieben: 'Ön m'avoit prié aussi de vous demander qvelqves nouvelles des Juifs ou Hebreux qv'on dit estre dans la Chine de temps immemorial. On souhaiteroit fort d'apprendre qvelqve chose de leur livres sacrés, sentiments et pratiqves.' Über D. E. Jablonski, dessen 'Ausgabe des Alten Testaments als eine tüchtige Leistung, die auf selbständigen textkritischen Studien beruht', gilt, s. A. Harnack a.a.O. I, 1. S. 112 f.

pp. 174-176. Konrad Mel, former court chaplain at Königsberg and later rector of the gymnasium at Hersford, was influenced by Leibniz. In 1700, on the occasion of the marriage of the landgrave of Hesse to the princess Luise Dorothea of Brandenburg, he sent a polyglot letter of congratulations, **Legatio Orientalis,** which contained eulogies in Hebrew and Chinese.

Mikami, Teichō 三 上 諦 聽:

開 封 猶 太 敎 徒 の 現 狀 報 告. (Report on the actual conditions of the Kaifeng Jewish community.) *Shina Bukkyo Shigaku* 支 那 佛 敎 史 學, Tokyo, 5:1, June 25, 1941, 76-77.

The author visited Kaifeng on Oct. 3, 1940, and inquired into the conditions of the local Jews, possibly in some official capacity, although the historical part of this article is rather slipshod, it contains the latest authentic information regarding the community.

According to Mikami there are about 100 Jews left. They belong to the families of Ai 艾, Chang 張, Chao 趙, Chin 金, Kao 高, Li 李, and Shih 石. The Li family has two branches, thus proving the popular saying, ch'i-hsing pa-chia 七 姓 八 家, or "seven [clan] names or eight families." The whereabouts of the Chang family are unknown. They actually left after having been involved in a feud with their co-religionists.

Milne, William, see *Philip, Robert: The life and opinions of the Rev. William Milne.*

* Minakata, Kumagusu 南 方 熊 楠:

"The Story of the 'Wandering Jew'." *Nature,* LIII, 1895-96.

Cf. Cordier, B.S., III, 1880.

Möllendorff, P.G. von, see *Edkins, J.: "Connection of the Chinese and Hebrew."*

* Montuclat:

"Those from the Land of Sinim." *La Chine,* no. 5, 15 oct. 1921, pp. 314-318.

Cf. Cordier, B.S., V, 3999.

Navarra B[runo]:

China und die Chinesen. Shanghai-Bremen, 1901. (Max Nössler & Co.) pp. 435-439. "Eine versprengte Judenkolonie".

Useful summary of the history of the Kaifeng community, but without indication of sources.

Navarrete, Domingo Fernandez (1610-89):

Tratados historicos, politicos, ethicos, y religiosos de la monarchia de China ... Madrid, 1676. (Imprenta Real.) Ch. IX, p. 80, col. 2, par. 2.

"La principal, y secta mas antigua, y graue, es la de los Letrados. Ha auido Missionarios, que han dicho, tener los Chinas muchas cosas de los Iudios. Y vno curioso apuntò, tener esta nacion mas de quarenta ceremonias Iudaycas. Auer muy muchos años, que llegaron Iudios a quella Region, es muy cierto, si bien no falta quien lo nigue; tambien lo es, que la China es muy antigua, que la dispersion de los doze Tribus, para que nadie diga, que los pobladores de China, fueron las dos Tribus que se desaparecieron..."

The principal, oldest, and most important sect is that of the literati. I have heard missionaries say that the Chinese have many things taken over from the Jews. And it is indeed a curious fact that the Chinese have more than fourty Jewish ceremonies. It is certain that the Jews arrived in that region very many years ago, although there are not lacking those who may deny it. It is also true that China is older than the dispersion of the Twelve Tribes, so that it will not be possible for anyone to say that the inhabitants of China might be the Tribes which were lost...

* Palladius *the Archimandrite* (Piotr Ivanovitch Kafarov, 1817-78):

"Starinnje sledj khristianstva v Kitaye." (Ancient traces of Christianity in China.) *Oriental Record,* St. Petersbourg, v. I, bk. 1, 1872.

The late John C. Ferguson in his obituary, "Palladius", in **The China Journal,** Shanghai, 11:4, Oct., 1929, p. 176, no. 15, mentions that the above article contains important references to the Jews in China. Cf. also Cordier, B.S., II, 771.

P'ang Yen-hsi 彭 炎 西 :

Hsi-chiao tung-lai k'ao-lüeh 西 教 東 來 考 略. (8) *K'ai-feng ku-Yu-t'ai-chiao pei-chi* 開 封 古 猶 太 教 碑 記 *Chung-kuo hsüeh-pao* 中 國 學 報, Peiping, 3:4, Ap. 15, 1945, 45-46.

Brief history of the Kaifeng Jews, based on the article by Ch'en Yüan 陳垣 (cf. old bibliogr., title no. 37) and on the stone inscriptions. According to the author there still live more than 100 Jews in Kaifeng on the north bank of the Huangho.

* Paravey, *(Chevalier)* de: see also *Riambourg: Traditions chinoises.*

Traditions primitives. De quelques faits bibliques retrouvés dans les hiéroglyphes chinois, et réfutation de quelques assertions de M. Renan.

Ext. des **Annales de philosophie chrétienne.** Ce Mémoire a été reproduit dans **La France litteraire,** Revue de Lyon, dirigée par Adrien Peladan. (Cf. Cordier, B.S., I, 574-575.)

* — "Dissertation sur le Ta-tsin et le nom hiéroglyphique donné en Chine à la Judée." *Annales de Philosophie chrétienne,* 1ère série, XII.

Cf. Cordier, B.S., IV, 2630.

* (?) Parrat, H.:

Les tons chinois sont sémitiques. Pièce in-4 oblong de 4 ff. n.c. autog.

"On lit au bas de la dernière page: Porrentruy, 8 novembre 1854, H. Parrat, anc. Profr." (Cf. Cordier, B.S., III, 1580).

Pelliot, Paul:

"Mémoires sur les coutumes du Cambodge, par Tcheou Ta-kouan 周 達 觀 traduits et annotés par M. P. Pelliot." *Bulletin de L'Ecole Française d'Extreme-Orient,* Hanoi, 2:2, Ap./June, 1902, p. 146, fn. 1.

Note about the hsi-yang-pu 西 洋 布. "...L'inscription de K'ai-fong-fou de 1489 (Tobar, Inscript. de K'ai fong fou, p. 43) fait mention de ces étoffes et c'est par négligence qu'essayant (B.E.F.E.O., I, 263) de fixer les étapes de la colonie juive de

K'ai-fong-fou, nous avons négligé de faire état de ce passage capital, où, disant leur loi originaire de l'Inde (出 自 天 竺), ces Juifs déclarent avoir offert à l'Empereur Song des toiles des mers d'Occident (進 貢 西 洋 布 於 宋); la voie maritime nous paraît décidément celle par laquelle ils sont venus."

Philip, Robert:

> The life and opinions of the Rev. William Milne, D.D., Missionary to China, illustrated by biographical annals of Asiatic Missions from primitive to Protestant times. New York-Philadelphia, 1843. (Appleton.) Ch. 17, 239-247. "Jewish witnesses in China."

Pingré, see l'Isle, de: Description de la Ville de Peking.

Pinot, Virgile: see also Fréret: Documents inédits.

> La Chine et la formation de l'esprit philosophique en France (1640-1740). Paris, 1932.

The compiler has a note indicating that this book contains a statement by some early etymologist that the I-ching 易 經 was composed by Enoch. But owing to the Pacific War the work is not now available locally and the compiler was unable to check the facts.

Purchas, Samuel:

> Hakluytus Posthumus or Purchas his Pilgrimes. Glasgow.

v. 8, 1905, ch. 5. "The Peregrination of Benjamin the sonne of Jonas, a Jew, written in Hebrew, translated into Latin by Arias Montanus. Discovering both the state of the Jewes, and of the world, about foure hundred and sixtie yeeres since." (Benjamin travelled during the years 1160 to 1173.)

p. 584. "Countrey of Sin." (Cf. Rabbi Benjamin of Tudela, old bibliogr. no. 15.)

v. 11, 1906, ch. 11. "The relation of Galeotto Perera, a Gentleman of good credit, that lay prisoner in China."

p. 576. "The Moores, Gentiles, and Jewes, have all their sundry Oathes." This passage refers to the hearings of evidence before Chinese judges. Perera, a Portuguese, was in China from 1549 to 1561.

v. 12, 1906, ch. 7. "A Discourse of the Kingdome of China, taken out of Ricius and Trigautius etc."

pp. 467-468. Early report on the Jews in Kaifeng and Hangchow.

Reichelt, Karl Ludvig (Ai Hsiang-te 艾 香 德); transl. from the Norwegian by Kathrina van Wagenen Bugge:

> Truth and tradition in Chinese Buddhism. A study of Chinese Mahayana Buddhism. Shanghai, 1st ed. 1927, 2nd ed. 1928, 3rd ed. 1930, 4th enlarged and revised ed. 1934.

1st-3rd ed., pp. 192-193; 4th ed., pp. 177-178. Bodhidharma (P'u-t'i ta-mo 菩 提 達 摩), the 1st Chinese and the 28th Indian patriarch after Buddha, arrived in China in 527. His "strong Jewish characteristics have been pointed out."

[187]

4th ed., p. 307. Chang Shun-i 張 純 — is the exponent of a group of modern
Buddhists who recognize Christianity as a special school within Buddhism. They plan
a new translation of the New Testament, because they think "that the real meaning of
Christ's teaching could not adequately be expressed in the poor and faulty language
and in the undeveloped milieu of the old Jewish nation."

Riambourg; notes by de Paravey:

"Traditions chinoises mises en rapport avec les traditions bibliques."
Avec notes de M. de Paravey. *Annales de Philosophie chrétienne,*
1ère série, XII.

Cf. Cordier, B.S., I, 574.

Ricci, Matteo, English translation from the *Opere storiche,* see *Appendix II.*

Rockhill, William Woodville:

"Notes on the relations and trade of China with the Eastern
Archipelago and the coast of the Indian Ocean during the
fourteenth century." Part I. *T'oung Pao,* v. 15, 1914, p. 435, end
of fn. 3 from p. 434.

"The only references I have found to Jews in the Yüan shih are two in number;
in 1330 (must read 1329; comp.) it was ordered that Buddhist priests, Tao-ssü, Yeh-li-
k'o-wên, Chu-hu, and Ta-shih-man were to be considered as traders and pay taxes in
accordance with the old regulations (of 1276?) Yüan shih, 33, 7b. In 1354 there is
(43, 11b) a reference to wealthy Moslims and Chu-hu, all of whom were ordered to
come to the Capital." Reference to Bretschneider, **Mediaeval Researches,** I, 268, and
JNCBr, RAS, n.s., X, 120.

— (transl. and editor):

*The journey of William of Rubruck to the Eastern parts of the
world, 1253-55, as narrated by himself, with two accounts of the
earlier journey of John of Pian de Carpine.* Translated from the
Latin, and edited with an indroductory notice. London, 1900.
Printed for the Hakluyt Society. pp. xvi-xvii and p. 114, end of fn.
1 from p. 113.

p. xiv. "Matthew Paris, under date of 1240, gives ... a full description of this
new people [the Tartars], embodying practically all the earliest information possessed
in western Europe ... that I will translate it in full." (**Introductory Notice.**)
[Matthew of Paris, an English monk and chronicler, died in 1259.]

p. xvi. "It is believed that these Tartars, of cursed memory, are of the ten
tribes who, (p. xvii) having forsaken the Mosaic law, followed after the golden calves,
and whom Alexander the Macedonian endeavoured at first to shut up in the rugged
mountains of the Caspians with bitumen-covered rocks ... It is written in sacred
history that they shall come out toward the end of the world, and shall make a great
slaughter of men. There arises, however, a doubt whether the Tartars now coming
from there be really they, for they do not use the Hebrew tongue, neither do they
know the laws of Moses, nor have they laws, nor are they governed by them. To

which it may be answered that, notwithstanding this, it is credible that they may belong to those who were shut up, and to whom reference has been made ..."

p. 114, end of fn. 1 from p. 113. "Whatever the opinion concerning the origin of the name, nearly all Christians in the first half of the thirteenth century believed that the Tartars were of the lost tribes of Israel. So strong was this belief that the Tartars were of Jewish descent, that we are told that the Jews of Europe, especially those of Germany, thinking that the Mongols were sent by God to free them from the oppression of the Christians, endeavoured in 1241 to smuggle arms and provisions to them (Matth. Paris, op. cit., iv, 131-138)."

Saeki, P. Y(oshirō) 佐 伯 好 郎 :

The Nestorian documents and relics in China. Tokyo, 1937.

p. 85. Mention of the Jewish stele of Kaifeng containing the name of Abraham.

pp. 125-160. Translation of the "Jesus-Messiah Sutra" (Hsü-t'ing Mi-shih-so ching 序 聽 迷 詩 所 經) which Saeki dates between 635 and 638. In it the Ten Commandments have been rendered. The translation was previously published in the J.N.C. Br., R.A.S., v. 63, 1932, pp. 31-45.

pp. 238-241. Saeki asserts that the term shih-hu 石 忽 in "The Lord of the Universe's Discourse on Alms-giving, Part III" (Shih tsun pu shih lun ti san 世 尊 布 施 論 第 三) applies to Jews. He dates the Ms. in 641.

Cf. also the review by Otto Franke, "Die Spuren der Nestorianer in China", in Ostasiatische Literaturzeitschrift, 42: 4, Ap., 1939, col. 201-209. — The Japanese original of the work appeared in Tokyo in 1936, under the title of Keikyō no Kenkyū 景 敎 の 研 究 .

— *The Nestorian monument in China.* London, first publ. in 1916; repr. in 1928. (Soc. for Promoting Christian Knowledge.)

p. 207. "We feel certain from the other part of this inscription, as well as from Prof. Pelliot's recent discovery, that the Bible, or at least a great part of the Holy Scriptures, must have been translated into Chinese by the end of the eighth century A.D."

pp. 224-225. Mention of the Jewish stele of 1512 at Kaifeng.

Santa Maria, Antonio de (Franciscan monk) :

"Fr. Antonio de Santa Maria. Epistola ad P. Provincialem, 3. ian. 1653. (Cinan (fu), provincia de Chantung.)" In *Sinica Franciscana,* II, Florence, 1933, p. 424.

This letter, dated Tsinanfu, Shantung prov., Jan. 3, 1653, contains the following passage: "En otro tiempo, 600 años despues, estuvo otro sacerdote, hebreo de nacion, y aunque parece entonces hubo mas dilatada christiandad..."

At another time, 600 years later, there was another priest of Hebrew origin and even though there was then apparently a more numerous Christian community...

This priest, tó whom the Franciscan father Santa Maria refers, must have been a Nestorian. He would have come to China during the 7th century, 600 after the alleged arrival in China of St. Thomas the Apostle.

[Scarth, John] A British Resident (pseudonym) :

Twelve years in China. By A British Resident. Edinburgh, 1860. (Thomas Constable & Co.)

p. 75. "The Taouists, it is said, heard of the birth of the Messiah, and sent some of their 'wise men of the east' to learn something of the new religion. Their emissaries, it is supposed, never reached Jerusalem, but on their way picked up the principles of the Buddhist doctrine, and returned with them to China."

pp. 90, 93, and 171-172. Brief statements pertinent to the Kaifeng Jews.

Schereschewsky, (Bishop) Samuel I. Joseph (1831-1906) :

("Obituaries." Cf. Cordier, *B.S.*, IV, 3134-35.)

Regarding the Protestant Bible translation and Schereschewsky's share in it, cf. Marshall Broomhall, **The Chinese Empire**, London (pref. 1907), pp. 18, 110, 374, 384, 386, and 414.

Schurhammer, G. (*S.J.*) :

"Der 'Tempel des Kreuzes'." *Asia Major*, 5:2, 1928, 247-248.

Information given to Francis Xavier during his stay in Malacca by a Portuguese merchant. The text is given in full in **Appendix IV.**

Sem[m]edo, Alvaro (Alvarez de; Tseng [or Lu] Te-chao (Chi-yüan) 曾 （魯） 德 照 （ 糤 元 ）; at the beginning he was called Hsieh Wu-lu 謝 務 祿 ; Portug. Jesuit, 1585-1643, arr. in China in 1613) :

Relacao Da Propagacao Da Fé No Reyno da China et outros adjacentes. Lisboa, 1642.

According to Pelliot nobody ever saw a Portuguese edition of the work. He assumes that Semedo arrived in Portugal in 1640 with the Portuguese Ms. of his work. Perhaps he published an extract from it, the **Breve Recopilaçao** of 1642. Manoel de Faria y Souza had a complete copy of the Ms., translated it into Spanish, changing the order of the materials and the style. He published this translation in Madrid in 1642 under the title of **Imperio de la China.** This Spanish adaptation of Faria y Souza had a second edition in 1642 which was reprinted in Lisbon in 1731.

When Semedo went to Rome in 1642, he took his Portuguese text with him. The Italian translation is based on his Portuguese text. It appeared in Rome in 1643 and was reprinted in Bologna in 1678. Under a different title it was also reprinted in Rome in 1653.

The French edition of 1645 is likewise based on the Italian edition. A new French translation appeared at Lyons in 1667.

The English edition of 1655 is translated from the Italian edition of 1653.

"Ainsi, sauf éventuellement l'extrait de Lisbonne, 1642, on ne connaît ni une édition ni un mss. du texte portugais original de Semedo." (p. 82.) Cf. also Pfister, **Notices biogr. et bibliogr.**, I, 146, no. 3, which was reviewed by Pelliot in the **T'oung Pao,** XXXI, 1935, 80-82.

[190]

The compiler has consulted the following editions:

(1) **The history of that great and renowned monarchy of China...** London, 1655, pt. I, ch. 30, pp. 153-154. — This edition contains on its title page the erroneous remark: "Lately written in Italian by F. Alvarez Semedo, a Porthugess."

(2) **Histoire universelle de la Chine...** transl. by Gilbert Girault, S.J. Lyon, 1667, pt. I, ch. 30, pp. 221-224. (Cf. Sommervogel, VII, 1114.)

(3) **Relatione della Grande Monarchia della Cina.** Transl. by Giovanni-Battista Giattini, S.J. Romae, 1643, pt. I, ch. 30, pp. 193-194. (Cf. Sommervogel, VII, 1114.)

(4) **Imperio de la China, y cultura evangelica en el.** Spanish transl. by Manoel de Faria y Souza, S.J. Lisboa, 1731. (This is the 2nd ed.; the 1st ed. appeared in 1642. Cf. Streit-Dindinger, Bibl. Miss., VII, 274, 3154.)

The text of the English ed., 1655, is reproduced in Appendix V.

Shih Ching-hsün 時 經 訓:

Ho-nan ti-chih 河 南 地 志. Kaifeng, n.d. (pref. 1919). pp. 60-61. *Yu-t'ai-chiao* 猶 太 教; with photograph of the inscr. of 1489 (4th plate, not numbered).

This brief section does not contain any indication of sources. The author mentions the hua-wen-pu 花 紋 布, or "cloth with decorative patters", introduced by the Jews.

The Jewish-Mohammedan relations were good during the Yüan period until the last part of the Ming time; then they began to deteriorate. Formerly the Jews frequently intermarried with the Mohammedans, later on with the Chinese; they are now assimilated.

The stone lions, which formerly stood in front of the synagogue, are sold to the monks of the shih-fang-yüan 什 方 院, a temple outside of Ts'ao-men 曹 門.

* — *T'iao-chin-chiao k'ao* 挑 筋 教 考. (?)Honan, before 1932.

Quoted by Wang Yu-ch'iao 王 幼 僑: Ho-nan fang-yü jen-wen lüeh-chih 河 南 方 與 人 文 略 志. Peiping, 1932. (Pei-p'ing Hsi-pei shu-chu fa-hang 北 平 西 北 書 局 發 行.).

* Slousch, N.; d'après Ibn Khordadbeh:

"Itinéraire des marchands juifs et russes qui se rencontrent dans les parages de la mer Caspienne." *Revue du Monde musulman*, Juin 1910, pp. 273-274.

Cf. Cordier, B.S., V, 400L

Smith, F. Porter:

A vocabulary of proper names in Chinese and English of places, persons, tribes, and sects. Shanghai, 1870. (Presbyterian Mission Press.)

p. 16. Ju-te-ya 如 德 亞, name for Syria and Palestine (Judaea) in Chinese and Japanese works.

p. 22. **Chiu-chiao** 舊 敎 , ancient faith

p. 33. **Man-la** 滿 喇 , Mullah, used for the Jewish Rabbi at Kaifeng.

Smith, George (Bishop of Victoria) ed.; the Rev. W.H. Medhurst transl.:

The Jews at K'ae-fung foo. Shanghae, 1851.

This report is based on the diaries of the two Chinese emissaries, Chiang Jung-chi 蔣 榮 基 and Ch'iu T'ien-sheng 邱 天 生 , an abstract of which appeared in the **Chinese Repository**, 20:7, July, 1851, Art. 7, pp. 436-466. (Cf. old bibliogr., no. 178.)

The original Chinese diary of Chiang Jung-chi is preserved in the University of Cambridge, England. (Cf. A.C. Moule, T'oung Pao, II 28, 1931, p. 128, and White, Chin. Jews, I, 132.)

Sogabe, Shizuo 曾 我 部 靜 雄 :

開 封 の 猶 太 人, ("The Kaifeng Jews.") *Revue Diplomatique* (*The Gaiko Jiho* 外 交 時 報), Tokyo, 97:4 (869), Febr. 15, 1941, 65-67.

The author visited Kaifeng in 1940. He went to the **Chiao-ching Hu-t'ung** 敎 經 胡 同 which is now divided into North 北 and South 南 . It is also called the T'iao-chin-chiao Hu-t'ung 挑 筋 敎 胡 同 .

The author claims that about 180 Jews have survived; 80 of them are supposed to be residing in Kaifeng and 100 in Shanghai or other centres. His informant, a member of the Chao 趙 family, told him that in 1918 a foreigner bought a family register, a **chia-p'u** 家 譜 , from them. That refers presumably to the Ms. in the possession of the Hebrew Union College, Cincinnati (Ohio), which has been described by Berthold Laufer.

Spinoza, Benedict de (1632-77) :

The chief works of Benedict de Spinoza, transl. from the Latin, with an introd. by R.H.M. Elwes. Rev. ed. 2 vols. London, 1900-01. "A theologico-political treatise (*Tractatus Theologico-Politicus,* first publ. in 1670'." v.l, ch. 3, p. 56.

"The sign of circumcision is, as I think, so important, that I could persuade myself that it alone would preserve the [Jewish] nation for ever. ... they may even, if occasion offers ... raise up their empire afresh, and that God may a second time elect them ..."

"Of such a possibility we have a very famous example in the Chinese. They too, have some distinctive mark on their heads which they most scrupulously observe, and by which they kept themselves apart from everyone else, and have thus kept themselves for so many thousand years that they far surpass all other nations in antiquity. They have not always retained empire, but they have recovered it when lost, and doubtless will do so again after the spirit of the Tartars becomes relaxed through the luxury of riches and pride."

Storfer, A.J.:

"Die Juden von Kai-Feng Fu. 'Die Sekte derer, die die Sehnen herausreissen'." Gelbe Post, Shanghai, 1:1, 1939, 12-14, with illustr.

Strauss, Victor von:

> *Laò Tsè's Taò Tĕ Kīng.* Aus dem Chinesischen ins Deutsche über-
> setzt, eingeleitet und commentirt. Leipzig, 1924. (Verlag der
> "Asia Major"; photolithographic reprint.) Ch. 14, fn. 1, pp. 61-73,
> and p. 75, fn. 2.

Strauss attempts to prove that the three characters i 夷, hsi 希 , and wei 微
occuring in the Tao-te-ching, represent the name of "Jehovah". He believes it possible
that the Jews entered China during the 7th century B.C.

Tafel, Albert:

> *Meine Tibetreise.* Stuttgart-Berlin-Leipzig. (Union Deutsche Ver-
> lagsgesellschaft.) I, 115-116.

p. 114. Im Chinesentum geht ja alles Fremde unter, wie auch vor einigen
Jahrhunderten in Ho nan, Tsche Kiang und anderen (p. 116) Provinzen grössere echte
Judengemeinden existierten, die heute bis auf ganz geringe Reste sich unter der anderen
Bevölkerung verloren haben. (fn. 1)

> fn. 1. Von der einst grossen Judengemeinde in Kai föng fu sind heute nur noch
> fünf oder sechs Familien übrig geblieben. Die Männer sehen aber heute
> vollkommen chinesisch aus und wissen von ihrer Religion so gut wie
> nichts mehr. Namen wie Tscha ka ba (Jacob?), Tschu da se (Judas?)
> mögen noch am meisten an ihren ursprünglichen Stamm erinnern.

* Tcheng Ki-tong (Ch'en Chi-t'ung 陳 季 同 ;general):

> "Les Juifs en Chine." *Le Gaulois,* Sunday, Febr. 2, 1890.

This article was reprinted in a book by the same author Mon pays. — La Chine
d'aujourd'hui, Paris, 1892. (Charpentier.) pp. 219-229.

To no. 46 of the previous bibliogr.; cf. Cordier, B.S., II, 1358, and III, 1840.

Tenney, Charles D. (*American Chargé d'Affaires*):

> ('The Jewish colony at Kaifeng." *Millard's Review of the Far
> East,* Shanghai, 12:1, March 6, 1920, pp. 6, 8, 10-12.

The above adress was delivered by Dr. Tenney at the Medical Conference held at
Peking during the previous week.

The author, who visited the Kaifeng community in 1918, "was disappointed in
finding so few remaining." His lecture represents a critical, but now obsolete study
which is largely based on the inscriptions of 1489 and 1512. He mentions the term
T'iao-chin Hui-hui 挑 筋 回 回 as one of the appellations for the Jews (p. 11).

* Terrien de Lacouperie, Albert Etienne Jean Baptiste de:

> "The Land of Sinim, not China." *Babylonian & Oriental Record,*
> 1:11, Sept., 1887, 183-191.

Cf. Cordier, B.S. III, 1919.

* — "The Sinim of Isaiah not the Chinese." *Babylonian Record,* no.
3, Jan. 7, 1887.

[193]

Reprinted in London: pièce in-4, 2 ff. ch.. (Cf. Cordier, B.S., III, 1919.)

* — "Wheat carried from Mesopotamia to Early China." *Babylonian & Oriental Record*, London, Sept., 1888.

Cf. Cordier, B.S., I, 6 578.

T'ien-hsia ti-i shang-hsin-jen 天 下 第 一 傷 心 人 (pseudonym, "the most unhappy man of the world"):

T'ien-chu hsieh-chiao ju Chung-kuo k'ao-lüeh 天主邪教入中國 考略. In: *P'i-hsieh chi-shih* 辟邪紀實. (?Nanking) Hsien-feng 11th year (1861), *chüan* 1, fol. 7a-8b.

The author of this violently anti-foreign work is a hsiu-tsai from Hunan. The section under discussion is directed against the Catholics. It has been translated into French by Henri Havret, S.J., under the title of "Recherches sur l'introduction en Chine de la religion du Seigneur du Ciel" in his work, La stèle chrétienne de Si-ngan-fou, IIème partie, Shanghai, 1897, (Var. sin. no. 12), pp. 287-289; the Chinese text is reproduced on pp. 387-388.

The author, whose scholarship was none of the best, confounds the Nestorians and Catholics with the Jews. He confuses the Nestorian stele of Sian with that of the Jews at Kaifeng 1489. From the latter he extracted most of his facts using them for invectives against the Catholics.

The biographical data about the author the compiler owes to Prof. Teng Chih-ch'eng 鄧 之 誠 of Yenching University.

* Timkowski, George (Timkovskii, Egor Fedorovitch):

Travels of the Russian Mission through Mongolia to China. London, 1827.

Timkowski says: "The physiognomies of the Tibetans are like the physiognomies of the Gypsies," to which the editor in a marginal note remarks, "This opinion corresponds to the observations of Thomas Maning, who also visited Lhasa, he maintains that the * Thibetan physiognomies are not of the Mongolian type but resemble more the Jewish type." (Quoted in Perlmann, **History of the Jews in China**, pp. 30-31.)

* Tonn, Willy:

"Eine jüdische Inschrift der Synagoge zu K'ai-feng-fu aus dem Jahre 1512." *Gemeindeblatt der Jüdischen Gemeinde*, Berlin, Aug., 1930, v. 20, pp. 360-364, with 3 illustr.

The article deals with the history, customs, and ethics of the Chinese Jews. It also contains the first German translation of the inscription of 1512.

[Torrance, Thomas:]

"The Chiang tribes of Western Szechwan." *Jl. of the North China Branch, R.A.S.*, Shanghai, v. 66, 1935, p. 126.

Lecture, delivered before the N.Ch. Branch of the R.A.S., Shanghai, on Dec. 6, 1935; a continuation of a lecture, delivered before the Society in 1923. The main points of the paper are to show: (1) that most of the aboriginal tribes in West Szechwan came from Asia Minor; (2) that the religion of the Chiang tribes closely resembles the religion of the ancient Hebrews.

Verhaeren, H. (*C.M.*) :

"Tchang Keng et la religion de la croix." *Le Bulletin catholique de Pékin,* 32:380/381, April-May, 1945, 218-230 & 272-281.

This article treats of Chang Keng 張 賡, a follower of the Shih-tzu-chiao 十 字 教, a sect which the author identifies as Nestorian.

The historical data of the article are largely based on Ricci's description of the visit by the Jew Ai T'ien 艾 田 on July 1, 1605, who on the following day introduced his friend Chang Keng. (Cf. Ricci, **Opere storiche**, I, 86-88 & 468-473; II, 290-293).

On p. 224, the author describes the relations between the Jews and the followers of the Shih-tzu-chiao according to a letter dated 1610 by the Jesuit father Nicolo Longobardi (cf. Appendix III). Father Verhaeren was the first to draw attention to this letter in connection with the Kaifeng Jews.

Vishnitser, M.L. — , and S.G. Lozinskii :

"Istoriya Evreev v Kitaye." (The history of the Jews in China.) In *Evrejskaya Entsiklopediya,* St. Petersbourg, 1901-06. (Brockhaus-Efron.) v. 9, pp. 491-501.

Copied by the courtesy of Mrs. Isabel Boyarsky.

*Weber, Harald :

"China und die Juden." *Hammer,* 35:810, 1936, 218-220.

From the Ostasiatische Rundschau, 17:16, 439.

Weng Tu-chien 翁 獨 健 :

Wo-t'o tsa-k'ao 斡 脫 雜 考 ("A study of wo-t'o.") *The Yenching Journal of Chinese Studies* 燕 京 學 報, Peiping, no. 29, June, 1941, 201-210.

Among the problems concerning the term wo-t'o, treated by the author, comes first "the wrong identification of the name with the Jews." (202-204). The author quotes several Chinese sources, where they have been wrongly identified.

* Werner, Matthias :

"Jüdische Gemeinden in Innerchina." *Rasse,* 6:5, 1939, 190-191.

From the Ostasiatische Rundschau, 20:19/20, 432.

* Weston, Stephen :

Siao çu lin or A small collection of Chinese characters, analysed and decompounded, with the English prefixed In the order of the Alphabet, By way of Introduction to the Language of China, Also. The Elementary characters as they are pronounced at Pekin & Can-

ton with a preface & notes of Construction.   To which is added the
Chines (sic) Genesis & its agreement with the Mosaic account.
Contentus paucis. Hor.   By Stephen Weston, BD. FRS. SA. RLH.
In-8, s.d., gravé sur cuivre. (1812.)

Cf. Cordier, B.S., III, 1712.

* White, (Bishop) William Charles (Huai Lü-kuang 懷 履 光):

"An attempt to reorganize the Chinese Jews of Kaifeng."   The
Chinese Recorder, Shanghai, 50:11, Nov., 1919, 780-782.

Cf. title no. 216 of the previous bibliography.

* — "A Chinese-Hebrew Codex." Asia, v. 42, Aug., 1942, 457-458.

The register of the Kaifeng community which is in the possession of the Hebrew
Union College at Cincinnati and was described by B. Laufer in his article, "A Chinese-
Hebrew manuscript."

* — "Chinese Jews." Transactions of the Royal Society of .Canada.
Third Series, Section II, Vol. XXXVIII, 1944.

* — "The Jews in China." Hebrew Standard, New York, June 4, 1920.

* — "K'aifeng Fu and the Chinese Jews." China, the Quarterly Record
of the Christian Literature Society for China, London, Jan., 1913,
no. 42.   (Taken from the North China Herald.)

— Chinese. Jews.   A Compilation of Matters Relating to the Jews of
K'aifeng Fu. 3 vols.   Toronto, 1942.   (The University of Toronto
Press.) Part I. Historical. xvii+211 p., with 5 sketch maps and 31
illustr.; Part II. Inscriptional. xii+184 pp., with 31 illustr; Part
III. Genealogical. Publ. in collaboration with Ronald James William.
xiii+226, with 35 illustr.

Reviewed by L. Carrington Goodrich in the Jewish Social Studies, 6: 1, Jan., 1944,
70-72; by R. Löwenthal in The Yenching Journal of Chinese Studies 燕 京 學 報, Peiping,
no. 30, Aug., 1946, 317-320.   Two more reviews are in the press: by Nieh Ch'ung-ch'i
聂 崇 岐, in the literary suppl. of the Yi-shih-pao 益 世 報, Tientsin, Aug., 1946, and
by Henri Bernard, S.J., in the Bulletin Catholique de Pékin, Sept., 1946.

Vol. I.   Historical. — The "Historical Outline" (8-28) is rather slim and primarily
limited to a description of the synagogue and its implements, part of which were
acquired by the author for his mission.

The rest of the volume contains extracts from various sources: (2) An excerpt
of Ricci's writings taken from Moule; (3) the letters by Gozani; (4) the memoir of
Brotier; (5) the correspondence of a number of Europeans with the Kaifeng community
(76-94); (6) the "Journal of the Chinese Delegates", Ch'iu T'ien-sheng 邱 天 生 and
Chiang Jung-chi 蔣 榮 基, ed. by Smith and Medhurst in Shanghai, 1851, in abridged
form (97-133); (7) Godboy, The Lost Tribes a Myth, excerpts from ch. XIII; (8) articles
by David A. Brown, an American Jew, who visited the community in 1933 as a guest of

Bishop White; (9) "Cullings" from nine different sources, mostly modern, incl. two on
the Chinese Mohammedans; but these are rather loosely attached and not brought into
direct connection with the problem under discussion.

Vol. II. Inscriptional. — This volume contains the translations, notes, and original
Chinese texts of the fundamental historical sources. They include the four stone
inscriptions dating from 1489, 1512, 1663, and 1679. The last one was almost
obliterated by children tossing coins against it, but was partly restored by Chinese
scholars. In addition, the Chinese archway inscriptions (p'ai-fang 牌坊), the inscriptions of the horizontal (pien 匾) and the vertical (lien 聯) tablets, and the Hebrew
writings and scriptures of the synagogue have been dealt with. A list of classical
quotations and allusions conclude this volume.

Vol. III. Genealogical. — This volume starts with the only Chinese-Hebrew
manuscript in existence, a kind of community register, in which the Chinese and
Hebrew names of 453 men and 259 women are listed. It was first described by Laufer
(1930), whose article, together with a note by Pelliot and further remarks by White,
precede the translation, annotations, and text of the Codex.

Then follows a Hebrew-Persian colophon, appended to the Genesis section-book
of the Torah, with translation and notes. This was also reproduced in the works of
Koegler (1801) and Finn (1843).

The rest of this volume is devoted to biographical notes on the Kaifeng Jews
from the Codex, the stone inscriptions, the wooden tablets, the local gazetteers, etc.

The magnificent photographic plates in the three volumes help to illustrate the
text.

Wilhelm, Richard:

Laotse Tao Te King. Das Buch des Alten vom Sinn und Leben.
Jena, 1921, p. 24, fn. 14.

Wilhelm rightly rejects the view, held by V. von Strauss in his translation and
by others, that the Chinese characters, i 夷, hsi 希, and wei 微 are the equivalent
for the Hebrew name of Jehovah.

Yang Yü 楊 瑀 :

Shan-chü hsin-hua 山 居 新 話 . In: *Chih-pu-tsu ch'i-ts'ung-shu*
知 不 足 齋 叢 書, *ti shih-erh chi* 第 十 二 集, fol. 7a. (Preface
dated 1360.) Reprinted in Shanghai, 1921, by the *Ku-shu liu-t'ung
ch'u* 古 書 流 通 處; photolithographed from the woodblock ed. of
Pao T'ing-po 鮑 廷 博.

"The officers of the Hangchow Sugar Bureau were all wealthy merchants of
Jewish (? and Mohammedan) extraction," 杭 州 砂 糖 局 煎 黎 之 用 糖 官 皆 主 鶻 回
回 富 商 也.

The term Chu-hu Hui-hui 主 鶻 回 回 may be tautological and simply apply to
"Jews" (cf. Yüan-tien-chang, 57, 16r-17r, Chu-hu Hui-hui 朮 忽 回 回, where the whole
term has been used to designate the Jews), or it may mean "Jews and Mohammedans".
Although grammatically both views are tenable, the compiler is inclined to the first
alternative.

[197]

Yü Cheng-hsieh 俞 正 燮 (1775-1840):

Kuei-ssu ts'un-kao 癸 巳 存 稿. The 1st ed. was publ. posthumously in 1849; the ed. consulted was publ. in Shanghai, 1941. (Commercial Press.) *tse 2, chüan* 13, fol. 397.

The section on Islam contains the following passages: "After Mu-sa 母 撒 (Moses) came the T'iao-chin-chiao 挑 筋 教 (Jewish religion)... The Scripture of Mu-sa is the T'ao-la-t'e 討 拉 忒 (Torah), the name of the synagogue is: the temple of the chu-hu 廄 虎 or chu-hu-te 廄 乎 德.

ANONYMOUS TITLES

"Chinese lad of Jewish descent chooses to become a priest." *Benedictine Orient*, Lisle, Illinois, 5:3, Ap., 1941, 1-2, with 2 photos.

A summary of the above article appeared in the Catholic Lumen News Service, Peiping, June 20, 1941. — Paul Shih Chung-yang, a descendant of the Kaifeng Jews, was baptized in 1924 and his son, Louis Shih Kai-ling, enrolled in 1941 in the local theological seminary, but left soon afterwards. It is said that he became a Buddhist.

Ju-meng-lu 如 夢 錄. Reprinted in 1921 by the Honan Provincial Library.

Ch'ang Mo-lai 常 茂 徠, the editor of an earlier edition of this description of Kaifeng, states in his preface of 1852 that for 30 years he had been unable to find this work. According to the tradition, Li Kuang-t'ien (Hsi-liang) 李 光 墅 (熙 亮) is the author, but the book was apparently compiled after Li's death in Nanking (around 1650).

f. 35a-b. On the south side of the Earth Street (T'u-chieh 土 街) there is a small shop for eye medicines belonging to the Ai 艾 family. ...In addition there is a general pharmacy belonging to Ai Ying-k'uei (Wen-so) 艾 應 奎 (文 所).

f. 40b. In the Hsien-erh Li-chia Hu-t'ung 線 兒 李 家 胡 同 there is a synagogue (Li-pai-ssu 禮 拜 寺) of the T'iao-chin-chiao 挑 筋 教.

* "Juden in China." *Jüdisches Litteraturblatt*, Ap., 1884.

According to Friedrich Hirth in his "Bibliography", Jl. of the North China Branch, R.A.S., XX, 1886, p. 260, no. 249.

"The levirate in China." *The China Review*, Hongkong, 10:1, July, 1881, p. 71.

"Semitic traces in China." *The China Review*, Hongkong, 13:6, June, 1884, 430.

"The second of the beautiful religious poems of the fourth century B.C., known as the 九 歌, suggests connection with Semitic thought. The high priest was in the habit of presenting himself in sackcloth and ashes before God [太一]. The exact words of the commentator are 垢 身 蓬 頭 着 敝 衣 以 為 禮. The modern sackcloth, which may be seen on the backs of chief mourners in China any day, reminds one of David and Joab 'girding themselves with sackcloth to mourn for Abner'."

[198]

"Sinagoga degli Ebrei cinesi." In *Scelta di lettere edificante* ....
Traduzione dall'originale francese. Milan, 1827, IV, 107.

Italian ed. of the Lettres édifiantes. Facing p. 107 is a hand-coloured imaginative illustration of the "Synagogue of the Chinese Hebrews."

["Terms for 'circumcision'."] *Mesny's Chinese Miscellany, Shanghai,* 2:8, May 14, 1896, p. 148, notes no. 556-562; cf. also 4:4, Jan. 21, 1905, p. 75.

Two American journalists, Mr. Jimmy Burke and Mr. Archibald Steele, visited Kaifeng on July 10, 1946, and wrote articles on the Kaifeng Jews for the Liberty magazine and the New York Herald Tribune respectively. So far the compiler has been unable to obtain copies of these articles.

APPENDIX I

Emmanuel Diaz: *Relatione delle cose più notabili scritte ne gli anni 1619, 1620 et 1621 della Cina.* Roma 1629. pp. 38-42.

p. 38. Four Jesuits went from Hangchow to Shensi province (p. 39) at the request of Philipp Wang, but the situation was so unfavourable that they did not stay there. On their way back two of them, namely, Father Longobardi with Brother Jean Fernandey, passed through Honan in order to search there for "the worshipers of the Cross."

In Honan they found a great mixture of religions:

(1) Mohammedans who enjoyed a rather high esteem;

p. 41. (2) Jews, "who at the beginning amounted to only 5 or 6, [but eventually] reached the number of 10,000. Their religion is mixed with paganism and they compete for literary degrees, but they are less esteemed than the Mohammedans.

(3) Christians....

A Jew stated that he had seen in the hands of a small boy among these Christians a book containing an image of the most saintly Madonna with the Infant Jesus in her arms and another image of two Saints, the one holding a sword and the other an object which he did not quite recall: doubtlessly these were the Apostles Peter and Paul.

Moreover, these Christians are so hardened in their errors (p. 42) into which they have fallen for lack of guidance that the Chinese are not on such a [low] level as they. Hence, our people, when they realized that they did not harvest any fruit, returned from there to Hangchow in spite of all the hardships which they had endured in order to help them.

APPENDIX II

De l'Isle & Pingré: *Description de la Ville de Peking.* Paris, 1765, pp. 29-30.

p. 29 *Du Fan-king-tchan (Fan-ching-ch'ang* 番 經 厰)

Nous avons dit que le lieu étoit le magazin des livres classiques étrangers, & qu'il étoit situé près de n° 5, à l'entrée du Palais Impérial. On a cru que la Sainte

Bible étoit conservée dans ce magazin: toutes lés recherches qu'on a faites à ce sujet, n'ont servi qu'à rendre le fait au moins extrêmément douteux.

Les Juifs établis à Cai-fong-fou, Capitale du Honan, dirent en effet aux Jésuites Missionnaires, que l'on conservoit une Bible hébraïque au Fan-king-tchan de Peking; les premiers Missionnaires arrivés à Peking, ou avoient entièrement perdu de vue cet avis, ou negligèrent d'en profiter. Mais cela n'échappa point à la vigilante attention du P. Bouvet, Jésuite François; il voulut à cet effet visiter le Fan-king-tchan. Le lieu où l'on avoit précédemment conservé les livres étrangers étoit détruit, & ces livres avoient été déposés dans un Miao voisin, sous la garde de quelques Bonzes. Le P. Bouvet vint à ce Miao avec deux autres Missionnaires de son Ordre & de sa Nation; il n'y trouva que l'Alcoran, avec des fragmens de livres classiques des Indiens, (p. 30) & les livres classiques des Lamas, le tout en mauvais état. Il croyait avoir entrevu dans un vieux coffre des caractères Chaldaïques, Syriaques & Hébraïques; le Bonze ne voulut point permettre la visite du coffre. Quelque temps après, le P. Bouvet étant retourné au Miao, le coffre fut visité, on ne trouva rien: l'Empereur avoit ordonné aux Bonzes de ne rien céler au P. Bouvet. Tous les livres classiques ont été transportés depuis dans l'interieur du Palais, le Miao a été démoli, & il ne lui est plus resté que le nom de Fan-king-tchan. Quand le P. Gaubil passa par Cai-fong-fou; les Juifs en presence du P. Gozani qui lui servoit d'interprète, l'assurèrent qu'il trouveroit la Bible dans le Fan-king-tchan; mais ces Juifs n'avoient jamais été à Peking: ils ne parloient qu'en conséquence d'une vieille tradition, qui pouvoit n'être pas bien certaine dans son origine. En effet, le P. Gaubil a fait à Peking toutes sortes de recherches par lui même, il en a fait faire par d'autres, & le tout inutilement; la Bible n'a pas été trouvé. Il y a environ cent ans que l'on comptoit à Peking quelques familles Juives; elles ont embrassé depuis le Mahométisme. Un Mahométan, homme d'esprit, dit plusieurs fois au P. Gaubil, que c'étoit parmi ces Mahometans, originairement Juifs, qu'il falloit chercher quelque exemplaire de la Bible: ce Mahometan fit même des recherches a ce sujet, le P. Gaubil en a fait de son côté; les unes & les autres on été jusqu'à présent infructueuses. Il paroît donc qu'il n'y a à Peking d'autres exemplaires des saintes Ecritures, que ceux qui y ont été portés par les Chrétiens Européens, ou qui y ont été peut-être imprimés par leur soins.

Copied by the courtesy of Dr. George R. Loehr of Yenching University in the Zikawei Library, Shanghai, February 22, 1946.

APPENDIX III

Nicolò Longobardi S.I. — Sciaoceu, 23 novembre 1610.

Al P. Claudio Aquaviva Prep. Gen. S.I. a Roma.

In *Opere storiche* ... Macerata, 1913, II, 493.

Di Xauceo, 23 di novembre del 1610.   Figlio nel Signore

Nicolao Longobardo

7.   Aiuti da darsi agli ebrei della Cina, per attirarli al cristianesimo.

Post scripta. Intesi che quei christiani della croce per amor che adorano. l'istesso Dio con li Giudei vanno a far oratione nella sinagoga, et i Guidei glielo concedono per il detto rispetto; anzi come più in numero, dignità e facoltà nella Cina, si danno come per suoi protettori. Per il que saria molto a proposito mandar qua V.P. uno o due padri periti dalla lingua hebrea per aiutar prima ai Giudei che tengono la scrittura hebrea e non l'intendono già per esser morti i suoi rabbini che la sapevono; anzi udendo dire ai nostri che venne già il Messia al mondo, dicono che lo vogliono seguire, adorar la sua imagine &c. Vengano dunque questi padri, che sono moltissimi in molte provincie della Cina, e giontamente si reduranno quei della Croce.

From Shao-chou 韶 州, Kwangtung prov., November 23rd, 1610.

....   Son in the Lord

....   Nicolao Longobardo.

7. Help to be given to the Jews of China in order to draw them to Christianity.

Postscript. I have been informed that those Christians of the Cross, owing to the love with which they worship the same God as the Jews, go to offer their prayers in the synagogue; and the Jews allow them [to do this] because of this [common] reverence. In addition, since the Jews surpass them in numbers, rank, and wealth in China, they undertake their protection. Hence, it would be very advisable, Ven. Father, to dispatch one or two Fathers, versed in the Hebrew language, because they possess the Hebrew Scriptures but do not understand them since their rabbis who knew Hebrew are dead. In fact, having heard us say that the Messiah had already come to the world, they say that they are willing to follow Him, to worship His likeness, &tc. May, therefore, these Fathers come, as there are so many Jews in several provinces of China; and those of the Cross will be retrieved together with them.

APPENDIX IV

G. Schurhammer, S.J.: "Der 'Tempel des Kreuzes' 十 字 寺 (Shih-tzu-ssu)." *Asia Major*, 5:2, 1928, 247-248.

p. 247. Als der hl. Franz Xavier im Jahre 1545 von Indien nach Malakka kam, traf er dort einen portugiesischen Kaufmann, der soeben aus China zurückkehrte und ihm mitteilte, er habe dort (die Portugiesen, denen der Zutritt ins verschlossene Reich der Mitte verboten war, trieben auf den einsamen Inseln vor Kanton Schleichhandel mit den Chinesen) einen sehr vornehmen Chinesen getroffen, der vom Kaiserhof in Peking kam und ihm erzählte, in seinem Lande in einem Gebirge wohnten viele Leute getrennt von den andern, die kein Schweinefleisch ässen und viele Feste feierten, aber keine Mohammedaner seien. Franz Xaver, der schon damals an die Möglichkeit einer Missionsfahrt nach China dachte und sich für dies geheimnisvolle Volk äusserst interessierte, schrieb darüber fünf Monate später aus Amboina am 10 Mai 1546 an seine Mitbrüder in Europa:

"In Malakka traf ich einen portugiesischen Kaufmann, der aus einem Lande mit grossem Handel kam, das China heisst. Dieser Kaufmann sagte mir, ein sehr angesehener Mann, der vom Hofe des Königs kam, habe ihn viele Dinge gefragt, darunter habe er sich auch erkundigt, ob die Christen Schweinefleisch ässen. Der portugiesische Kaufmann antwortete ihm mit Ja und frug, warum er sich danach erkundige. Der Chinese antwortete ihm, i n s e i n e m L a n d e w o h n t e n v i e l e L e u t e i n e i n e m G e b i r g e , g e t r e n n t v o n d e n a n d e r e n L e u t e n , d i e k e i n S c h w e i n e f l e i s c h ä s s e n u n d v i e l e F e s t e b e o b a c h t e t e n . Ich weiss nicht, was für Leute das sind, ob es Christen sind, die das alte und das neue Gesetz beobachten, wie es jene des Preste Juan[1] (fn. 1. in Abessinien) tun oder ob es die Stämme der Juden sind, von denen man nichts mehr weiss, denn sie sind keine Mohammedaner, wie alle sagen.

[201]

Von Malakka fahren alle Jahre viele Schiffe der Portugiesen zu den Häfen Chinas. Ich habe vielen empfohlen, sie sollten über jene Leute Erkundigungen einziehen, indem ich sie darauf aufmerksam machte, sie sollten sich eingehend über die Zeremonien und Gebräuche unterrichten, (p. 248) die unter ihnen beobachtet würden, um daraus erfahren zu können, ob es Christen oder Juden sind. Viele sagen, der Apostel Sankt Thomas sei nach China gegangen und habe viele Christen gewonnen..."

In seinen späteren Briefen kommt Xaver nicht mehr auf dieses Volk in den Bergen Chinas zurück, wohl weil seine Gewährsmanner ihm keine neue Kunde darüber berichten konnten.

Mohammedaner schliesst er selber aus. Juden scheinen kaum in Frage zu kommen, denn die Bemerkung, jene Leute wohnten in den Bergen, schliessen die Hafenorte Kanton, Hang-chou, Ning-po, das am Unterlauf des Yang-tsu gelegene Nanking (wo die letzten Juden erst 1677 zum Islam übertraten), das in der Ebene gelegene Peking und wohl auch das im Tal des Huang-ho gelegene, durch seine Judenkolonie berühmte Kai-feng-fu aus, die einzigen Orte, wo Juden erwähnt werden...

APPENDIX V

The History of that great and renowned Monarchy of China ... Lately written in *Italian* by F. Alvarez Semedo, a *Portughess*, after he had resided twenty two yeares at the Court, and other Famous Cities of that Kingdom. Now put into *English* by a person of quality ... London, 1655, pp. 152-154.

p. 152. "There are, moreover, in **China, Moors** in great abundance, not in all the Provinces, nor in evry City, but yet in the more principal. They speak the language of the Countrie, and know nothing of their own tongue, a few words only excepted. * They are acquainted also with many things of the holy Scripture."

* The Spanish and Italian editions agree with the English text, but the French translation has instead of "Moors", i.e., Mohammedans, "Juifs". That is evidently a mistake; French ed., pp. 221: "De plus il y a des Juifs en grand nombre, non pas à la vérité dans toutes les Prouinces, n'y dans toutes les villes; mais aumoins dans les principales, qui, parlent la langue du pays, sans auoir rien retenu de la Iudée, que certains mots, & beaucoup de choses de l'Escriture Sainte."

In the next paragraph, the French translator wrongly renders as "Synagogues" and "la loy de Moyse" the terms which in the English, Italian, and Spanish editions are mentioned as "mosques" and "their own law" (i.e., the religion of Islam). In the same paragraph, with reference to the Mohammedans, the following phrase, not contained in the other editions, is inserted in the Spanish edition: "Like the Hebrews in Spain, (they are Merchants, Physicians, &c.)."

Similarly, in the following paragraph, "Iuifs & (des Mores)" has twice been added in the French edition, to remain in keeping with the previous interpolations, although in the other editions the Jews are not mentioned in the corresponding passages.

p. 153. "There are likewise **Jews** in **China**, although at this time no great number of them: but when or how they came thither I am not able to say. Anciently there was a great store of them, but they have been diminished by little and little, many of them turning **Moors**. There live more of them in the Province of Honan, in the capital City thereof, called **Cai Fum Fu**, than in any other place. They have there a **Synagogue**, well built and adorned in the fashion of a great Chappel, and set out with curtaines. They say they have there a very ancient Hebrew Bible. Father

Julius Alenes, one of our company, was among them for some time: they shewed him their Synagogues, but would not draw their curtaines and let him see the Bible. Father Matthaeus Riccius affirmeth, that according to the relation which the Jews themselves made to him thereof in Pekim, it was not at all differing from ours. They have no knowledge at all of Christ, so that it seemeth, they were entered into China before he came into the World; or at least, if they have ever heard of him, the memorie of it is quite lost: and therefore it would be of great consequence to see their Bible: for perhaps they have not corrupted it, as our Jews have done, to obscure the glorie of our Redeemer.

p. 154. These, as they are in no great number, so it is not probable they should long preserve themselves. They who at the Court had some discourse with our Fathers, did much lament that they had lost themselves for want of the Hebrew Tongue, and by the little knowledge they had of their law, and said, that after some time they should all become either Moores or Gentiles: that the ruler of their Synagogue at that time was a decrepit old man, and his sonne, who was to succeed him in his Office, young and ignorant of the things of their law, and that indeed there were very few among them, who were zealous observers of it.

Moreover these Jews did seem to be much troubled and weary of the reproaches which the Gentiles laid upon some ceremonies of their law, which is a sign they have no great affection for it: as, their not eating of Swines flesh, their not touching a beast, which hat been killed by the hand of a Gentile, but especially the circumcising of their Infants on the eighth day; which their wives and Chinesse kindred tell them, is a cruell and barbarous thing.

At this time we have, in that City of Cai Fumfu a house and a Church; and (when I left that Kingdome) a good number of Christians, which daily encreased, not without hope also, that some good may be done upon those Jews, who, being so ready to change their religion, will more easily embrace the true one, which hath more conformitie to theirs, than any other."

APPENDIX VI

Opere storiche del P. Matteo Ricci S.I. Edite a cura del Comitato per le Onoranze Nazionali con prolegomeni note e tavole dal P. Pietro Tachi-Venturi S.I. 2 vols. Macerata, 1911-1913.

Vol. I., pp. 86-87 and 468-473.

p. 86. *Mohammedans, Hebrews, and Christians in the Middle Kingdom.*

We have likewise discovered, as will be explained below, Jews who are living according to the ancient law of Moses. But they number only a few families and. as far as we know, they have no synagogues elsewhere (p. 87) except in Kaifeng fu, the capital of Honan province, and in Hangchow fu, the capital of Chekiang province. In it (in the Kaifeng synagogue; tr.) the Pentateuch of Moses is preserved with great veneration. It is written in Hebrew script without vowel signs, on sheep-skin parchement rolled up according to the old fashion. They do not have other books from the Old Testament and also did not know which ones they did not possess. They have preserved the ceremony of circumcision and, moreover, they abstain from eating porc and any kind of meat with sinews according to their ancient ritual.

It was only a few years ago that we learned for certain that there exist also Christians, especially in the northern provinces, who are called worshippers of the cross (shih-tzu-chiao 十字教 ; tr.). Sixty years ago they flourished to such an extent

in regard to the number of their families, and their literary and military abilities
that the Chinese became suspicous of them; they were perhaps instigated by the
Mohammedans, who everywhere are our enemies. The Chinese, therefore, wanted to
catch them and thus they all went into hiding, some of them as Turks (Mohammedans;
tr.) or Jews, but most of them became gentiles (Chinese Confucianists, Buddhists, or
Taoists; tr.). Their churches were changed into temples of idols and their descendants,
although many preserved the custom of making the sign of the cross over their food
and drink, remained so afraid that they did not want to confess to be the progeny of
the followers of the cross; and there is nobody, either among them or others, who
knows of any occasion to make these crosses. But this symbol of theirs clearly
demonstrates that they are the offspring of alien people in China...

The Chinese call all these foreigners hui-hui 回 回 , from which name we cannot
learn their origin. The Mohammedans they call the hui-hui of the three laws; the
Jews they call the hui-hui, who extract the sinews from the meat which they eat; the
Christians they call the hui-hui of the word for ten, because the Chinese character for
ten forms a perfect cross (shih 十 ; cf. above shih-tzu-chiao; tr.) and there exists
neither a name nor a use for the cross.

vol. I, p. 468. *The conversation of Ricci with the Israelite Ai* 艾
The Hebrews in China.

This book reached also the hands of a Jew by nationality and profession [of
his faith] from the province and capital of Honan (Kaifeng; tr.), whose surname was
Ai. He had already obtained the rank of licentiate in Chinese literature and he came
during this year to Peking for the doctoral examination. Having read in this book
that we were not followers of the Law of the Saracens (Islam; tr.), like the majority
of those [foreigners] staying in China, and that we worshipped only the King of
Heaven, he was convinced that we were followers of his Mosaic law. He very
cheerfully entered the home of the fathers, saying that he belonged to our creed. His
face was quite different from that of a Chinese in respect to his nose, his eyes, and
all his features.

Father Matteo led him immediately to the chapel. There, on the occasion of
the festival of S. Giovanni Battista, a beautiful altar-piece of the Madonna had been
newly placed on the altar; on the one side, the Madonna had the Infant Jesus and, on
the other, S. Giovanni Battista, who worshipped the Infant on his knees.

The Jew, who had come with the idea of having discovered people of his faith,
did not in the least doubt that it was the picture of Rebecca with her sons Jacob and
Esau. He thus instantly offered reverence to it saying: "I do not wish to worship
images, but I wish to venerate these, who were of my race and kindred." And, as
on both sides of the chapel there were also the Four Evangelists, the Jew asked
whether these were some of the twelve sons of the one who was standing on the altar:
The father, thinking that he meant the Twelve Apostles, replied in the affirmative.
He then led him into (p. 469) his room in order to examine him further and to find
out what sort of man he was. Gradually, however, he began to realize that he was
a Jew, though Ai did not use that term, because he did not know the designation of
Jew, but only that of Israelite. I showed him the Bible of Plantinus in Hebrew and
he at once recognized his Scripture, although he could not read it.

From this, our people in the capital of Honan, i.e., Kaifeng, knew that there
lived ten or twelve Jewish families with a very beautiful synagogue. This had been
recently repaired at a cost of 10,000 ducats. In the synagogue the Jews kept with
much veneration the Pentateuch of Moses, written on sheepskin parchment, rolled in
five scrolls. They lived there for 500 or 600 years and many more families of their

co-religionists with a synagogue stayed in Hangchow, the capital of Chekiang, and also in other parts, but [there] without a synagogue. However, they gradually vanished by dying out. As they do not eat pork, the Chinese make little distinction between them and the Saracens of the Law of Mohammed, although these Jews feel unfriendly towards that sect and abhor it.

p. 470. This man called the Saracens (Mohammedans; tr.) san-chiao 三 教, i.e., of the three laws (creeds; tr.), kept by the Jews, the Christians, and the gentiles (Chinese; tr.) respectively; and so, he claimed, they were [also] called by the Jews. But, as we know from the following, the Chinese distinguish these three creeds by other names; namely, they call the Saracens "the people, (p. 471) who do not eat pork", the Jews, "the people, who do not eat nerves (sinews; tr.)", because they observe until now the ancient law of extracting the sinews of all the animals which they eat; and the descendants of the Christians [they call] "the people, who do not eat round-hoofed animals", because the Moors (Mohammedans; tr.) and the Jews and all the Chinese eat the meat of horses, mules, and other similar animals, while the descendants of the Christians do not eat it according to the custom of their homeland.

Further information concerning the Hebrews of Kaifeng.

This Jews told many stories of the Old Testament, like those of Abraham, of Judith, of Mordecai, of Esther, and others; although the sound of the proper names was quite different and, possibly, his [pronunciation] was more apt and closer to the Hebrew. For instance, Jerusalem he called Hierusoloim and the Messiah, who, he said, was still to come, he called Moscia. He told the father that in Kaifeng there were many who knew Hebrew and that among them was one of his brothers, but that from his youth he had devoted himself to Chinese literary studies. He, therefore, had not learned Hebrew. He also gave to understand that by following the affairs of the Chinese literati, he had been expelled from the synagogue by the Grand Rabbi, its head, and had become half excommunicated. He would readily abandon this creed if he could obtain the doctor's degree, as was done by the Saracens, who, once they had received their doctor's degree, were no longer afraid of their mullah and gave up their faith.

Efforts to trace the Christians and the Hebrews of Kaifeng
rendered useless.

Three years later Father Matteo sent one of our Chinese brothers, together with one of the literati of that region, who had received holy baptism in Peking, to this city in order to inquire what relics of Christianity existed there and also to see what kind of scriptures they were using. But there he was better received by the Jews than by the worshipers of the cross. The latter did not want to admit to the brother to be descendants of the worshipers of the cross...

p. 472. He got copied the beginning and the end of the Hebrew books which the Jews kept in the synagogue; in these were used the same letters as those of our Pentateuch, but without [vowel] signs beneath the letters according to the ancient custom.

Father Matteo had written a letter in Chinese to the Grand Rabbi. In it he said that he had with him in Peking all the books of the Old Testament and also the New [Testament] about the life of the Messiah who had already come into the world. But he (the Grand Rabbi; tr.) replied to the brother that the Messiah would come 10,000 years hence. And, because they had heard of the very great and good reputation of the father, they sent to say that, provided he would refrain from eating pork and would stay with them, they would make him their Grand Rabbi.

Later on three other Jews from that locality came to Peking. They were so disposed to become Christians that they would readily have received holy baptism, if they could have stayed a few days longer. One of them was a nephew of the licentiate Ai, the son of one of his brothers. The fathers arranged a great feast for them, explaining many things of their (of the Jewish; tr.) law which neither they nor their teachers knew; also that the Messiah had already come and that his image was the one which they had seen in our church. All three of them worshiped it kneeling, as if they were Christians. They also took with them [copies] of the **Dottrina Christiana** and other books on our activities rendered into Chinese.

These three were very sad seeing that their sect was thus to be extinguished, because nobody knew its scriptures, and that they would have to become either gentiles or Saracens, like the Christians who in olden times lived in this city. They said that their old Grand Rabbi, who had some knowledge, had already died and that one of his (p. 473) young sons had succeeded him through inheritance. But he knew nothing of the law and it seemed very bad in an extremely well built temple which they had, that there was no image; neither was there any image in their chapels nor in their houses. If they had placed an image of the Saviour in their temple and homes, it would have greatly blessed all the people. And especially Ai complained of the restrictions which the Grand Rabbi had placed on them, such as not eating any meat of animals which had not been killed by his own hand, saying that here in Peking, if they had wished to abide by this regulation, they would have died of hunger; and also the circumcision of babies eight days after their birth, which seemed very cruel to their gentile wives and relatives. They concluded that they would follow our law, provided we abolished these ceremonies, because it would not be very difficult [for them] to eat pork.

Therefore, Father Matteo decided to send at the first opportunity a father there to stay permanently, in order to discover gradually the local Christian relics and also to bring about the conversion of the Jews. But he could not do this immediately, because in that city was then a governor, who was not well disposed, or rather hostile, towards Christianity.

Vol. II, pp. 289-293.   Letter no. 35 to the P. Claudio Acquaviva, Prep. Gen., S.J., Peking July 26, 1605.

p. 289.   *Families descended from ancient Christians in Honan province.*

A few days ago we learned that in the central region of China there lived for 500 years a considerable number of Christians and that there have remained important traces of them in many places. During the past three years I have written to you, Venerable Father, that (p. 290) we had discovered a Christian community in territory conquered by China, but [they lived] outside of the Great North Wall. Until now, for the lack of a few ducats to undertake this trip, we have not sent anybody to investigate how many there are and where they came from. Now we know that in the central part of China, half a month's [travel] from here and equally far from Nanking, there live five or six Christian families in Kaifeng fu, the capital of Honan province. But, what little there existed of Christianity is almost entirely extinguished due to the fact that already several years ago their church was changed into a temple of idols, called **Quanguam**. * What prevented us until now from knowing of it was that they did not call themselves by the name of Christians, but people of **Terza**: ** according to the name of the kingdom from which they came to China and from the law of the **shih-tzu** 十字, i.e., from the character for ten. This character forms a perfect cross, in this way +. Because of their general features and because of the fact that they did not worship idols they resembled the Moors and Jews.

We learned this through a Jew by profession of his faith (literally: "law"), nationality, and features, who came to visit me during the past days because he had heard of my reputation (p. 291) and because of the many printed books concerning our activities. He, therefore, understood that we were neither Moors nor gentiles and thought that we were of his faith. This man, whose surname was Ai 艾, lived in the capital of Honan province. His father had three sons. He [himself] had studied Chinese literature and thus graduated as a licentiate. He was already sixty years old and had come this year to ask for an office which he was given in a school in the city of Yangchow. His two brothers studied Hebrew and are, apparently rabbis in the Jewish community. Ai said that on their land there was a great synagogue on which 10,000 ducats had been spent and that six or eight families of his co-religionists were living there.

He came to our house during the octave of St. John the Baptist and we had placed a large and beautiful image of the Madonna with the Infant on one side of the altar and, on the other, of St. John the Baptist. This man did not know the designation of Jew, but called himself only Israelite. When he saw the image, he thought that it represented the two children, Jacob and Esau. He, therefore, said: "Although I do not worship images, I want to offer reverence to my earliest ancestors." Therefore, he knelt and worshiped. At the beginning of the conversation he told that the head of his sect had twelve sons, so that I thought he was a Christian and that he spoke of the Twelve Apostles. Ultimately I discovered that he was not a Christian, but was not much opposed to Christianity; because he admitted to me that they were unable to keep their law in China, owing to the fact that the circumcision, the purification, the [eating of] pork, and other things impeded their relations with others, especially for those, who wanted to become officials. He also gave us to understand that **factus erat extra synagogam** [he had been excluded from the synagogue] and did not know much, although he told many stories from the Old Testament, of the Twelve Tribes, of Moses, [down] to the story of Haman and Mordecai. He also stated that his brothers knew everything written in the books of his law and I think that they also had other books dealing with superstitions.

He said that they had preserved the tradition that many Moors, Christians and Jews had come with the king Tamerlane, when he conquered the whole of Persia and also China 800 years ago (p. 292) and that the Moors were predominant, while the Christians and Jews remained [only] a few. In the Honan region, however, there existed all of the three sects, although the Christian one was almost extinct. But among them there were many literati and high officials. Among the others there lives now a Nanking **shang-shu** 尚書 *** by the name of Chang Meng-nan 張孟男, a good friend of ours when we stayed there. He was extremely friendly, as he was with the Nanking fathers. He stated that the descendants of Christians did not want to admit this fact, because in China it is deemed little honourable to be of foreign descent. This Chang Meng-nan, from his appearance, looked like one of our people.

The following day the Jew brought to our house somebody from his region by the name of Chang [Keng] 張 [庚] who, he said, was a descendant of the Christians and was likewise to receive an office, which he [actually] obtained in Shensi province.

p. 293. *China and the famous Cathay of Marco Polo.*

From this we understand that it is now much less doubtful that China is identical with the Cathay of Marco Polo, the Venetian. Marco Polo is also right when he says that there are Christians in Cathay, although in his time there would not have been many. This Jew made me also consider whether or not it was the late Tamerlane, as we call him, who established the Chinese empire 500 years ago   As we know that the one who invaded China was the son of the conqueror of Persia; because, although the father did not conquer China, everything is attributed to him.

    * Kuan-wang 關王; the name of the temple is Kuan-ti-miao 關帝廟. Cf. A. C. Moule, Christians in China before the year 1550, London, 1930, p. 10, fn. 11.

    ** Terza is tarsä, a word applied by Moslems to Christians and other non-Moslems. Ibid.

    *** President of a Board; there were altogether six Boards with a Manchu and a Chinese President each.